WHAT PEO
ABOUT JAILBREAK

MW01108244

"This is a powerful book that's anointed by God! The mix of Scripture, commentary, quoted content, probing questions, and prayers are fabulous and effective! It's also great to have both the male and female perspectives. While I don't have a porn issue, there are other areas these principles apply. I believe many will experience supernatural healing and deliverance while reading it."

—Susan Hutchison
Editor, Joyce Meyer Ministries

"On the outside, you might view the Newfields as the ideal couple. *Jailbreak* is their personal story of struggles and liberation from the enslavement of pornography. Not only is it their story, but also a wonderful teaching manual of how to be set free from this addiction. Clearly, one of the best sources of information on the subject of sexual dependency I have ever read."

—C. R. Kersten
Executive Director, Teen Challenge of St. Louis

"Your book—wow! The insight is incredible. And to have the wife's perspective in each chapter is something I've never seen in any book before. The application features add movement that brings freedom instead of just information. Without question, *Jailbreak* will help and equip many in our society and the church."

—Ed Shirrell
Senior Pastor, Faith Community Church

JAILBREAK

Cover Design: TMD Creative, Timothy Moore@www.tmdcreative.net
Interior Design: Greg Holtzmann
Illustrations: Bryanna Newfield
Editorial Consultants: Chad R. Trafton and Susan Hutchison

NEW FIELDS CREATIVE SERVICES
www.newfieldscreativeservices.com

www.xulonpress.com

JAILBREAK

breaking free from
the prison of **porn**

by vincent & allison newfield

PRESS

ACKNOWLEDGEMENTS

I (Vincent) want to thank you, Allison, for your incredible, selfless love throughout our journey to freedom. Next to God Himself, you are the reason I walk in freedom today. Your prayers, patience, and companionship are priceless. Thank you for writing this book with me and motivating me to press toward the finish line. I love and value you more than words can express, my Love!

To our fabulous four daughters, you are such a treasure to us! We are honored to be your father and mother and so grateful for your tender love. You each hold a special place in our hearts. Thank you for your enduring patience throughout all the many challenges while writing this book. Each of you shares in the rewards of the lives healed, restored, and freed.

To my mom and dad, Frank and Claudia, thank you for pioneering the path of Christian living before me and for your continued prayers and support. What a blessing you are! We love you. To Carolyn and Tom Seely, our tireless cheerleaders and the greatest in-laws one could hope for, thank you for your love, prayers, and support.

To my uncle and friend, Frank Sampere, who has been there for me and our family through many highs and lows, thank you for your prayers and words of wisdom! To Randy and Brenda, Frank and Tanya, thank you for your unfailing prayers and support.

A special thank you to our cherished friends Chad Trafton, Susan Hutchison, Greg Holtzmann, and Tim Moore for lending your incredible gifts to the creation of this book. Your sacrificial investment of time, talent, and energy has been noted in Heaven!

And **thank You**, Father, for doing a work in me and Allison that we could never do on our own. You are our very best Friend, and we are so grateful to be doing life with You!

WE DEDICATE THIS BOOK...

To you, the war-weary man who has battled lust and porn and been held captive in its grip... To you, the prisoner who has longed to escape but been unable to find the Way... Now is the time! Today is the day your salvation begins! May the eyes of your heart be opened like never before. ...May you encounter the Answer and experience true, lasting freedom in Him!

To the precious wives and children...the families who've been shattered and ripped apart by porn's devastating fallout...to the girls who are victims of sex slavery and their families... May true, lasting freedom be found. May hope, healing, peace, and total restoration be yours as we push back the darkness and release the Light!

Holy Spirit, saturate these pages with Your supernatural presence. May Your power, peace, and personal revelation be with every reader. May the truth herein go viral, becoming even more accessible than porn itself. In Jesus' name!

A Special Note...

A portion of the profits from the sales of *Jailbreak* will be given to organizations bringing hope and freedom to the victims of sex trafficking. Together, we are creating a circle of freedom for men, women, and children! **Thank you** for helping us make this message go viral!

INTRODUCTION

IMPRISONED. From my pre-teen years to my early twenties, I had a growing addiction to porn. Little by little, lust and impurity tightened its grip on my soul and body. Yes, I was a Christian. But my perceptions and practices regarding sex were under the influence of a different spirit. I longed to be free but did not know how to experience it.

Getting married, I thought. *That's when this will end.* Oh, how wrong I was. Not only did the addiction continue, but I also inflicted great pain on my wife, Allison. Guilt, shame, and condemnation hung over me like a dark cloud. I was plagued by bouts of fear and anger. *Will I ever be free?* I cried. *Can God break this horrific cycle of sin? Can He give me healthy sexual desires?*

Yes! God *can* break the cycle of sin! And He *can* give you healthy sexual desires. **I am free**. My life is proof. This is our story...a candid glimpse of Allison and mine's journey to freedom. In *Jailbreak*, we each share our heart and offer a proven pathway to freedom through relationship with Jesus. At the close of each chapter, you'll find *Encouragement from the Heart of a Woman*. This is my wife, Allison's, eye-opening perspective written directly to men.

Please know that your journey to freedom will be as unique as your own fingerprints. As author John Eldredge put it, "There are no formulas with God. The way in which God heals our wound is a deeply personal process. He is a person and he insists on working personally." So as you carefully read thru each chapter, *pray*. Ask the Holy Spirit how the truths apply to you specifically, and be open to what He reveals and willing to do what He instructs.

Don't rush. Take your time. Answer the questions honestly, chew on the scriptures, and pray from your heart. And *take notes*. God **will** speak to you. He will show you things about yourself and about Himself that you've never seen before. These revelations are *priceless*, so take time to write them.

This book is written to married, Christian men.

To Single Men: Wherever you see the word "wife," insert "future wife." Realize the way you manage your sexual appetite *before* marriage is the way you will manage it after you're married. *Now* is the time to learn to discipline your eyes, mind, and heart by the power of the Holy Spirit.

To Women: Statistics reveal that one out of three porn-site visits are by women. If this describes you, *Jailbreak* can help. Wherever you see the word "wife," insert "husband" or "future husband."

To Those with Other Addictions: The amazing thing about being in relationship with Jesus is that He gives us freedom from **all** bondages. Whatever the habit—alcohol, drugs, food, porn—the *Jailbreak* principles apply. Wherever you see the word "porn," insert the name of what you're facing.

Before you begin, Allison and I offer this prayer for you:

Spirit of the Living God,

*Thank You for our brother who desires to be set free from the prison of porn. From the start, we pray that Your presence will be with him every step of the way. Open his spiritual eyes and ears to see and hear what You're speaking. Saturate him with the truth or Your Word, and reveal to him the truth about his life—truth that will set him free. Give him a heart of humility, a heart of brokenness, and a heart that is willing to obey Your promptings. May his craving for porn be uprooted and replaced with cravings for Christ and the bride You have favored him with. May this journey catapult him into a relationship with You like never before. **Prove Yourself** to Your son—that You are real, that You love him intensely, and that he can experience freedom and purity in a relationship with You. In Jesus' matchless name, Amen!*

CONTENTS

PART I: SETTING THE STAGE

The Naked Truth about Porn and Sex

"How Did I Get Here?" Discovering Your Roots

CONTENTS

PART 2: THE GREAT ESCAPE
21 STEPS TO FREEDOM

PART 1

SETTING THE STAGE

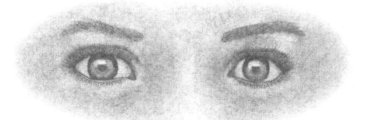

The Naked Truth
About Porn and Sex

ONE BROTHER TO ANOTHER

"Pornography is from the Greek word pornos (the same word used...for an adulteress or a prostitute) and from the word grapho, which means to write. Thus, pornography refers to the writings or reflections about prostitution. This means that when an individual meditates on the writings or the photography contained in pornography, it is the equivalent of committing mental prostitution."

— Rick Renner[1]

Sparkling Gems from the Greek

Chapter 1

WHAT IS PORN?

"...A spirit of prostitution leads them astray.
They commit adultery by giving themselves to other gods."

Hosea 4:12 GW

I know. You know what porn is. That's why you picked up this book... because you're trying to break free from its grips. But let's take a closer look at what the word porn means, how long it's been around, and what God has to say about it.

By Definition...

Pornography is "any representation of sexual behavior in books, pictures, statues, movies, and other media that is intended to cause sexual excitement."[2] Makes sense so far, right? Nothing you didn't know. Interestingly, the word pornography originated in the mid-19th century and is derived from two Greek words: *porne*, which means "prostitute," and *graphein*, which means "to write." The compounding of the two words is *pornographos*, which literally means "writing about prostitutes."[3]

A prostitute is a woman (or man) who engages in sexual acts for money. It's estimated that the annual revenue generated globally from prostitution is over $100 billion.[4] The word *prostitute* originated in the early 1500s and was taken from the Latin word *prostituta*, which carries the meaning "to expose for sale."[5] All that said, modern-day pornography in magazines, movies, and on the Internet is essentially *prostitution on paper, on film and on the computer.*

How Long Has Porn Been Around?

Contrary to what some think, pornography did *not* originate in 1969 when Bob Guccione published his first *Penthouse* magazine. Nor did it start with Hugh Hefner, the founder of *Playboy*, who printed his first issue in December 1953 and sold over fifty thousand copies. Pornography, like prostitution, has been around in some form since the earliest civilizations. From early cave paintings of human genitalia to sexual acts depicted on Egyptian papyrus, from erotic Greek and Roman statues and artwork to sensual pictures painted on colored woodblocks in Japan…name the nation, and it had porn.[6] Some things never change.

What *has* changed over the years is porn's availability. With each technological advance, the proliferation of porn has increased. Inventions like the printing press in the mid-1500s, photography in the 1830s, and motion pictures in the mid-1890s made the availability and quantity of prostitution on paper and in film grow dramatically. An even greater dispersion of porn began through the launch of cable and satellite television, which began in the late 1970s, coupled with the invention of video cassettes in the 1980s and DVDs in the 1990s.[7] However, the greatest exponential expansion of porn to date has resulted from the public debut of the World Wide Web in the late 1980s/early 1990s. Nothing has made porn more accessible.

How Extensive Is Porn's Reach?

Check out these facts and figures: At the time of this writing, 50-60 percent of all Christian men are struggling with porn. About 43 percent of all Internet users view pornographic material. About 40 million Americans are regular visitors to porn sites, watching an average of 15 minutes per session; two out of three are men. The day of the week online porn is most viewed is Sunday. Internet porn alone in the U.S. pulls in $2.8 billion a year; globally, it produces $4.9 billion annually.[8]

How much has the porn industry grown? In 2001, Forbes Magazine revealed that the *entire* porn industry produced $2.6 to $3.9 billion annually.[9] Currently, porn pulls in a whopping **$97 billion a year** — that's twenty-five times more money than just over a decade ago. That's about $259 million a day, $11 million an hour, or about $3,000 spent **every second** around the world on porn.[10] The U.S. alone annually spends over $13 billion on porn and is the biggest producer. Nearly 90 percent of all porn films are produced in the San Fernando Valley, with 20,000 new releases each year.[11] Tragically, the nation birthed to be a lighthouse of the gospel has become the greatest peep show on earth. May God have mercy on us.

What Does God Say About Porn?

You won't find the word pornography anywhere in Scripture. However, with the understanding that pornography is essentially *prostitution*, you will find countless warnings and instructions from Genesis to Revelation about it. Words synonymous with prostitute found in Scripture include harlot, whore, loose woman, adulteress, and fornicator. When you take the word pornography and plug it in place of these words in Scripture, your eyes will be opened to its destructive nature and how it grieves God's heart.

If there was anyone who could offer some sound advice on porn, it's King Solomon. He had 700 wives and 300 concubines, which is another name for mistress. His unchecked appetite for women proved to be his downfall. The ungodly women he married *turned his heart away from God* and toward other gods (see 1 Kings 11:3-4). Solomon offers men of all generations life-giving words of warning in Proverbs 5, 6, and 7. We'll explore the core of God's message through him in the chapters ahead.

If you think about it, Solomon had access to more women than he could handle. His lifestyle is very similar to today's porn-addicted man. Porn creates an increasing appetite for women that cannot be satisfied. This sexual vice drives men to view hundreds if not thousands of images. In most cases, he visualizes and fantasizes about having sex with each one while masturbating. Researchers have found that after about three exposures to the same image, coupled with manual release, it's as if the man has actually had intercourse with the woman he's fantasized over.

God states we are not to have any gods before Him nor make any graven images to worship (see Exodus 20:4). Jesus reiterates this commandment, saying we are to love God with *all* our heart, soul, mind and strength (see Mark 12:30). To *worship* literally means "to give worth to." This includes our time, attention, and devotion. Along my journey to freedom, God showed me that each woman's picture I had fantasized over in magazines, movies, etc., was an image I was worshipping. Sex had become an idol, taking my time, attention, and devotion. On top of that, He said every woman I had imagined having sex with while "doing my thing" was as if I had actually done it. The same is true for you.

The Bottom Line

Viewing porn and relieving yourself sexually is just like joining yourself to a prostitute. Yes, this is strong, candid, and in your face. But in God's eyes, "...anyone who even looks at a woman with lust has already committed adultery with her in his heart" (Matthew 5:28 NLT).

Sobering, isn't it? Don't feel condemned, but definitely feel convicted. Let godly sorrow move you to prayer. Confess and repent of your sin and receive God's forgiveness and grace. **Thank God** for His mercy, His forgiveness, and His power to heal and change you. As you humble yourself and walk through this study, He will teach you how to live clean, pure and free!

Encouragement from the Heart of a Woman

Man of God, what you are coming out of is painful and powerful. The behavior is negatively impacting every area of your life. But you were born for more than this defeated lifestyle. As you need to heal from your past entanglements, so does your wife. As you need God's forgiveness, patience, and healing, your wife needs it too. She is hurting and probably unable to effectively communicate herself to you. Just as she does not understand your sexual drive and need for release, you will most likely not understand the depth of pain your actions have caused her.

Each time Vincent gave himself to a woman portrayed in porn, I was robbed of his attention and affections—even when I was unaware of his sin. His one need that I alone am supposed to have the privilege of fulfilling was stolen from me repeatedly. This was most painful. It caused me to be distant and to distrust him. The same is true for you and your wife. Imagine how you would feel if she slept with your best friend, brother, or father.

I pray that you will allow the deep love of our Great Savior to lead you to repentance. As you submit yourself to Him and flee from this immoral lifestyle, He will heal you and your loved ones and grant you His power to defeat the enemy. Pray for your wife to be healed and made whole as you walk into the freedom Jesus died to give you. Realize that you cannot heal her and it's not your responsibility. Only Jesus can repair that which has been broken. Receive the victory Jesus died to give you. I speak strength to you in the name of Jesus and call you an overcomer in Him!

Sum It:

Pornography is any representation of sexual behavior in print, in movies, on the Internet and any other media that's intended to cause sexual excitement. Modern-day porn is essentially *prostitution on paper, on film, and on the computer.* Viewing porn and relieving yourself sexually is just like joining yourself to a prostitute. If this describes you, confess and repent of your sin and receive God's forgiveness and grace.

Study It:

Proverbs 5, 6, and 7; 1 Kings 11:3-4; Exodus 20:4; Mark 12:30; Matthew 5:27-30

Apply It:

1 What eye-opening information did you learn about porn? *What does the fact that porn literally means "prostitute" say to you about viewing it?*

_____

_____

_____

_____

_____

2 Carefully read Proverbs 5, 6 and 7, substituting the word *pornography* in place of adulteress and prostitute. What are you seeing in these passages? What is the Holy Spirit speaking to you?

_____

_____

_____

_____

_____

3 What's your greatest takeaway from this chapter? How are you challenged? What action(s) is God prompting you to take?

_____

_____

_____

_____

_____

Pray It:

"Father, please forgive me for supporting and advancing the pornography industry in any way. Forgive me for being unfaithful to You and my precious wife. I never knew looking and lusting over porn was the same as joining myself to a prostitute. Wash me clean with the blood of Jesus. Uproot from me every desire to look at porn in any form. Help me, Lord, to redirect my passion toward You and my bride. I love You, Lord, and I thank You for Your mercy, patience, and forgiveness. In Jesus' name, Amen."

ONE BROTHER TO ANOTHER

"...Pornography is a destructive phenomenon. We understand that it does not contribute anything to society but, rather, takes away from and diminishes what we regard as socially good."

— C. Everett Koop[1]
Surgeon General
United States of America, 1982-89

Chapter 2

READ 'EM AND WEEP

For a prostitute will bring a man to poverty,
and an adulteress may cost him his very life.
Proverbs 6:26 TLB

The stats don't lie. The price tag on porn is greater than you can imagine. Sin will take you farther than you want to go, keep you longer than you want to stay, and cost you more than you want to pay.

In 1985, President Ronald Reagan authorized a second commission to study the effects of pornography on individuals, families, and society at large.[2] For one year, testimony was taken from victims of pornography, police officers, FBI agents, social scientists, and the producers of hard-core materials. While the findings of porn's damaging influence were clear, "there was not a single secular publisher in America who would print the report," said Focus on the Family founder, Dr. James Dobson, who served as one of the eleven commissioners. "Nor would network television present the facts."[3]

Therefore, in this chapter we present sound, scientific findings that became a part of the Attorney General's Commission on Pornography released in 1986. These studies were carefully conducted by doctors, psychologists, and college professors to determine porn's effects. Time and space don't permit a detailed explanation of all the variables and controls used in each experiment. What we will provide is the pertinent information and findings essential to your journey to freedom.

Porn's Pattern: Fulfillment Fades, Addiction Grows

The use of porn is destructive to healthy sexuality. Victor Cline, a specialist in the treatment of sexual deviances at the University of Utah, states without reservation that exposure to pornographic materials has a *distinct pattern*: fulfillment fades, addiction grows. The user experiences sexual stimulation from the materials that quickly replaces normal sexual activity. This leads to addiction. A tolerance for porn then develops, requiring the user to see progressively stronger images to achieve the same "kick" or high.[4]

As a young man once imprisoned by porn, I confirm this to be fact. The viewing of pornography *desensitizes* the viewer. The more it is watched, the less the watcher is upset, offended, or aroused by what is seen. With few exceptions, viewers of nonviolent, common (or "soft") porn end up becoming consumers of more potent, hard-core porn, including violent pornography. Frequent viewing not only desensitizes viewers to the violence against women but also diminishes their perception of what is degrading to women.[5]

Over time, people become bored by ordinary porn and develop an appetite for stronger, more bizarre versions. I experienced this firsthand. With each additional exposure, I became dissatisfied with what I was familiar with. The usual was no longer good enough, and I craved something more. The "more" was bizarre sexual images. Can you identify? This highly significant finding was discovered by Dr. Dolf Zillmann at Indiana University, his colleague Dr. Jennings Bryant at the University of Houston, and their associate James Weaver at the University of Kentucky. The same conclusion was replicated by Dr. James Check at York University in Canada and by Dr. Gene Abel at Emory University in his studies of jailed sex offenders. [6]

"Like the addiction to drugs, alcohol, or food, those who get hooked on sexually explicit materials become obsessed by their need," affirms Dr. James Dobson. "In time it encompasses their entire world. These images can also interfere with normal sexual relationships between husbands and wives, since nothing in reality can possibly compete with airbrushed fantasies."[7]

Without question, porn's distinct pattern is: *fulfillment fades, addiction grows.*

Porn Damages and Distorts Your View of Women and Children

There are unspoken values and standards that permeate porn and leave a measurable impact on its viewers. Doctors Zillmann and Bryant discovered this. In one experiment, they exposed one group of men and women to six hours of prime-time situational comedies and another group to six hours of X-rated, nonviolent porn purchased at a typical video store. Each group watched one hour per week. What did they discover overall?

Exposure to porn clearly makes people more likely to believe that...

- The greatest sexual joy comes *without* enduring (lasting) commitment.

- Partners expect each other to be unfaithful.

- There are health risks in repressing (limiting) sexual urges.

- Promiscuity (immorality, lustfulness) is natural.

- Children are liabilities and handicaps.[8]

Ironically, never in pornography is there a hint that sexual intercourse produces children, whose rearing requires commitment and financial sacrifice on the part of parents. Never in porn is there an idea that sexual acts with multiple partners dramatically increase the likelihood of acquiring sexually transmitted diseases (STDs). Never in porn is there a trace of the mental, emotional, or physical scars that are often left on those who participate in sex outside of marriage. There's no bad breath, no BO, no menstruation, no sickness, no financial pressure, and no pressure at work. All that is presented is a lustful illusion of sexual fulfillment. But that's all it is—an *illusion* with a very high price tag.

Make no mistake: *Porn damages and distorts your view of women and children. If you're married, your wife and kids suffer greatly.*

Porn Decreases Your Sexual Satisfaction

Continuing their search for answers, Zillmann and Bryant carefully conducted another experiment. In a controlled environment similar to the previous study, one group of men and women were shown innocuous (harmless) movies and another was shown common pornography. Both groups viewed an equal number of hours over a six-week period. What were their overwhelming findings?

Viewers of porn have...

- An overall *decrease in satisfaction* with their present intimate relationship.

- A *diminished satisfaction* with the physical appearance of their partner.

- A *reduced satisfaction* with their partner's affection as well as their sexual behavior, curiosity, and innovations.

- A greater level of importance of sex *without* emotional involvement.[9]

Overwhelmingly, Drs. Zillmann and Bryant determined that after repeatedly viewing pornographic films, sexual satisfaction decreased—just as much in women as in men. The scientific evidence shows that viewing even nonviolent porn alters perceptions and influences the attitudes of people.[10] "Whatever the specific contents of standard pornography," states Zillmann, "there can be no doubts that effects are created, and consistently so. There can be no doubt that pornography, as a form of primarily male entertainment, promotes the victimization of women in particular."[11] Sadly, in some cases, men have so programmed their bodies to respond to porn that they become unable to experience an erection and intercourse with their wives.

There's no doubt about it: *Viewing porn decreases your sexual satisfaction.*

The Effects of Viewing Violent, Nonviolent, and Massive Amounts of Porn

Canadian researcher James Check took his research a step further. He experimented to compare the effects of viewing nonviolent porn to violent porn. Using 436 males, Check divided them into groups, including a control group, and showed each group films with three types of sexual material: simple erotica (such as used in sex-Ed type films), nonviolent porn, and violent porn (women being brutally forced into sex acts). He discovered that viewing nonviolent porn increased the likelihood that subjects would commit rape and other forced sexual acts *to the very same extent* of violent porn.[12]

Another study done by Zillmann and Bryant revealed that people who had massive exposure to pornographic films thought that unusual sex practices were more common than the people who had minimal or no exposure to porn. These unusual practices include anal sex, group sex (orgies), sadomasochistic sex (pleasure derived from pain), and sex with animals (bestiality). These findings clearly show that the use of pornography leads people to grosser forms of sex, and it changes their attitudes about bizarre sex practices.[13]

Here's the biggest shocker: Zillmann also noted that men and women who had massive exposure to porn *viewed rape as a trivial matter*; it was considered a lesser crime, and in many cases not a crime at all.[14] Psychologist Edward Donnerstein of the University of Wisconsin came to the same conclusion through his experiments.[15] A study by Malamuth and Feshback at the University of California at Los Angeles also confirmed these results. Their research showed that 51 percent of male students exposed to violent pornography indicated a likelihood of raping a woman if they could get away with it.[16]

All these studies by Zillmann, Bryant, and Weaver, along with those by Check, Malamuth, and Donnerstein, taken together, establish valid "laboratory" evidence. Closely controlled and scientifically sound, they verify that pornography alters perceptions and influences the attitudes of people.[17] These findings were instrumental in helping the Attorney General's Commission on Pornography to conclude that *degrading pornography—both violent and nonviolent in form—is harmful.*[18]

What Does All This Mean to You?

The evidence is clear: The path of porn leads to destruction. Stop and ask yourself, *Do I want to pay the high price of porn? Do I want to continue viewing it and become addicted and desensitized to what I'm seeing—desiring and requiring stronger, more perverted and violent images to achieve the same high? Do I want to view women as sex objects, disrespecting and devaluing them as God's creation? Do I want to continue experiencing less and less satisfaction with my wife's appearance, affection, and sexual expressions? Do I want to see my kids as a handicap? Do I want to become so twisted in my thinking that I view rape as trivial or even acceptable, if I could get away with it?* If your answer is no, you need to get off porn's path.

Friend, sexual fulfillment via the view of porn is fleeting and ultimately fatal to your well-being. "For a *prostitute* {porn} will bring a man to poverty, and an *adulteress* may cost him his very life" (Proverbs 6:26 TLB). If you are imprisoned in this pit, it's time to escape! The fact that you're holding this book is evidence of God's hand of mercy and grace being extended. Take hold of it and give yourself fully to Him. He will set you free and place you on the path of purity and sexual fulfillment like you've never dreamed!

Encouragement from the Heart of a Woman

Rape…trivial? Man of God, rape is no trivial matter. It is a horrible act of violence that ravages women in indescribable ways. Imagine this: A man in your neighborhood is attacked in his home by an unidentified woman. She ties him up, brutally rapes him, and then castrates him just before leaving the scene. Reports like these begin to surface all over your state and the country. Then it happens to your brother, followed by your son.

How would you feel? Vulnerable? Upset? Wouldn't you want there to be a public outrage? What if it had happened to you? Do you think it is important for a man's body to be valued and protected? I do! Likewise, I feel it's important to protect and value a woman's body. The fact that pornography degrades women to the point of viewing rape as trivial should alarm you! Sex was never designed to be a conquering event. It is meant to be a mutually gratifying and powerfully unifying experience!

Listen! Can you hear the cry of your wife...your daughters...your granddaughters? They're all saying, "Protect me, please! Defend and guard my life!" Man of God, you were made for more than this. You were not called to experience or be associated with the facts this chapter exposes. You are called to love and protect your wife and the women in your life—just as Jesus loves and protects the Church. Rise up and be the protector you were created to be.

Think seriously about the choices you're making, and realize you will give an account for your actions. I believe in you, and this book is not in your hands by accident. This is your appointed time of freedom! Repent for your actions and allow the strength and love of Jesus Christ to bring forth freedom in your life. Freedom to love genuinely and selflessly, freedom to experience sex the way God intended, freedom to be at peace, free from guilt and condemnation. Trust God with your sexual desires and He will strengthen you and fulfill your greatest needs.

Sum It:

There's a high price tag on viewing porn. It destroys a healthy sex life while producing a distinctive pattern: fulfillment fades, addiction grows. Each viewing desensitizes the viewer to the value of human life and requires progressively stronger, more perverted and violent images to achieve the same "high." Porn—violent and nonviolent alike—decreases your sexual satisfaction and distorts and degrades your view of women and children, especially your wife and kids. The more you're exposed to porn, the more likely you are to view rape as trivial and even acceptable, if you could get away with it.

Want current porn stats? Check out www.jailbreakthebook.com.

Study It:

Proverbs 2:12-19; 5, 6, and 7; Leviticus 19:29; 1 Corinthians 6:12-20

Apply It:

1 Carefully reread porn's effects on your level of *sexual satisfaction*. Can you personally identify with any of these? If so, which ones? What do your answers and the evidence presented in this chapter say to you?

_____

_____

_____

_____

2 Reread porn's effects on your *view of women and children*. Can you identify with any of these, especially regarding your wife and kids? If so, which ones? What does the evidence presented and your answers say to you?

_____

_____

_____

_____

3 After hearing the scientific research on porn's addictive nature and all its negative tendencies, which is *most concerning* to you? Why? How has your view of pornography changed as a result?

_____

_____

_____

_____

4 What is your greatest takeaway from this chapter? What scriptures, principles, or ideas spoke to your heart most? How do they challenge you? What action(s) is God prompting you to take?

_____

_____

_____

_____

Pray It:

"Father, forgive me for giving place to porn in my life and believing the enemy's lies over the truth of Your Word. I don't want to continue down this path. I don't want to have a distorted, devalued view of women and children—I don't want to be dissatisfied with my wife or see my kids as handicaps. They are Your priceless gifts to me. And I never want to see rape as trivial. Help me, Father, to rise up and become the protector and defender You created me to be for my wife and the women in my life. Without You, I am powerless to change. But with You, I can do all things— including live free from porn! Thank You, Lord! In Jesus' name, Amen!"

ONE BROTHER TO ANOTHER

"You live in a world awash with sensual images available twenty-four hours a day in a variety of mediums: print, television, videos, the Internet—even phones. But God offers you freedom from slavery of sin through the cross of Christ, and He created your eyes and mind with an ability to be trained and controlled. We simply have to stand up and walk by His power in the right path."

— Stephen Arterburn[1]

Every Man's Battle

Chapter 3

THE ENEMY'S ULTIMATE GOAL

The thief's purpose is to steal and kill and destroy....

John 10:10 NLT

Steal, kill, and destroy—that's the enemy's mission. Satan, the thief, comes to steal your purity, kill your physical union with your wife, and destroy your family. Methodically, he baits each trap, gaining territory with each pornographic escapade in which you engage. Slowly and steadily, he expands his control over your mind, heart, and body as you yield to his temptations. Like a marionette puppet, he seeks to master your every move until his ultimate goal is achieved—enslavement.

Jesus Christ is the answer! He's the way—the only way—to freedom. While the thief comes only in order to steal, kill, and destroy, Jesus came that you may have and enjoy life, and have it in abundance—to the full, till it overflows (see John 10:10 AMP). The question is, whose mission are you helping to fulfill?

I Was Bound but Blind to It

I didn't see the bondage I was in for a long time. I blindly believed I was in control of myself, but eventually it became clear that I wasn't. Every time I gave in to the temptation to look at and lust after women in porn and relieve myself sexually, I *gave place* to the enemy and he gained a little more control over my soul—my mind, will, and emotions.

His *perverted* influence began to dominate my thinking, decisions, and feelings about sex and women. He constructed a *stronghold* of sexual immorality in my life. His behavior became my behavior. Looking for pornographic images when I was alone became an automatic, second-nature response. I had allowed him to get his hooks in me and I couldn't break free.

As a boy, I used to fish with my dad and brothers. We often used treble hooks that were excellent at catching fish. They have three sharp prongs attached to one eyelet, and when a fish swallows the bait attached to one of these, it is extremely hard for him to break free. Treble hooks are so apt at snagging things, I had to be very careful while casting my line not to snag somebody's head.

In a similar way, when I was trapped in the prison of porn, I felt as if the enemy had huge hooks anchored in my mind, will, and emotions. And whenever he wanted me to look at and lust after something, all he had to do was jerk back on his "porn" pole, set the hook, and reel me in. He had me hook, line, and sinker.

Initially, the lingerie section of catalogs and swimsuit magazines provided the perfect "pop." Eventually, these became old news, and a Playboy-grade of porn took its place. But all too soon, they became uninteresting too. "More, more!" something within me cried. So I got ahold of something racier. A new high was reached, but it too was temporary. My flesh was never satisfied. Enough was never enough. As Richard Exley noted in his book *Deliver Me*, "The more we attempt to appease our lust, the more demanding it becomes. There is simply not enough erotica in the world to satisfy its insatiable appetite."[2]

As strange as it may seem, I also had a genuine desire in my heart to serve God at this time. Before long, my love for Him began to collide with my flesh's craving for porn. A violent inner storm began to rage, producing fierce feelings of guilt, condemnation, shame, and anger. Looking back, I am grateful for the storm and the prayers of my parents and friends. I believe they kept me from sinking deeper into depravity and sin. Only God knows how low a man will go, but history reveals a man influenced by porn can sink extremely low.

Remember Ted Bundy?

Ted was a man who grew up in a loving Christian home, and he did not experience sexual abuse. What he *did* experience was regular viewing of pornography. He admitted that as a boy, he started looking at common porn, but it eventually became more hard-core and bizarre in nature. Time passed and he began acting out his evil fantasies. Before he was finally caught by authorities in 1978, Bundy became one of America's most feared serial killers responsible for beating, raping, and murdering no less than thirty girls and women between the ages of twelve and twenty-six.

The day before Ted was executed, he was interviewed by Focus on the Family founder Dr. James Dobson. During the discussion, he talked in detail about his involvement with porn, confirming its pattern of fading fulfillment and growing addiction.

"Once you become addicted to it, and I look at this as a kind of addiction," said Bundy, "you look for more potent, more explicit, more graphic kinds of material. Like an addiction, you keep craving something which is harder and gives you a greater sense of excitement, until you reach the point where the pornography only goes so far.... The most damaging kind of pornography—and I'm talking from hard, real, personal experience—is that that involves violence and sexual violence. The wedding of those two forces—as I know only too well— brings about behavior that is too terrible to describe."[3]

Interestingly, Bundy added, "I'm not blaming pornography. I'm not saying it caused me to go out and do certain things. I take full responsibility for all the things that I've done. That's not the question here. The issue is how this kind of literature contributed and helped mold and shape the kinds of violent behavior."[4]

When Dr. Dobson asked about the untold damage porn is causing, Bundy said, "I'm no social scientist, and I don't pretend to believe what John Q. Citizen thinks about this, but I've lived in prison for a long time now, and I've met a lot of men who were motivated to commit violence. *Without exception, every one of them was deeply involved in pornography—deeply consumed by the addiction.* The F.B.I.'s own study on serial homicide shows that the most common interest among serial killers is pornography."[5]

On January 24, 1989 Ted Bundy was executed for his crimes.

What about Jeffrey Dahmer?

It seems Dahmer picked up where Bundy left off. He committed his first murder in 1978 at the age of 18. Nine years later, he began a string of horrific killings. By the time of his final arrest in 1992, Dahmer was a convicted child molester and confessed homosexual who had lured 17 young men to his apartment, had sex with them, then killed them and dismembered their bodies. Some parts of his victims' bodies he ate, while others he dissolved in acid or stored in his refrigerator— specifically their heads.[6]

What was one of the significant findings in Dahmer's Milwaukee apartment where he performed most of his killings and cannibalistic acts? According to local and national newspapers, *massive quantities of hard-core pornography* and videotapes were found.[7] Was pornography the only cause of Dahmer's behavior? No. Was porn a major influence behind his activities? Absolutely.

The FBI has found that an overwhelming majority (nearly 80 percent) of twentieth century mass murderers used pornography extensively and as an integral part of their murderous, sexual activity. The FBI and police nationwide have also reported finding extensive porn collections in the homes of virtually every mass-murderer and child molester that they arrest.[8]

Dozens of studies, including the landmark Attorney General's Commission on Pornography in 1986, have shown that dangerous offenders are likely to precede their violent acts with the extended use of pornographic materials. These include child molesters, killers, and rapists.[9]

"Pornography is harmless," an enraged porn supporter and businessman snarled at me before a city council hearing. That's the argument the porn industry persistently spouts. They claim that there is no "extensive" proof that pornography is even causally related to sexual crime. How they come to this conclusion is beyond understanding. While some secular sources try to "spin" away or minimize any connection between porn and sexually abusive and violent behavior, the facts don't lie.

Human Trafficking Is Modern-day Slavery

Included in Satan's ultimate goal is the enslavement of women, children, and men. There are more slaves in the world today than at any other point in human history, with an estimated 27 million in bondage across the globe. Every number represents a life. These people are being exploited primarily for sexual activity against their will. About every 30 seconds, someone else becomes a victim, and their average age is twelve years old.[10]

According to A21 Campaign, an organization mobilized to abolish injustice in the 21st century, human trafficking is the second largest global organized crime today. It generates over $31 billion annually—about $28 billion is exclusively from sex trafficking. Sex trafficking operates by the law of supply and demand. As the demand for women, children, and men for sexual exploitation increases, the supply of slaves must also increase to meet the demand.[11]

Without question, there is a direct connection between porn, prostitution, and sex trafficking. The more enslaved a man becomes to porn, the more deviant his desires grow. This creates a rippling effect of demand and pushes him and others closer and closer to Satan's ultimate goal. Some will argue against this, but it is true. When you lay out all the pieces of the puzzle, the connection is clear. Oh, there are many steps from the starting point of a boy discovering his first centerfold and masturbating... to a man paying for forced sexual favors from an enslaved thirteen-year-old girl. But there is a connection.

What Does This Mean to You?

The findings are clear: Viewing porn in any form degrades your value of women, children, marriage, and family, and decreases your sexual satisfaction. Will you become another Ted Bundy or Jeffrey Dahmer? I don't know. But their lives are a major red alert that no one is immune to the deadly allure and influence of porn. As Pastor Mark Driscoll put it, "Lust is an insatiable parasite that you must not feed, lest it grow and lead to death."[12]

I ask again, whose mission are you helping to fulfill? If you're watching and paying for porn, you're supporting the industry and helping to spread its horrific effects. Even if you get your porn fix for free, your participation serves to strengthen these spiritual forces of darkness on the earth. Just as God works through men and women to advance His kingdom, Satan does likewise. Stop and ask yourself, *Is this what I want to be a part of? Do I want to help empower demonic forces of sexual immorality, sexual violence, and sexual enslavement on the earth? What am I going to do?*

My friend, "God paid a high price for you, so don't be enslaved by the world" (1 Corinthians 7:23 NLT). And don't be a part of the world's enslavement. It's time to break free and help others break free too! Today is the day of salvation!

Encouragement from the Heart of a Woman

Man of God, I pray that you have ears to hear, eyes to see, and a heart that will respond to the things the Spirit of God is saying here. The enemy's ultimate goal is to enslave you and then use your enslavement to enslave others. Freedom from sin and right standing with God is what Jesus died to give you and everyone slse. And it's your freedom that Satan is after.

Please wake up! We're in a war. Our enemy is cunning, subtle, and persistent. He has an army and a carefully calculated plan. I believe his plan ultimately culminates in the horrific industry of sex slavery—men paying to have sex with sex slaves. My heart is especially broken for underage slave girls. The evils these precious young girls endure is heartbreaking. Incredibly, their average age is about twelve years old, and girls as little as four years old have been eslaved for sex. Yes, four!

Many of these girls are abducted; some are deceived into thinking they are being offered good-paying jobs or an education, and some are sold by their parents to pay for family debt. Once aquired, they are repeatedly beaten, gang-raped, and drugged into submission by their captors. In many cases, they are forced to service 20 to 100 men a day. This is a miserable existence.

Repulsive, right? The enemy knows no boundaries and has no compassion for anyone. If you choose to remain in slavery to porn, I assure you, you will do things that you thought you'd never do, if you haven't done them already. You might say, "But wait, I would never rape a four-year-old little girl. All I do is look at pictures, watch a few movies, consume Victoria's Secret magazines, and masturbate. I'm not hurting anybody!" Well, maybe not directly. But when you aline yourself with the enemy—agreeing with him and participating in his activities, choosing to do things the way he does—you are actually strengthening and becoming a part of his army.

Resist this, Man of God! Don't associate or join forces with the army of darkness. Surrender yourself to Jesus and demand the enemy to repay you for what he's stolen. Rise up and take your place in the kingdom of Light! Then wreak havoc on the kingdom of darkness. I call you blessed and free!

Sum It:

Steal, kill, and destroy is the enemy's mission. As you yield to his temptations, he slowly and steadily expands his control over your mind, heart, and body. He seeks to master your every move until his ultimate goal is achieved—enslavement. Only God knows how low a man will go, but history reveals a man influenced by porn can sink extremely low. Whether you're paying for porn or getting it free, your participation serves to strengthen the spiritual forces of darkness in the earth—including the enslavement of men, women, and children. Don't be a part of enslavement. Break free and help others break free too!

Study It:

Jesus: John 3:17; 10:10; 12:46-47; 14:6; 1 John 3:8 **The Enemy**: John 8:44; 1 Peter 5:8-9; Revelation 12:10 **Sin**: Romans 6:23; 1 Corinthians 7:23

Apply It:

1 After hearing the stories of Ted Bundy and Jeffrey Dahmer and the crime connection stats, what is your reaction? How are you moved? Does it change your view of porn? If so, how?

_____

_____

_____

_____

_____

2 In light of the overall message of this chapter, whose mission would you say you're helping to fulfill? Whose side are you on—Satan's or Jesus'? What evidence in your life backs this up?

_____

_____

_____

_____

_____

3 What is your greatest takeaway from this chapter? What principles or ideas spoke to your heart most? How do they challenge you? What action(s) is God prompting you to take? Write them down.

_____

_____

_____

_____

_____

Pray It:

"Father, I repent for playing right into the enemy's hands. By viewing porn and masturbating, I've not only strengthened his hold over my life, but also over the lives of others. Please forgive me. I do **not** want to help strengthen the forces of darkness on the earth. I want **no part** in spreading sexual immorality, violence, or enslavement. I want to see it crushed. I want to help fulfill Your mission of freedom! Please destroy the lustful desire for porn in me and give me a passionate desire for You. In Jesus' name, Amen!"

ONE BROTHER TO ANOTHER

"God created marriage in a place called Eden, which means 'pleasure and delight'... God created sex for pleasure and lifelong enjoyment in marriage. ...The devil didn't create sex. ... Your genitals were created by God, and He created sex {to be} enjoyable because He's a great God and a fun God. ...{He} wants you to enjoy sex in marriage!"

— Jimmy Evans[1]
Marriage on the Rock Curriculum

Chapter 4

SEX: GOD-CREATED...
GOD-APPROVED

God created human beings in his own image. In the image of God he created them; male and female he created them. Then God blessed them and said, "Be fruitful and multiply. Fill the earth and govern it...." Then God looked over all he had made, and he saw that it was very good....

Genesis 1:27-28, 31 NLT

God created sex and it is spectacular! It is the foundation of all life and extremely precious in His eyes. By definition, the word sex is from the Latin word *seco*, meaning "to divide, the distinction between male and female."[2] When God created humans, He created us *in His image*, male and female. There is no "in between" category. There are no "shims"—just male and female. Both are equal in God's sight and reflect specific characteristics of who He is.

Immediately after He made the first man and woman, God blessed them and said, "Be fruitful and multiply...." What was He saying? "Have sex! Make love! Enjoy each other fully and produce children from your sexual intimacy." With this instruction, God spoke a blessing on their sexual union. Wow! God blesses sex within the confines of marriage. It's His divine design. With His blessing come purity, pleasure, health, strength, satisfaction, safety, and so much more.

Sex Was Created Before the Fall

Please note, God created sex and blessed sex *before* sin entered the world. He created male organs and female organs to anatomically fit together and bring pleasure and produce children before man disobeyed and fell into sin. And sex God's way carries *no shame*. When God brought Eve to Adam to consummate the marriage, "The man and his wife were both naked, and they felt *no shame*" (Genesis 2:25 NIV).

How did God feel about what He had made? Scripture says, "And God saw everything that He had made, and behold, it was **very good** (suitable, pleasant) and *He approved it completely*" (Genesis

1:31 AMP). God thinks sex between a husband and wife is awesome and approves of it completely! He has given us sex for intimate communication, celebration, pleasure, and creation of new life.

Why Is Sex Such a Big Deal?

Pure, clean sex within marriage produces **life**—life in the form of deeper love and greater overall health for both husband and wife. Studies reveal that the most enjoyable, satisfying sex is experienced between married, heterosexual couples.[3] Regardless of how Hollywood tries to market sex, they cannot manufacture true fulfillment. Yes, sex outside of marriage, including pornography with masturbation, is pleasurable—but only for a season. It is *not* blessed by God. Ultimately it produces disease and death in the form of guilt, shame, depression, loneliness, suicide, and broken lives.

Pure, clean sex within marriage also produces new life in the form of children. Don't miss this point. Scripture says, "God, not you, made marriage. His Spirit inhabits even the smallest details of marriage. And what does he want from marriage? Children of God, that's what. So guard the spirit of marriage within you. Don't cheat on your spouse" (Malachi 2:14-15 The Message).

What kind of children does God want? Children trained and raised to be godly.[4] This is one of the main reasons Satan fights so hard to pervert sex. He hates God and those created in His image. He knows that godly seed will advance God's kingdom and wreak havoc on his.

The sexual union between husband and wife is the most powerful connection on the face of the earth. It gives us the ability to create life—a life with an eternal spirit that will live forever. Just as the Father created us in His image, He empowers us to create children in our image and then train them to be godly. Life—not just temporary but *eternal*—comes through sex. What an awesome privilege...what an awesome responsibility.

Sex Is the Ultimate Connection

Sex is the most intimate level by which we can know another person. God-created, God-blessed sex is an expression of deep, sincere love and devotion that involves every part of who we are. Through sexual intercourse, a man and woman not only connect in *body* but also in *soul* and *spirit*. Your soul is your mind, will, and emotions. During sex, your thoughts, desires, and feelings are engaged and yielded to the other person. Likewise, your spirit, the deepest part of who you are, is also fused together with your mate.

God, speaking through Paul, declares, "There's more to sex than mere skin on skin. Sex is as much spiritual mystery as physical fact. As written in Scripture, 'The two become one.' Since we want to become spiritually one with the Master, we must not pursue the kind of sex that avoids commitment and intimacy, leaving us more lonely than ever— the kind of sex that can never 'become one'" (1 Corinthians 6:16-17 The Message). What a clear description of a person addicted to porn: no real intimacy and lonelier than ever. Been there. Done that. Never want to go there again.

Remember, God said it is *not* good for man to be *alone* (Genesis 2:18). This includes being alone and relieving yourself sexually while looking at porn. God's divine design is for you to enjoy sexual fulfillment *within marriage*. There is no stronger, life-giving bond than sex God's way. My friend, hear and heed God's warning: "Run from sexual sin! No other sin so clearly affects the body as this one does. For sexual immorality is a sin against your own body" (1 Corinthians 6:18 NLT).

Keep the Fire in the Fireplace

Picture this: A roaring flame, the crackling sounds of solid oak burning, glowing embers radiating shades of red, all carefully contained within the rugged walls of a stone fireplace. Ahhh... Few things are more welcome on a bone-chilling day! If we keep the fire in the fireplace, it provides warmth, enjoyment, and heat for cooking. Remove the fire from the fireplace and it will burn the house down.

The same is true with sex. Within the boundaries of marriage, sex provides warmth, enjoyment, and helps keep a couple cooking in red-hot love. Remove sex from the marriage bed and the fire of lust will burn out of control and destroy lives. This is why God says, "Honor marriage, and guard the sacredness of sexual intimacy between wife and husband. God draws a firm line against casual and illicit sex" (Hebrews 13:4 The Message).

Sex outside of marriage in any form is a counterfeit and will eventually bring destruction. This includes *fornication*, sex between two unmarried people; *adultery*, sex with a married woman or man; *homosexuality*, sex between two men or two women; and *viewing pornography* while masturbating. Again, God's divine design is sex within marriage—one man and one woman for life. It is God-blessed and God-approved. And "because God created this organic union of the two sexes, no one should desecrate his art by cutting them apart" (Mark 10:9 The Message).

Encouragement from the Heart of a Woman

*Sex, God's way, is a beautiful thing! As a woman who is married to a man who had a pornography issue, I can tell you firsthand that sexual gratification achieved outside of God's design equals heartbreak. God's way is **always** the best way. What He designs, He designs well! The counterfeit design of the enemy lacks everything of lasting value. Self-gratification through porn is shallow and leaves the victim—and a victim he is—shamed and guilt-ridden.*

God designed sex to be an act between two people connected on every level. As you have sought to receive sexual gratification through masturbation and pornography, you have removed your wife from her rightful position. She alone has been ordained by God to meet your sexual needs. When you take her out of the equation, you no longer have His blessing, and it is impossible for you to be satisfied. The outcome will always be frustration and loneliness, and your needs will never be met.

Think about it. Sex is the one need only your wife can meet so you can be blessed with guilt-free fulfillment. Everything else can be done by someone else. Someone else can cook and clean for you, purchase your clothes, write out the bills, keep your calendar, and even raise your kids. But sex is the one thing that only she has God's approval to do for you. As Eve was created to be a helpmeet for Adam, so was your wife created. She is truly a gift from God to you.

Please understand as you have struggled with sexual temptation, she has been intensely damaged. The only way I can describe it is this: Coming to grips with Vincent's porn issues was like him taking a machete and ripping through my flesh repeatedly. The violation and pain was deep and intense. Unfortunately, his "I'm sorry," was just not able to heal and restore me. Only Jesus could. The same is true for your wife. Only Jesus can heal her, your marriage, and your sexual union.

*Man of God, **pray** for her, and ask her to pray for you. Give her time to heal. In the meantime, treat her like the treasure she is. Ask the Lord to teach you how to value her for the gift she is intended to be. With Him, all things are possible, and no matter how badly your marriage has been damaged by sexual sin, He can restore your relationship. God restored the relationship between Vincent and me, and He'll do the same for you and your wife!*

Sum It:

Sex is God-created and God-approved. His divine design is one man and one woman for life, experiencing sexual ecstasy within the safety of marriage. Sex was created *before* sin entered the world, and it is the most powerful and intimate connection we can experience in this life. Hear and heed God's warning: "Run from sexual sin!"

Study It:

Genesis 1:27-28, 31; 2:21-25; Malachi 2:14-15; 1 Corinthians 6:16-20; Proverbs 5; 6:20-29; 7; Matthew 5:27-30; Mark 10:6-9; Hebrews 13:4

Apply It:

1 How do you see sex differently after reading this chapter? In your own words, describe sex the way God created it to be.

_____

_____

_____

_____

_____

2 Why do you think Satan fights so hard to entice you into the trap of pornography? What lies has he used to get you to give in? How can you guard yourself better in these areas?

_____

_____

_____

_____

_____

Pray and ask the Holy Spirit for His input. No one knows your heart like Him.

3 A major key to breaking free from the self-centered tendencies of porn is to get "you" off your mind. Realize your wife is hurting and needs healing. Get quiet before God and pray, "Lord, how can I value and appreciate my wife and sincerely express it in ways she can receive it?"

_____

_____

_____

_____

Be still and listen for what the Holy Spirit speaks to your heart. Write what He says.

4 What is your greatest takeaway from this chapter? What scriptures, principles or ideas spoke to your heart most? How do they challenge you? What action(s) is God prompting you to take?

_____

_____

_____

_____

Things I Want to Remember:

Pray It:

"Father, thank You for the gift of sex. Please forgive me for accepting and settling for the enemy's counterfeit version of porn. Forgive me for being self-centered and not valuing my wife. Give me wisdom and discernment to recognize and reject Satan's lies about sex—from the media, others, and even my own flesh. By Your grace I will run from every trace of sexual sin. Help me see and experience sex the way you originally intended...in all its beauty, strength, love, and pleasure. Help me to value my wife and see her as the gift she truly is. Help me express genuine love and appreciation to her. In Jesus' name, Amen."

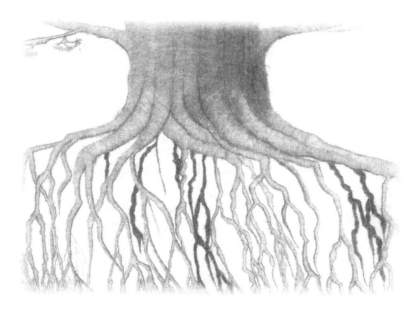

"How Did I Get Here?"

Discovering Your Roots

ONE BROTHER TO ANOTHER

*"The Lord knows very well that you cannot change your own heart and cannot cleanse your own nature. However, He also knows that He can do both. ...**All things are possible with God** (Matthew 19:26). He can reverse the direction of your desires and the current of your life. Instead of going downward from God, He can make your whole being tend upward **toward** God. ...If you yield yourself up to His divine working, the Lord will alter your nature. He will subdue the old nature and breathe new life into you. Put your trust in the Lord Jesus Christ."*

— Charles H. Spurgeon[1]
All of Grace

Chapter 5

EVERYONE HAS A STORY

*...I want to encourage you and give **my testimony**
that this is the true grace of God....*

1 Peter 5:12 GNT

Everyone has a story. My story begins with the fact that I always liked girls—always. I never went through a girl-hating stage. As far back as I can remember, I was chasing girls around the playground, playing house, and buddying up to the babysitter. Age didn't matter. If it was a girl, I liked her.

Exposed at an Early Age

It happened when I was about eight. I saw pornography for the first time. A "friend" called me and said, "You gotta come see what I found." When I arrived at his house, he showed me a huge footlocker filled with dozens of porn magazines—soft and hard-core. I can still smell the mildew-stained pages. Up to that point, I had never seen a naked woman. At first sight I was confused and grossed out. I didn't understand what I was looking at. After a few minutes of my friend showing me pictures, I had had enough and told him to put it away. Ironically, even though I was repulsed, I wanted to see it again.

Time passed. I was now about eleven. I spent the day at another friend's house across town. No one was home initially, so he took me into his parents' room, opened his dad's dresser, and "Jackpot!" Another pile of porn. A few months later, I was given my first centerfold. Oddly enough, it came from a girl I was working with at a Christian school work program.

Again and again, scenarios like these played out. In between early exposures, I discovered the lingerie section of the Sears and JCPenney catalogs. They became regular viewing. Access to porn increased as I took summer jobs at a seafood dock and the local mall. Every time I looked and lusted, uneasiness and guilt increasingly gripped my gut. I knew in my heart it wasn't right, but I couldn't stop. A monster had been awakened within, and I didn't know how to put him back to sleep.

Show and Tell

Interwoven among exposures to porn were a number of other "experiences." Sometime between the ages of six and eight, I was alone with two female cousins—one a year older and one a year younger. For some reason, the older one had the idea to pull down her underwear and show me how we were *different*. Her sister quickly followed suit. I got an eyeful.

A few years later, I was by a neighbor's house. She and her friend were having a sleepover and decided to get ready for bed early. Just before I went home, they called me into the bedroom. As I entered, I saw them laughing and jumping up and down on the bed. As their nightgowns went up and down, it quickly became apparent they had on no underwear. Again, I got an eyeful.

About the same time, there was a girl at school who really seemed to like me. Magnetically I was drawn to any cute girl who gave me attention. But this brief encounter was more than I expected. One day while sitting next to her in class, she took my hand and placed it between her legs. Nothing like that had ever happened before. I was dumbfounded and gripped with excitement simultaneously. This, coupled with a series of sensual gestures and handwritten notes, later revealed that this girl had done things of which I was clueless. Similar encounters took place years later in seventh grade and again when I was a senior. In most cases, my "inexperience" quickly diverted each girl's attraction to another guy. Although I was heartbroken then, I realize now it was God's mercy.

As I moved into junior high, my hormones kicked into high gear. Uniforms were required. This meant the girls wore skirts, creating an opportunity for a "free show" as we climbed the stairs between classes. I learned to position myself just far enough below the pretty girls every chance I got. Boy, I thought I was clever. But all I was doing was playing right into the enemy's hands. Lust and lasciviousness became a major stronghold in my life, a stronghold that would hold me captive for years to come.

Mesmerized by Music, Magazines and Movies

Add to all of this a strong love for music. Unfortunately, a lot of the music I listened to was ungodly. From the summer of '81 until the spring of '89 when I met my wife, Allison, pop rock was a staple in my diet. I listened to the radio for hours on end all summer long and after school. The majority of the lyrics were laced with lust and sexual innuendos, and I knew them by heart. Songs like "Body Language," "Like a Virgin," and "I Want Your Sex" stirred up impure desires and cemented sinful patterns in my life.

By my late teens, I had developed an irregular appetite for porn. Some days I would stay clean, going a week or more without looking at anything immoral. Then something would catch my eye and the urge would surge within me to see some skin. From exercise shows and music videos on TV to swimsuit, lingerie, or soft-porn magazines...I would feast my eyes on whatever I could get my hands on. It actually seemed easier to rent or buy a soft-porn movie at the local video store than a magazine at the mall.

Amidst all this, I was going to church twice a week and trying to live for God. In my heart, I loved Him and wanted to be clean, pure, and free. And He loved me. His Spirit living in me was deeply grieved every time I gave place to porn. On days when I was overwhelmed by guilt and shame, I would take the magazine or movie I had, sneak outside at night and stuff it underneath all the trash. But often, if the garbage man hadn't come yet, I would return a couple of days later to retrieve the porn for one more fling. I felt like Dr. Jekyll and Mr. Hyde. It was a love-hate relationship. *Getting married*, I thought. *That's when all this will stop.* Again I was wrong. It didn't just go away. I brought it with me and inflicted deep pain on my precious bride. Freedom eventually came but not without a fight—a fight we would win together.

Why Share All This?

It's imperative to see how the enemy works. God says *do not be ignorant of Satan's devices* (see 2 Corinthians 2:11 KJV). The word *devices* is the Greek word *noema*, which basically means "thoughts with an evil purpose" strategically brought against you.[2] Satan's top target is children, as we'll see more clearly in the next chapter. The two devices he uses most effectively to gain control of kids' hearts are the media and their friends. Satan masterfully manipulates the media and our relationships to produce and plant his perversion. Negative peer pressure compounds and reinforces the media's affects. Add to this mix a lack of godly instruction from the Word, and you have a recipe for disaster.

So what's *your* story? How did you grow up? What kinds of movies, music, magazines, and TV shows did you feed your spirit? Who did you hang around? What kind of things did you experience? We don't look back to cast blame. We look back to learn how the enemy got in. Each ungodly choice we make is a point of entry for the enemy. To move forward in freedom, we must repent of our actions and ask God to clean and heal us within. We don't want to dwell on the past, but we certainly want to learn from it and not repeat it.

Your story is still being written, and so is mine. As I have surrendered my life to God, He has set me free from the prison of porn. He has taught me several principles from His Word to gain and maintain purity. That's what we will explore together through the remainder of this book. God is not mad at you. He loves you intensely! His arms are open wide for you to enter and receive His love. You **will** overcome…by the blood of the Lamb and the word of your testimony (see Revelation 12:11). Your story is your testimony. God wants to begin writing a new chapter of freedom in your life…starting today!

Encouragement from the Heart of a Woman

*When Vincent and I got married, I knew **nothing** of his porn issues. I found out about three months into our marriage. I was shocked and ready to leave! I felt completely betrayed and was overwhelmed with feelings of inadequacy and loneliness. I took his issues and made them mine. I became self-focused and **believed** the problem was all about me. While he felt condemned, shameful, and guilt-ridden, I was angry, hurt, and frustrated. We were both self-focused, trying to fix ourselves—the perfect ingredients for strife and discord to flourish. We were playing right into the enemy's hands, working his plan perfectly.*

After years of crying and praying to God for help, I finally heard Him say something that changed the way I saw the situation. That day, my precious Counselor, the Holy Spirit, told me, "Vincent's issue with porn is not about you. You are not the first one to receive hurt and pain from his sin. I am." In that moment, it was as if I could see Jesus, my Savior and his, standing between Vincent and me. And every time he violated himself and sought sexual release through porn, Christ was the first One to receive pain.

Jesus was actually shielding me from the full weight of it. After all, He was with Vincent each time he fell into the enemy's hands. It was not until I could see the situation through the eyes of Jesus—through the eyes of love—that I realized it wasn't about me at all. It was about a son of God that was entangled in a web of deception. He was being robbed of what God intended for him to have—true sexual fulfillment. With this new vision, I began to earnestly pray for Vincent's deliverance, healing, and freedom. And in the process, I received the same.

Man of God, what do you want? More sexual frustration, guilt, condemnation, and shame? A greater chasm of separation between you and your wife? That's not the life Jesus died to give you. He has a much better plan. Make prayer a priority, especially prayer for your wife! Ask the Lord to help you see her and your situation through His eyes, the way He sees it. Realize she is hurting deeply and is in need of Jesus' healing power and restoration, just as you are. Only He can go to the innermost part of where she hurts and you hurt and bring healing. You are in this together. As you get your attention off yourself and onto Christ and your wife, your healing will begin!

Sum It:

The media choices you feed on and the people you hang around are two of the greatest influences shaping who you are. They help reveal how the enemy entered your life in the past and how he is influencing you today as an adult. To move forward in freedom, repent of any wrong actions. Ask God to clean and heal you within. Surrender yourself to Him and let Him begin writing a new chapter of freedom in your life today.

Study It:

Media Choices: Romans 12:2; Proverbs 4:14-15, 23 **Relationships**: Proverbs 22:24-25; 24:1-2; 1 Corinthians 15:33; 2 Corinthians 2:11; 6:14-18 **Healing for Soul & Spirit**: 2 Timothy 3:16-17; Hebrews 4:12; James 1:21; Psalm 119:9

Apply It:

1 What's *your* story? How did you grow up? What kinds of movies, music, magazines and TV shows did you feed your spirit? Who did you hang around? What kind of things did you experience? Get quiet before God. Write what He is showing you about your life.

_____

_____

_____

_____

_____

All these things combined contribute to the way you view sex and/or your addiction to porn.

2 How is the enemy currently using your friends and the media [movies, music, TV, Internet, etc.] to plant and expand his perversion in your life? Pray and ask the Lord to help you see things through His eyes, the way He does. What "way of escape" from these devices is He showing you?

_____

_____

_____

_____

_____

Read 1 Corinthians 10:13 for God's promise to provide a "way of escape" from every temptation.

3 What is your greatest takeaway from this chapter? What scriptures, principles, or ideas spoke to your heart most? How do they challenge you? What action(s) is God prompting you to take?

_____

_____

_____

_____

_____

Things I Want to Remember:

Pray It:

"Father, thank You for loving me and not rejecting or condemning me. You know all the things I've experienced while growing up that have made me who I am. Please show me anything I need to know about my past that will empower me to live a pure life in the present and future. Reveal any patterns of behavior in my choices of media and friends that are causing me to self-destruct. I surrender myself to You. And Lord, I pray for my wife. Please forgive me for causing her so much pain. Heal her where she hurts emotionally, mentally, and spiritually. Help me to get 'me' off my mind and be mindful of You and her. Flood our hearts with Your love and grace. We will overcome by Your strength! In Jesus' name, Amen!"

ONE BROTHER TO ANOTHER

"You must think in terms of legacy. More than just a good time, you should seek a good legacy. Who do you want your sons and daughters, grandsons and granddaughters to marry? How do you want them to treat others and be treated sexually? How you behave today sets in motion a future for sexual freedom or slavery, life or death—a future not only for your life but also for the generations that will follow in your wake."

— Mark Driscoll[1]

Real Marriage

Chapter 6

LIKE FATHER...LIKE SON

The Lord is slow to anger and filled with unfailing love,
forgiving every kind of sin and rebellion. But he does not excuse the
guilty. He lays the sins of the parents upon their children; the entire
family is affected—even children in the third and fourth generations.
Numbers 14:18 NLT

Satan has studied mankind for over 6,000 years. This includes your family. He knows the weaknesses of your parents, grandparents, and the generations before. He knows what "buttons" to push to increase the likelihood of you giving in to sin. He doesn't miss a trick. He initiates his attacks when we are infants—even from the time we are in the womb.

Satan Goes After the Child

From the beginning, Satan has sought to destroy the seed of mankind. After man disobeyed God in the garden, God put hostility between our offspring and the enemy's offspring, and the war for our children has been raging ever since. Why? Because godly seed advances God's kingdom and destroys the kingdom of darkness.

Satan went after Moses as a child. When word of a deliverer for God's people got out, Satan moved on Pharaoh's heart to kill all the Hebrew boys (see Exodus 1:15-22). But Moses' parents sought God for wisdom, and He gave them a plan that saved Moses' life. History was made.

Satan went after Jesus as a child. When word of the Messiah being born in Bethlehem got out, Satan moved on King Herod's heart to kill every Jewish boy two years old and younger (see Matthew 2). But Jesus' parents heard from God and received a plan of direction that saved Jesus' life. History was made.

This pattern is repeated in the book of Revelation. Satan, the great dragon, is positioned in front of a woman in labor, waiting to devour her child when he is born. Again, his plan fails. God rescues the child and defeats the dragon (see Revelation 12). Again, history is made.

Satan is still after children today. Since 1973, he has moved on the hearts of millions, causing over 55 million children to be murdered by abortion in the U.S. alone.[2] And if he can't deceive parents to abort their children, he will try and get them to abuse them—verbally, physically, or sexually. Make no mistake: The enemy has had plans to destroy you since your conception.

But God has plans too! He has "plans for peace and not disaster, plans to give you a future filled with hope" (Jeremiah 29:11 GW). Look back over your life. Can you see the times when God made a way where there seemed to be no way? When He provided *what* you needed, *when* you needed it. When He protected you from imminent danger or even death just in the nick of time. God is the same yesterday, today, and forever! His plans will prevail as you stay in relationship with Him.

Plan "P"

Now if the enemy can't kill you at conception, he moves to Plan "P"—perversion. To *pervert* means "to turn from truth or proper purpose; to distort or twist from the true use; to turn from what's right."[3] Satan will pervert the truth about sex and everything else in life in an effort to dethrone God from your heart and destroy your life.

The most effective time for the enemy to pervert the truth is when we're young. Think about it. As children, we are like wet cement. Everything about us is moldable and pliable. The way we think, our perspective on life, our understanding of God, our personality... everything is taking shape. We are innocent, sincere, and very trusting. This "moldability" in the hands of God is great, but moldability in the hands of the enemy becomes *vulnerability*. If Satan can sow his seeds of error, perversion, and destruction in our hearts and minds, he can hinder our relationship with God and sabotage our destiny. And his most effective ammunition is to tempt us in the same areas of sin in which our ancestors struggled.

Your Family History Plays a Part

Do you remember going to see a new doctor? They handed you a form with umpteen questions about your family history. "Did anyone in your family have cancer, diabetes, heart disease" and on and on the list goes. Doctors know that if your parents and grandparents had certain problems, you are at a higher risk of having the same issues. You have a predisposition to develop the same diseases in your bloodline.

This principle holds true spiritually. Look at your family history—on both your father and mother's side. What sins are prevalent? Can you see any patterns? If your father or grandfather had problems with alcohol or drugs, the risk is high that you may have a weakness in the same area. Likewise, if your family members had problems with porn, adultery, or homosexuality, the risk is high that you too may have a weakness in one of these same areas. *You have a predisposition to develop the same sins in your family.*

This is what God means when He says "He lays the sins of the parents upon their children; **the entire family is affected**—even children in the third and fourth generations" (Numbers 14:18 NLT). This verse describes a *generational* curse—a sin pattern that is passed on from one generation to the next.

Abraham, Isaac, and Jacob give us a great example. In this family, lying was an issue. Out of fear for his life, Abraham asked Sarah to lie and say she was his sister (see Genesis 12:10-20). Isaac, Abraham's son, followed suit. For fear of his life, he lied to King Abimelech and said Rebekah, his wife, was his sister (see Genesis 26:7-10). Jacob, Isaac's son and Abraham's grandson, took lying to a new level. In order to get the firstborn blessing from his father who was blind and near death, he pretended to be his brother, Esau (see Genesis 27:1-36). Deception didn't stop there. Jacob's sons, the fourth generation from Abraham, lied to him and said their brother Joseph had been killed by a wild animal when they had actually sold him into slavery (see Genesis 37:12-36).

The point is, sin patterns not dealt with properly will be passed on from one generation to the next, often becoming more deadly. Lying, cheating, laziness, fearfulness, greed, drunkenness, worry, lust, perversion, and every other sin pattern *not repented of* will be passed on to your children and your children's children. How do you stop it?

Draw a Line in Your Bloodline!

If you're dealing with an addiction to porn, you probably have people in your bloodline who have battled sexual sin. While you can't do anything about the family members who have come before you, you can certainly do something to affect the ones who come after you. As a father and husband, you are the spiritual covering for your family. Your choices affect your wife, your children, and your grandchildren—for better or worse. Why not choose as Joshua did? Take a stand and side with God and say, "As for me and my family, we will serve the Lord" (Joshua 24:15 NLT).

Instead of passing on a generational curse, you can pass on a generational blessing! How? By bringing every sin pattern you know or feel may be operating in your bloodline to the cross of Christ. Get in agreement with God. Call sin, sin. Confess and repent of your family's sins and ask God to forgive you and wash you clean with the blood of Jesus.[4] He will forgive you and deliver you and your descendants from every generational curse that has plagued your family.

Interestingly, right after God told Moses and the Israelites about laying the sins of the parents upon their children to the third and fourth generations, He said, "But I lavish unfailing love for a *thousand generations* on those who love me and obey my commands" (Exodus 20:6 NLT). Wow! What a picture of God's merciful heart. He is always ready and willing to forgive, restore, heal, and love those who humble themselves before Him and repent of their sins.

Through Jesus Christ, **every curse is broken**. Scripture says, "Christ has rescued us from the curse pronounced by the law. When he was hung on the cross, he took upon himself the curse for our wrongdoing. For it is written in the Scriptures, 'Cursed is everyone who is hung on a tree'" (Galatians 3:13 NLT). What an awesome promise!

Friend, what are you passing on to your sons and daughters? How about your grandchildren? Help protect them from battling sexual sin. Instead of passing on a legacy of sexual perversity, pass on the righteousness of God in Jesus Christ! Make the decision to take responsibility for your actions and get in agreement with God. Call the sins of your family what God calls them—sin. Bring them to the cross of Christ and let them die there. Draw a line in your bloodline against sin, and you will not pass on the sin patterns of past generations.

Encouragement from the Heart of a Woman

Inheritance is a powerful thing. Bill Gates has three children who will likely never experience the financial stress and struggle that many do because of the inheritance he is passing on. They will probably be taught how to steward their finances in such a way that having money will not be a problem. Similarly, sex God's way is a beautiful gift we were all intended to inherit. You have the ability to pass this gift on to your children and grandchildren.

Man of God, you are not seeking sexual freedom or reading this book by accident. This is your hour to rise up and come forth in strength. We need you to fight! Your freedom matters—not only for you but for generations to come. Think about how free you would be if you would have never seen some of the things you've seen and done some of the things you've done. Like Vincent, you can choose to help guard your children from the enemy's traps. This is a priceless inheritance you have the privilege of leaving them.

Please don't allow your children and grandchildren to learn about sex from the world. Educate yourself on this stronghold that binds you and be the one who is willing to talk about it with others. Be a voice of change and a source of strength to all those around you. Give your sons and daughters and grandchildren the gift—the legacy—of sexual purity. Allow them to experience sex untainted by the enemy, in its purest, most rewarding form. As you stand and trust God for deliverance, He will grant it to you and your entire family.

Sum It:

Satan's most effective temptations against you are in the areas of weakness your ancestors struggled. You have a predisposition to develop their same sin habits. Sin patterns not dealt with properly will be passed on to the next generation. While you can't do anything about your ancestors, you can do something to help your descendants. Instead of passing on a generational curse, pass on a generational blessing! Draw a line in your bloodline. Repent of your family's sins, bring them to the cross of Christ, and the curse will be cancelled.

Study It:

Exodus 1:15-22; 20:5-6; 34:6-7; Numbers 14:18; Matthew 2; Revelation 12; Jeremiah 29:11; Genesis 12:10-20; 26:7-10; 27:1-36; 37:12-36; Galatians 3:13; Psalm 79:8-9; Proverbs 13:22; 1 John 1:9

Apply It:

1 Next to the media and your friends, the greatest influence that has shaped your life is your parents. The same holds true for your kids. What are you passing on to your sons and daughters and your grandchildren? What sin patterns or weaknesses do you see or sense operating in your bloodline?

_____

_____

_____

_____

_____

2 The best thing you can do to put a stop to the generational sins plaguing your family is to draw a line in your bloodline against the enemy. In your own words, explain how you can do this.

_____

_____

_____

_____

_____

3 Passing on a generational _blessing of purity_ is possible. In what ways might you encourage and promote sexual purity in your children, grandchildren, and others in your sphere of influence?

_____

_____

_____

_____

_____

Think about it. What do you wish you could have heard to help you avoid the trap of lust and porn? Are you willing to share this along with what God has taught you from your struggles? Pray and ask the Lord for His grace and timing to speak into the lives of your children and grandchildren.

4 What is your greatest takeaway from this chapter? What scriptures, principles or ideas spoke to your heart most? How do they challenge you? What action(s) is God prompting you to take?

_____

_____

_____

_____

_____

Things I Want to Remember:

Pray It:

"Father, thank You for saving me from a miserable life of sin through Jesus. He redeemed me and paid for my sins with His blood. I am Your heir and a joint heir with Christ. Since He lives in and through me, I have the right to overcome sin because He overcame. Please forgive me and my family for all our disobedience and sinful behavior. (Tell God any specific sin you see or sense operating in your family.) Jesus, You rescued us from every curse, taking them upon Yourself when You died on the cross. Therefore, I renounce and break every curse that has come into my life both generationally and through my own choices. By faith, I take back the ground my family and I have given to the enemy and I surrender it to You. From this day forward, help me build strongholds of righteousness in my life and the lives of my children and grandchildren. In Jesus' name, Amen!"

ONE BROTHER TO ANOTHER

"All transgression begins with sinful thinking. You who have come to Christ for a pure heart, guard against the pictures of lewdness and sensuality which Satan flashes upon the screen of your imaginations, select with care the books you read, choose discerningly the kind of entertainment you attend, the kind of associates with whom you mingle, and the kind of environment in which you place yourself. You should no more allow sinful imaginations to accumulate in your mind and soul than you would let garbage collect in your living room."

—Billy Graham[1]
The Secret of Happiness

Chapter 7

YOU ARE WHAT YOU EAT

For as he {a man} thinks in his heart, so is he.

Proverbs 23:7 AMP

The two greatest physical drives a man has are for food and sex. While our bodies are built by the physical food we eat, our spirits are built by the spiritual food we eat. *Everything* we take into our eyes and ears is food for our soul and spirit. The "food groups" from which we feed ourselves include the people we hang out with as well as our media choices—music, movies, magazines, television, books, the Internet, etc. In this chapter, we will focus on the latter.

What You See and Hear Influences What You Do

To savor the flavor of a thick, juicy steak, you open your mouth and take a bite. The entryway is your mouth, and the primary place of digestion is your stomach. With spiritual food, the entryways are your **eyes** and **ears**, and the places it's digested are your mind and heart. With our eyes and ears we take in images, sounds, and information. This includes philosophies, opinions, and ideas about sex. Our mind "chews" on them, and eventually they go down deep into our heart and become a part of who we are. And the way we think in our heart is what we become (see Proverbs 23:7).

Now, you may be thinking, *What I watch and listen to doesn't affect me.* I used to think and say that too. But the truth is *everything* you read, *everything* you watch, and *everything* you listen to has a definite degree of effect on you. Every image on the Internet and in movies, every story in a magazine or book, and every song on the radio or a CD is "food for thought." They shape your thinking and influence your actions more than you realize.

Advertisers are hip to the impact of what people see and hear. Companies like Anheuser-Busch, General Motors, and Walt Disney recently spent $3-4 million dollars a pop for every 30-second ad they ran during the Super-Bowl.[2] Yes, different things affect different people in different ways, and some things affect us more than others. But the point is, **everything** we see with our EYES and hear with our EARS has an effect on us.

World-renown evangelist Billy Graham said, "All transgression begins with sinful thinking. You who have come to Christ for a pure heart, guard against the pictures of lewdness and sensuality which Satan flashes upon the screen of your imaginations, select with care the books you read, choose discerningly the kind of entertainment you attend, the kind of associates with whom you mingle, and the kind of environment in which you place yourself. You should no more allow sinful imaginations to accumulate in your mind and soul than you would let garbage collect in your living room."[3]

Garbage In...Garbage Out

In my teen years and early twenties, I struggled greatly with lustful thoughts and keeping a pure mind. During that time, I was feeding my spirit junk food from the radio on a regular basis. Four to five days a week I pumped iron in my garage. When I did, the radio was on, and virtually every song I heard was laced with lyrics about sex.

Add to my choice of music a smorgasbord of junk food from TV and movies. Having a portable TV and hours alone at home gave me access to exercise shows, music videos, and programs with images I wish I could erase from my memory. Sneaking a peek at the Solid Gold Dancers, the babes on Baywatch, and the immorality on MTV was a secret pastime. I also viewed videos while at friends' houses that I knew in my heart I shouldn't be watching. Porn's power was fortified by images from R-rated box-office hits like *Stripes*, *Porky's*, and *Friday the 13th*. By today's standards, these may seem tame. Nevertheless, with each viewing I empowered impurity. A perverted image of sex and a degraded image of women grew stronger in my life.

As I said before, I was a Christian with a desire to keep my mind pure and free from lust and porn. But in my immaturity, I failed to see the connection between my struggles and my media choices. I didn't realize that the music, movies, and TV shows I was feeding my spirit were a steady diet of the deadly toxin I was trying to avoid. I'd go to church on Sunday, ask God to forgive me for entertaining filthy thoughts, and then go right back to feeding myself the same garbage days later. It's no wonder I couldn't break free.

By my late teens, my struggle for freedom was intense. God's Spirit living in me became more and more grieved every time I gave place to porn. He convicted me, bringing uneasiness within, but His voice was drowned out by the enemy's accusations of shame, guilt, and condemnation. That's when I cried out to God for answers, and He began to reveal the "WHY" behind what I was I thinking and feeling: "For as he {a man} thinks in his heart, so is he" (Proverbs 23:7 AMP).

Then I did the math. Each week, I was feeding my spirit 35 to 45 hours of immoral messages and images. They were poisoning my soul, negatively shaping my mind, will, and emotions to see evil as normal. At the same time, I was only feeding my spirit about 10 hours of healthy things, like God's Word, Christian teaching, and uplifting music and movies. The numbers were not in my favor. Now, I'm not saying God wants us to be in church every time the doors open or have our nose in the Bible from daylight till dark. I'm also not saying we can only watch Christian TV, listen to Christian music, and read Christian books. What I am saying is **we need to be aware of what we're feeding our spirit**—we need to guard our heart with all diligence and get rid of every sin and unnecessary weight that draws us away from God.[4]

What Are You Eating?

Stop and take an honest look at yourself. What are you feeding your spirit? What media choices are you selecting on the Internet, your cell phone, and TV? If Jesus was physically sitting next to you while you were watching and listening, would you do anything differently? The truth is, He is with you. If you're a believer and have surrendered your life to God, you are the home of His Holy Spirit (see 1 Corinthians 3:16; 6:18-20). He will never leave you (see Matthew 28:20). He is ready, willing and able to set you free from porn, but He will not force His will upon you. You must *choose life* so that you and your children can live!

Cakes, candy, soda, and chips may taste good while they're in your mouth, but a steady diet of these will eventually produce sickness and disease. Similarly, sexually-charged images are stimulating and satisfying—but only for a season. You cannot visually and mentally "chew" on scanty images of women and expect to have a pure mind and heart. Eventually, the results of such a diet will bring devastating consequences to those who eat it and affect those around them.

Don't let the devil dupe you another day. Accept responsibility for what you're feeding your spirit. Ask God to forgive you for giving the enemy an open door to operate in your life. Pray for His power and desire to exchange poor media choices for healthy ones. In the coming chapters, the importance of watching what you eat spiritually will become clearer as we talk about *starving your flesh, feeding your spirit, guarding your heart, and avoiding the scenes of temptation.*

Encouragement from the Heart of a Woman

Man of God, pray and ask God to reveal to you how much your media choices are affecting your life. As you realize their impact, you will be more likely to fight harder to make changes. What you choose to listen to, watch, and entertain is an example to all who are around you. Don't be duped into believing that what you do in secret doesn't affect others. The Bible says that our acts of worship are a sweet aroma to God (see 2 Corinthians 2:14-15). I can only imagine that the rest of our acts have an aroma as well. I'm going to go out on a limb and take a guess that our impurity stinks to Him! And this smell has a way of traveling and affecting everyone in close proximity.

As you seek and fight for your freedom, consider doing a fast from all media. "Really?" you say. "That sounds drastic." Well, how badly do you want to be free? The media you have chosen has dramatically impacted your situation in life. If doing a complete media fast seems impossible at this point, then do a partial fast. But by all means, change your media choices from negative to positive. Exchange the familiar with something new. After all, you cannot expect to get different results if you keep doing the same thing!

There are numerous good books, audio books, teachings, and music to choose from. Recently, I have been touched and challenged by the books and podcasts of Mark Batterson, John and Lisa Bevere, and Christine Cain. Music has also dramatically affected my life and the way I view things. I encourage you to connect with some new Christian artists. God has really poured out His amazing Spirit into the music we have today. Find some new songs to feed on. Ask a friend who is experiencing victory in this area of his life what kind of media he consumes. Remember to guard your heart, for it truly is the wellspring of your life!

Sum It:

You are what you eat—both physically and spiritually. Garbage in will produce garbage out. Be careful what you feed your spirit, especially your media menu choices. Everything you see with your eyes and hear with your ears has an effect on you. Guard your heart with all diligence and get rid of every sin and unnecessary weight that draws you away from God. Make life-giving choices, and you and your family will live!

Study It:

Proverbs 4:21-27; 23:7; Luke 6:43-45; 1 Corinthians 3:16; 6:18-20; Galatians 6:7-9; Deuteronomy 30:19; Hebrews 11:25; 12:1-2

Apply It:

1 What are you eating? What specific movies, music, magazines, and TV shows are you feeding your spirit? What are you ordering on your Internet, cell phone, and TV? (Be honest.)

_____

_____

_____

2 Do the math: How much time are you investing feeding your spirit *good* things? How about *unhealthy* things? Which has the upper hand? What is God showing you from this ratio?

_____

_____

_____

3 Ask yourself, *Is what I'm watching, reading, listening to, etc. strengthening my walk with God? Is this the kind of behavior I want to see in myself, my wife, and my children? What kind of effect is this entertainment having on me and my family—does it cultivate the fruit of God's Spirit or the desires of the flesh?* Answer each as honestly as you can.

_____

_____

_____

4 What is your greatest takeaway from this chapter? What scriptures, principles, or ideas spoke to your heart most? How do they challenge you? What action(s) is God prompting you to take?

_____

_____

_____

Pray It:

"Father, I've fed my spirit a lot of junk food over the years, and I had no idea what I was doing most of the time. Purge from my memory all ungodly images and messages with the blood of Jesus. Detox my mind, will, and emotions from the perversion and deception of the enemy and this world. If I own any immoral movies, music, magazines, etc., show them to me and give me the strength to get rid of them. Holy Spirit, help me be aware of my media choices. Sound an alarm the moment I begin to think of selecting ungodly entertainment, and give me the grace not to buy, rent, watch, or listen to it. Thank You for loving me and helping me make better choices. In Jesus' name, Amen!"

ONE BROTHER TO ANOTHER

"Sexual intimacy is a complex neurochemical and hormonal event. It is one of the most powerful God-given pathways by which men form attachments. In viewing and acting out to pornography, men form attachments to the images and not real people. ...Pornography enslaves the viewer to an image instead of bonding him to his wife."

—**William M. Struthers, Ph.D.**[1]

Chapter 8

THE LOOK IS THE HOOK

*…Your heart can be corrupted by lust even quicker
than your body. Those leering looks you think nobody
notices—they also corrupt.*

—Matthew 5:28 The Message

The eyes—no part of a man's anatomy draws him into sin faster. It's what drew King David into the sin of adultery and eventually murder. God's Word says, "…As he *looked* out over the city, he noticed a woman of unusual beauty taking a bath," and the rest is history (2 Samuel 11:2 NLT). Job knew the trouble the eyes can bring and the trap they can spring. That's why he said, "I made a solemn pact with myself never to undress a girl with my eyes" (Job 31:1 The Message). Indeed, *the look is the hook that leads to sin.*

Man Is a Visual Being

Man's extraordinary visual capacity was originally pure when God created it. Genesis 2:19 (GW) states, "The Lord God had formed all the wild animals and all the birds out of the ground. Then he brought them to the man to see what he would call them. Whatever the man called each creature became its name."

Don't miss this. Adam was immersed in a flawless environment—lush vegetation, pristine air, perfect peace, and a perfect temperature. He enjoyed face-to-face fellowship with the Father, and the Father was personally involved in Adam's work. One by one, the Almighty paraded each creature before Adam's eyes, and he *looked* at them and called them what they are. Wow! What extraordinary visual capacity. He had no courses in zoology or biology—no *National Geographic* or encyclopedia of animals to draw from. He was writing science by what he saw!

When there was no suitable mate for Adam, God put him to sleep and "built" him a loving companion from his own flesh. And boy was she built! When God brought her to Adam and he laid his eyes on her beauty, he shouted, "WO…MAN!" Adam looked at Eve's naked body and was astronomically aroused! His sensors were firing like never before, and it was *good—very good*. In fact, it was God-blessed!

Do you see the power of man's sight? God created an incredible neurological connection between our eyes and our brains. A connection so tight, as anatomist Dr. David Menton explains, that the eye is actually a "bud" off of the brain in our embryonic stage. As men, what we see stirs our soul—our *thoughts, feelings,* and *desires* are ignited and excited. Friend, this is how you were created *before* sin entered the world. You are wired to be aroused by what you see. Therefore, you must learn how to harness this incredible capacity and use it for good. How? By God's grace!

The Chemical Reaction from Sexual Attraction

God has wired men to be keenly sensitive to visual, sexual signals such as a naked, or partially naked, female form, *for the purpose of bonding*. These signals trigger neurological, chemical, and hormonal reactions that are the source of the sexual *rush*. The sight of a beautiful woman to a man is like lighting an internal fuse that quickly detonates a keg of dynamite.

The way we learn to respond to and manage this explosion of energy forms psychological and behavioral *habits*. These habits (repeated patterns of arousal and response) eventually form a neurological *pathway*—an established "road" within our central nervous system for impulses to travel on. This pathway then becomes the preferred route, or well-beaten path, you and I mentally and emotionally travel each time we are visually aroused.[2]

There are several regions of the brain that are involved when men act out sexually—the ventral tegmental area (VTA) is one of them. The VTA is a group of neurons (specialized cells that transmit nerve impulses) located in the midbrain close to the brain stem.[3] The midbrain is a part of the central nervous system that helps to relay information for vision, hearing, and arousal.[4] As a man, when you view pornography, there is an increase in the activity of your VTA cells, which means an increase in the production of the neurochemical *dopamine*.[5]

What's so important about dopamine? Dopamine is one of the major "feel good" chemicals our body produces and secretes. It is a neurotransmitter—a chemical released by nerve cells that sends signals to other nerve cells. Dopamine in the brain stimulates feelings of happiness and excitability and can improve your overall level of contentment. Several drugs, including cocaine and alcohol, act on the

VTA cells to release dopamine and create the sensation of happiness.[6] Dopamine is also the "craving" chemical activated when a man views porn or any sexually stimulating image.

The VTA, together with a handful of other brain regions, appear to be the sites responsible for the psychological experiences of craving and euphoria that underlie the sexual experience. When you act out sexually, your body releases the brain's natural chemical reinforcers: dopamine, endorphins, norepinephrine, and oxytocin. As this happens, *a memory of the event is chemically burned into your mind, and the memory binds you to the object you connect to the experience.*[7] Well-known author and speaker Stephen Arterburn confirms this saying, "Men receive a chemical high from sexually charged images—a hormone called epinephrine is secreted into the bloodstream, which locks into the memory whatever stimulus is present at the time of the emotional excitement."[8]

Within the boundaries of marriage, the release of all these "feel good" chemicals is awesome! Why? Because it burns a healthy memory of sexual intimacy in your mind and bonds you to your wife. Outside of marriage, which includes viewing porn while masturbating, this God-given function turns deadly. Instead of being bound to your wife, you become bound to the image you are focused on—porn. Pornography enslaves you, the viewer, to an image rather than binding you to your wife.[9] This memory branded on your brain subconsciously motivates you to keep recreating the same event so that you can experience the same "high" using the same methods. The result—bondage.

Hear and Heed Jesus' Warning

Are you beginning to see the light? Visual stimulation is sexual foreplay for men. It is a powerful part of our sexual fulfillment, and therefore, we must learn to control our look so we don't get hooked on the wrong thing. This is why Jesus warns, "You have heard that it was said, You shall not commit adultery. But I say to you that everyone who so much as *looks at a woman with evil desire* for her has already committed adultery with her in his heart" (Matthew 5:27-28 AMP). My friend, *the look is the hook!*

How are we to deal with it? Jesus continues, "...If you want to live a morally pure life, here's what you have to do: You have to *blind your right eye* the moment you catch it in a lustful leer. You have to choose to live one-eyed or else be dumped on a moral trash pile" (v. 29 The Message). Now, Jesus is not telling us to literally gouge out our eye if we're looking and lusting after women. He is telling us to take every necessary precaution to blind ourselves from looking at women on paper, on the computer, or in person as objects for sexual consumption. This includes replaying and fantasizing over past images you've seen. Only your wife deserves your gaze of desire.

Jesus doesn't stop there. He completes His prescription for pulverizing perversity by saying, "And if your *right hand* serves as a trap to ensnare you or is an occasion for you to stumble and sin, cut it off and cast it from you. It is better that you lose one of your members than that your entire body should be cast into hell (Gehenna)" (v. 30 AMP). Did you catch what He said? What do we usually end up doing with our *hand* while looking and lusting after women in porn? You got it—we masturbate. Could it be that Jesus is addressing this? For certain, He is saying, "Don't allow your hand to be an instrument of sin. Do whatever you need to do to not give in to temptation. It's deadly—so deadly it can eventually send you to hell." Men, we would do well to heed His instruction.

Develop a New Plan of Action!

Are you seeing things you've never seen before? Are you convicted in your heart of a lack of control over your eyes? It's time to develop a new plan of action! It's time to learn how to harness your gaze in a new direction. "We do this by keeping our eyes on Jesus, the champion who initiates and perfects our faith..." (Hebrews 12:2 NLT). With God's help, you can master the art of guarding your heart...you can imprison every impure thought and fix your eyes on God's heavenly prize—the wife of your youth. We will cover these points in the chapters ahead, so stay tuned!

Encouragement from the Heart of a Woman

Man of God, your sexual appetite is as normal as your physical appetite. You were created to desire/crave intimacy with a woman. How else could you fulfill God's very first mandate to "be fruitful and multiply" (Genesis 1:22 NLT)? Everything good comes from Him—and brother, sex is good. In fact, it's great when we operate inside the guidelines God lays out in His Word. However, doing anything less leaves us frustrated, condemned, empty, angry, and alone. These are the exact feelings both Vincent and I experienced when we first started coming out of this.

Guard your eyes, Man of God; this is where the battle begins. You were created to be aroused by what you see; guard your eyes to be aroused by only what you can have. Just as you wouldn't choose to satisfy your physical hunger with food laced with feces, don't choose to satisfy your sexual hunger with poisonous porn. Looking and lusting after women's bodies will always leave you lacking. Women have **many** gifts and talents that reach far beyond sexual fulfillment. When you only view women as sex objects, you miss out on everything else we bring to the table—this is especially true of your wife.

Train yourself to look beyond a woman's physical body and see the person she really is. This begins with your wife. God will help you, if you ask Him. His Holy Spirit will give you the ability to see all the skills, talents, wisdom, and creativity He has given her. If you have been chained up by porn for many years, this may take some time to accomplish, but with God all things are possible! (See Matthew 19:26.)

Realize you may be called upon by God to give an account for how you steward the gifts and talents entrusted to you in the form of your wife. She was created to be your helper. So look for ways to encourage her to flourish in her God-given gifts and talents. He has specific plans and purposes for her. She is so much more than your sexual fulfillment. Yes, train yourself to look to her alone for your sexual fulfillment, but also train yourself to really listen to her wants, needs, and dreams. Renew your mind with God's Word (see Romans 12:2). Your future is bright, Man of God. I call you blessed!

Sum It:

The look is the hook that leads to sin. Visual stimulation is sexual foreplay for men and a powerful part of our sexual fulfillment. Therefore, you must learn to control your eyes so you don't get hooked on the wrong thing. Allow your passion to bond you with your bride and burn memories in your mind of her alone. Make a covenant with the Lord, your wife, and yourself never to look upon another woman with lust in your heart.

Study It:

Genesis 2:18-25; Job 31:1; Proverbs 4:25-27; Matthew 5:27-30; Luke 11:34-36; Philippians 4:8; 1 Thessalonians 5:21-22.

Apply It:

1 What new insights have you learned about the visual capacity God has given you?

_____

_____

_____

_____

2 In your own words, describe your chemical reaction to sexual attraction—what happens in your body when you *see* a sexually-charged image and then act out sexually?

_____

_____

_____

_____

3 In light of the previous question, what is God's positive purpose in creating you this way? How does this knowledge motivate you to want to give your visual appetite exclusively to your wife?

_____

_____

_____

_____

4 Carefully reread Jesus' words in Matthew 5:27-30. What is the Holy Spirit showing you in verses 27-28? How about verses 29-30?

_____

_____

_____

_____

5 What is your greatest takeaway from this chapter? What scriptures, principles, or ideas spoke to your heart most? How do they challenge you? What action(s) is God prompting you to take?

_____

_____

_____

_____

Things I Want to Remember:

Pray It:

"*Father, forgive me. I've allowed myself to have a visual free-for-all, looking and lusting at women in porn and in person more times than I can remember. According to Your Word, I have committed adultery in my heart. Please forgive me and wash me clean. Change me! 'Turn my eyes from worthless things, and give me life through your word' (Psalm 119:37 NLT). Take away the impure desire to look and lust after other women, and give me desire for my wife alone. Heal the hurts I have inflicted on her. May I be visually stimulated and satisfied by her alone. Thank You for Your mercy, Your forgiveness, and Your grace! In Jesus' name, Amen!*"

ONE BROTHER TO ANOTHER

"...Clearly sex can take on all the characteristics of an addiction. All addictions have one thing in common: they function as an emotional anesthesia. They serve to kill the pain of unpleasant emotions or experiences. ...Because sex provides tremendous pleasure, it easily becomes a means of escape. It is both a tranquilizer for anxiety and a stimulant to provide a boost during a depressed mood. Either way, it provides an escape from some of life's more painful realities."

—Dr. Archibald Hart[1]
The Sexual Man

Chapter 9

IT'S THE FRUIT OF A DEEPER ROOT

The ax is ready to cut down the trees at the roots;
every tree that does not bear good fruit will be
cut down and thrown in the fire.
Luke 3:9 GNT

Lookin' for love in all the wrong places... There is a lot of truth in this best-selling song snippet by Johnny Lee. For me and countless others, I wasn't just looking for love. I was looking for acceptance, comfort, and relief from rejection. My addiction to porn and masturbation was not just a lust issue. It was a learned pattern of behavior I developed during puberty and young adulthood—it was my *coping mechanism* for dealing with stress.

Dr. William Struthers, associate professor of psychology at Wheaton College, reveals, "Pornography and the craving for sexual intimacy are rarely the root causes of the problems. As you dig deeper into the reasons someone looks at porn, you will find that it is a symptom of a much deeper, human problem. Enlightenment is an educational process whereby we identify the environmental, emotional, and psychological needs and triggers underlying the sin pattern."[2]

For years, I thought my porn problem was solely linked to lust, and I attacked it from that angle only. But that wasn't true. There were emotional needs and environmental factors involved that needed to be addressed. As author Randy Alcorn aptly said, when we turn to porn and masturbation, "...we are medicating a pain—maybe loneliness, discouragement, rejection, or fear. There is something deeper than just the obvious desire. We need to address the *root* issue, to ask God to meet the needs that make us vulnerable to the temptation."[3]

As strange as it may seem, I did not come to this *full* realization until I began working on this book. The fact is, many men battling porn are clueless to the deeper root cause. You may be one of them. In this chapter, we will explore the connection between porn addiction and our craving for comfort and emotional stability. We will also learn about the better way—God's way—of receiving comfort and peace.

What Strengthens Porn's Addictive Nature?

We live in a fallen world, and all of us have faced our fair share of discouragement, rejection, and abuse. Consequently, we each develop ways of handling these stressful situations. Many times porn and masturbation are unconsciously used to soothe our aching heart and help "process our pain." Porn addiction becomes our coping mechanism for dealing with discomfort.

Using his groundbreaking nationwide research, psychologist and acclaimed author Dr. Archibald Hart offers powerful insights in his book *The Sexual Man*. Explaining the sex addiction connection, Dr. Hart says,

> "...Clearly sex can take on all the characteristics of an addiction. All addictions have one thing in common: they function as an **emotional anesthesia**. They serve to kill the pain of unpleasant emotions or experiences. People resort to addictions to numb their pain or to escape from life's responsibilities.
>
> ...Because sex provides tremendous pleasure, it easily becomes a means of escape. It is both a tranquilizer for anxiety and a stimulant to provide a boost during a depressed mood. Either way, it provides an escape from some of life's more painful realities. And some men turn to sex to relieve their tension..."[4]

Just before I turned twelve, my father took on a new job that moved my family and me about twenty miles across town. It was away from everything and everyone I knew. I was entering middle school—sixth grade to be precise. Of all my school years, this was the worst. I had no friends, and instead of having one classroom with one teacher, I now had six. Wearing glasses, lacking confidence, and being fearful made me a prime target of bullies. Although I hated to fight, I found myself on the receiving end of someone's fist or foot about once a week. On top of all this, I was entering puberty, and as the son of a full-time minister, people had "great expectations" of me. Indeed, the stage was set for plenty of stress.

A myriad of emotions swirled within me. Rejection from peers, fear of being picked on, and anger against those mistreating me stewed in my soul like a pressure cooker. I craved comfort and acceptance. While I received healthy doses from my parents, for which I am extremely grateful, the deluge of difficulty I was dealing with became overwhelming. I turned inward and tried to handle things on my own. Without thinking, I began to relieve myself sexually while looking at porn. This practice became my *emotional anesthesia*—my way of escape from life's painful realities.

Time passed, and I took my coping mechanism for dealing with discomfort right into adulthood. As a newly married man, when rejection resurfaced or unsolvable situations at work began to stress me out, I unconsciously gravitated toward sexual release through porn. This is not uncommon. Dr. Hart shares that while some forms of stress serve to direct our sex drive toward a healthy expression, other forms—specifically worry and anxiety—point us in the wrong direction. He states:

> "It is the stress of being hassled, of having a boss on your back, of failing projects, or of difficult coworkers. This type of stress doesn't sublimate the sex drive; it makes it more intense. Sex becomes the only good thing left in life. It becomes a *pacifier*, a *security blanket*, a *nirvana*. And if men can't get it at home, they'll look for it somewhere else."[5]

Let me be clear. I am not trying to justify the use of porn and masturbation on the grounds of rejection, abuse, or any other stressful challenges one might face. I am simply exposing an often unidentified, yet very real, cause for porn addiction. Lust is not the only issue. It is merely the fruit of a deeper root. In order to eliminate the fruit, we must identify and deal with the root. Then freedom can be experienced.

Dr. Hart concludes that...

> "In the long run...addictive sexuality never lives up to its promises. No matter how exciting it may be, you still have to come back to earth and deal with taxes, freeways, bosses from hell, and old age. Unless sex is relegated to its proper place in human experience and used for healthy reasons, it will always end up being a disappointment."[6]

Take God's Way of Escape!

If you have taken the path of porn as a means of coping and finding comfort, you're not alone. More importantly, there is a better way—God's way! He says, "...The wrong desires that come into your life aren't anything new and different. Many others have faced exactly the same problems before you. And *no temptation is irresistible*. You can trust God to keep the temptation from becoming so strong that you can't stand up against it, for he has promised this and will do what he says. **He will show you how to escape temptation's power** so that you can bear up patiently against it" (1 Corinthians 10:13 TLB).

The first step to escape temptation's power and not use porn to medicate your pain is to *admit* and *confess* that what you have been doing is wrong. *Repent* of it as sin: Ask God to forgive you, and receive His forgiveness. Ask Him to create in you a "new-creation" response to stress (see 2 Corinthians 5:17)—a response in which you run to Him for comfort instead of running to sexual release through porn. For He is "...the *God of all comfort*, who comforts us in all our troubles..." (2 Corinthians 1:3-4 NIV).

Before Jesus went to heaven, He said, "I will ask the Father, and He will give you another **Comforter** (Counselor, Helper, Intercessor, Advocate, Strengthener, and Standby), that He may remain with you forever" (John 14:16 AMP). Who is this Comforter? He is the Holy Spirit—the Spirit of Christ Himself! As a believer, the Spirit of Christ is living in you. And He is passionately calling, "Come to Me! Come to Me! I am your Way out! I am your answer. I am your rest."[7]

We will talk more about the power and importance of your relationship with Jesus in the coming chapters. For now, I urge you to accept His awesome invitation! God's Spirit knows everything about you. He knows how you're wired and the root reason you turn to porn for comfort. Run to Him when you're hurting, and let Him comfort you. Like David, pray and ask God to show you what's going on inside. Say, "Search me, O God, and know my heart; test me and know my anxious thoughts. Point out anything in me that offends you, and lead me along the path of everlasting life" (Psalm 139:23-24 NLT). Once God shows you the root reason, surrender it to Him and ask Him to heal you. What He reveals, He intends to heal. There is no condemnation for you—just comfort as you cooperate with His Spirit.

Receive Comfort from Your Bride

Another way God desires to comfort you and help you cope with life's stresses is through the gift of your wife. Remember, even in man's most perfect state, *before* he fell into sin, God said, "...It is not good for the man to be alone. I will make a helper who is just right for him" (Genesis 2:18 NLT). God blessed and greatly comforted Isaac after the death of his mother through the gift of his wife Rebekah (see Genesis 24:62-67). Indeed, "The man who finds a wife finds a good thing; she is a blessing to him from the Lord" (Proverbs 18:22 TLB).

I have experienced this personally, and I'm eternally grateful for the gift of my Allison! For many of the early years of our marriage, I did not see her for the treasure that she is. In fear, I was often challenged by the input she offered. In pride, I resisted her loving embrace with which she wanted to comfort me. Regrettably, I held her at arm's length many times, leaving both of us in a state of lack. Over time, God has brought healing into our lives. As I have been open and honest with Him and her, I have received a genuine appreciation for the incredible strength and wisdom she brings to my life.

Now, you may say, "But Vincent, you don't know my situation. My wife is angry and hurt over what I've done. Getting comfort from her is not an option right now." I understand. Throughout our twenty-three years of marriage, there have been many times when Allison could not comfort me and I could not comfort her. It's in those times I learned to run to the Lord and rely upon His supernatural strength and comfort alone. I learned to pray for Allison to be healed and trust the Lord with our relationship. It is truly amazing how He has healed us and knit us together. And He desires to do the same for you!

God-Created, God-Approved Sex Provides Healthy Comfort

As a man, one of the many blessings that comes through sexual intimacy with your wife is a physiological feeling of comfort and safety. God in His infinite wisdom created you that way. He also knew the sexual struggles you and every other man would face. So He said, "Because there is so much sexual immorality, each man should have his own wife, and each woman should have her own husband. The husband should fulfill his wife's sexual needs, and the wife should fulfill her husband's needs. **Do not deprive each other of sexual relations**, unless you both agree to refrain from sexual intimacy for a limited time so you can give yourselves more completely to prayer. Afterward, you should *come together again so that Satan won't be able to tempt you* because of your lack of self-control" (1 Corinthians 7:2-3, 5 NLT).

Brother, don't foolishly try to go it alone. I know men who went weeks and months at a time without sexually connecting with their wives. In every case, the results were eventually disastrous. This is sexual insanity—especially knowing that the average man's seminal vesicles fill to capacity within about 72 hours, creating a heightened hormonal sensitivity to all sexual stimuli and an increased sexual hunger.[8] Without regular times of true sexual fulfillment with your wife, you are setting yourself up for failure on multiple levels.

Do what God says—**don't deprive each other of sexual relations**, unless you both agree to it and it's only for a short time. Why? *So that Satan won't be able to tempt you* because of your lack of self-control. If you are having marital struggles, get help. There are many awesome resources available to help you create a marriage that thrives (visit www.jailbreakthebook.com). Humble yourself before your wife, apologize for the wrong choices you've made, and receive her loving embrace. Stoke *your* fire of pure desire and enjoy your wife sexually! Not only will you be blessed, but she will be blessed too!

Encouragement from the Heart of a Woman

When I was a little girl, I was not one to dream of one day meeting a prince, falling in love, and getting married. I was never a girl looking for a boyfriend, nor did I grow up and become a woman looking for a man. I never really wanted to get married. While I enjoyed putting on make-up and dressing up to go out with my friends, it was never my intention to attract men. However, it seemed inevitable.

With few exceptions, the men that I met had one thing on their mind. And quite honestly, it disgusted me! I really didn't know how to cope with their inappropriate advances. No one had ever taught me about stewarding my influence or beauty, nor about speaking strength to people. Therefore, I was left to cope with this the best way I could. Unfortunately, my coping mechanism for dealing with difficulty was not godly. The best way I knew to manage these situations was to use my mouth to degrade, belittle, and verbally abuse men in hopes that they would quit propositioning me. I was mean, hateful, and very angry. This became my automatic response to most men.

Through my years of being in relationship with Jesus, He gently exposed and addressed the root issue I was dealing with—fear. In His amazing faithfulness, He has taken my mouth, cleaned it up, and is now allowing me the privilege to speak to you. I want you to know that I don't take this privilege lightly. I consider it an honor to be able to speak strength, hope, healing, and restoration to you.

Man of God, don't use porn as your coping mechanism. God has a better way. As the Holy Spirit reveals to you how this habit developed and became rooted in your life, cooperate with Him. Repent for any wrong, willful choices He shows you and receive His strength and wisdom. Continue to surrender yourself to Him daily, and His great plan for you will unfold. I call you blessed and victorious in Him!

Sum It:

Your addiction to porn and masturbation is likely not just an issue of lust. It is the fruit of a deeper root. Many times it is an unconscious attempt to soothe your aching heart and cope with emotional discomfort. Like any addiction, it serves as emotional anesthesia to kill the pain and escape unpleasant experiences. But this so-called medicine will never bring the healing you need. There's a better way—God's way! He will comfort you and help you escape temptation's power. And if you let Him, He will make your bride a source of great comfort. Not only will you be blessed, but she will be blessed also!

Study It:

A Way of Escape: 1 Corinthians 10:13; Isaiah 30:21; 42:16; Psalm 25:4-5, 9; 32:8 **God Comforts**: 2 Corinthians 1:3-4; John 14:16-17, 26; Matthew 11:28-30; Isaiah 51:3, 12; 66:13; Psalm 34:17-22; 145:18-19 **God Reveals Roots**: Psalm 139:23-24; Jeremiah 17:9-10; Hebrews 4:13; Daniel 2:22 **Your Wife Is a Blessing**: Genesis 2:18; Proverbs 5:15-19; 18:22; 31:10-29; 1 Corinthians 7:2-5; Psalm 128:3

Apply It:

1 Only God knows your heart. Stop and pray, "Lord, is there a deeper root reason I'm imprisoned in porn? Is there a painful experience, past or present, that I'm trying to cope with improperly? If so, what is it?" *Be still and listen.* What is He revealing? Surrender it to Him; ask Him to heal you.

_____

_____

_____

_____

Check out: Psalm 139:23-24; Jeremiah 17:9-10; Hebrews 4:13; Daniel 2:22

2 There is something that God wants you to be *rooted* in. Carefully read Ephesians 3:16-19; 1 John 4:15-18 and Romans 8:35-39 and identify it. What is He speaking to you in these passages?

_____

_____

_____

_____

3 God, through His Holy Spirit, is your *Comforter*. Carefully read Matthew 11:28-30; Psalm 34:17-22; 145:18-19. What is He revealing? How do these verses comfort and encourage you?

_____

_____

_____

_____

4 God has given you your wife as an expression of Him—to be your *helper.* Read Psalm 128:3; Proverbs 5:15-19; 18:22; 19:14; 31:10-29; 1 Corinthians 7:2-5. What is He showing you in these verses?

_____

_____

_____

5 What's your greatest takeaway from this chapter? What scriptures, principles, or ideas spoke to your heart most? How are you challenged? What action(s) is God prompting you to take?

_____

_____

_____

Things I Want to Remember:

Pray It:

"Father, thank You for revealing that there is a deeper root to this rotten fruit in my life. Please forgive me for taking matters into my own hands and trying to comfort myself. I don't want porn to be my pacifier or pain reliever any longer, but only You can make this happen. Holy Spirit, You are my Comforter! You know the specific emotional pain I've been trying to medicate. Please reveal the root causes so that I may surrender them to You in prayer and experience true healing. And forgive me for not allowing my wife to comfort me as You created her to. Heal our marriage. Help us to humbly appreciate each other and grow in love. I bless our communication and our sexual relations with health and life. In Jesus' name, Amen!"

ONE BROTHER TO ANOTHER

"For men, the spiritual battle is often won or lost on the battlefield of sexual temptation. And when we lose a battle, the enemy wants us to give up the fight. Can I remind you of something the enemy knows all too well? You may lose some battles, but the war has already been won. And while the Enemy never stops accusing us, our Almighty Ally never stops fighting for us, never gives up on us."

— Mark Batterson[1]
The Circle Maker

Chapter 10

YOUR FREEDOM HAS BEEN PAID FOR!

Christ purchased our freedom [redeeming us] from the curse (doom)
of the Law [and its condemnation] by [Himself]
becoming a curse for us....

Galatians 3:13 AMP

Did you know that your freedom has been paid for? Your freedom over porn and every other sin known to man has been purchased by Jesus—but you must *believe* it in order to *receive it.*

While Satan's ultimate goal is *enslavement*, which leads to death, God's ultimate goal is *freedom* that produces life. Your heavenly Father wanted you to be free and back in relationship with Him so much that He didn't wait for you to ask for it. While you were still a sinner, He sent Jesus to die in your place and pay the penalty for your sins; by this He demonstrated His immeasurable love for you (see Romans 5:8).

Friend, "God has rescued us from the power of darkness and has brought us into the kingdom of his Son, whom he loves. His Son *paid the price to free us*, which means that our sins are forgiven." This is God's Word to you in Colossians 1:13-14 (GW). Verse 14 in The Message says, "The Son who got us out of the pit we were in, got rid of the sins we were doomed to keep repeating." Praise God! Jesus paid the price to free us from the pit of porn and the sins of looking, lusting, and relieving ourselves sexually—sins we were doomed to keep repeating. Praise His Name!

What Are You Believing and Speaking About Yourself?

Now you may be thinking, *Vincent, that sounds good, but I am not free. I am still struggling with porn. What am I missing?* Well, let me answer your question with a question: What are you *believing* and *speaking* about yourself? Do you believe and say things like, "I'm just a sinner saved by grace. I can't do anything right. This will never change. I don't think I'll ever be free from this." *Or* do you believe and say what God says about you in His Word?

You *were* a sinner, but if you have repented of your sins and welcomed Jesus into your life, you are a brand-new creation. "When someone becomes a Christian, he becomes a brand-new person inside. He is not the same anymore. A new life has begun!" (2 Corinthians 5:17 TLB). When God looks at you, He doesn't see the sin-stained man you used to be. He sees a brand-new person in Christ Jesus. If fact, He sees you as *righteous.*

Second Corinthians 5:21 (NKJV) declares, "For He made Him who knew no sin to be sin for us, that we might become the righteousness of God in Him." Using verses like these, you can begin to *believe* and say things like, "I am a brand-new person inside. My old life is gone. Jesus has purchased my freedom from porn! I am *not* doomed to keep repeating past sins. I am the righteousness of God in Jesus. I am free!" This is the way God sees you and what He says about you. So this is what you need to believe and say about yourself.

What you believe and say about yourself defines who you are and determines what you become. Except for your parents' words in your formative years, no one's words (and thoughts) hold a greater impact on you than your own. I can speak 150 to 200 words a minute to you, but you speak to yourself at a rate of 500 to 600 words a minute— nearly three times more. It's called *self-talk,* the continuing internal conversation that you have with yourself. Since you speak to "you" more than anyone, you need to be telling yourself the truth about who you are in Christ, how much God loves you, and how free you are in Him. Remember, what you think in your heart is what you become, and the power of life and death is in *your* tongue (see Proverbs 18:21; 23:7).

Sin's Power Over You Is Broken!

What else does God say about your freedom that Christ paid for? He says that sin's power over you has been *broken.* This is vital for you to know and believe. There are three opposing forces trying to keep you from becoming like Jesus and living the life He died to give you: they are the world, the flesh, and the devil. These three work together and are often inseparable. We will talk at length about living free from the world's temptations and overcoming the power of the enemy in the chapters ahead. For now, let's focus our attention on the flesh—all that we are *apart from God.*

There is only one way to live free from the demands and cravings of your flesh; it must be *crucified.* No, I don't mean you should build a cross and have someone nail you to it or perform some type of self-mutilation. Crucifying the flesh is a figure of speech. When Christ was crucified, He took all our sins upon Himself. When we repent of our sins and welcome Him into our lives, our flesh—our old sin nature—is symbolically crucified with Him. Paul, through the power of the Holy Spirit, makes this clear:

> "For sin's power over us was broken when we became Christians and were baptized to become a part of Jesus Christ; through his death the power of your sinful nature was shattered. Your old sin-loving nature was buried with him by baptism when he died, and when God the Father, with glorious power, brought him back to life again, you were given his wonderful new life to enjoy. For you have become a part of him, and so you died with him, so to speak, when he died; and now you share his new life and shall rise as he did. Your old evil desires were nailed to the cross with him; that part of you that loves to sin was crushed and fatally wounded, so that your sin-loving body is no longer under sin's control, no longer needs to be a slave to sin" (Romans 6:2-6 TLB).

Meditating on this passage and speaking it out loud over my life has been one of the most freedom-producing habits I've ever developed. I've reread these verses countless times and personalized them as a declaration of freedom. The verse I quote most is verse 6: *"My old evil desires were nailed to the cross with Christ; that part of me that loves to sin was crushed and fatally wounded, so that my sin-loving body is no longer under sin's control and no longer needs to be a slave to sin."* I also personalize Galatians 2:20: *"I have been crucified with Christ and I, my flesh, no longer lives. But Christ lives in me! And the life I now live in this body, I live by faith in Jesus, the One who loves me and gave Himself for me."* Meditating on and speaking verses like these will change who you are and how you see yourself.

See Yourself Dead to Sin but Alive and Free In Christ!

Five verses after Paul explains how sin's power has been broken, he reveals a major key to victory: "Even so *consider yourselves also dead to sin* and your relation to it broken, but alive to God [living in unbroken fellowship with Him] in Christ Jesus" (Romans 6:11 AMP). Consider yourself *dead to sin*. To *consider* means "to think, believe, or see." God wants you to see your "SELF"—your old, sinful nature or flesh—dead to sin. No one in a casket has a problem with lust anymore; they are dead. In the same way, see your flesh as dead and in a casket.

Not only are we to see ourselves as dead to sin, but also *our relation to sin broken* (AMP). This paints a powerful picture. Before I met and married my wife, Allison, I dated a girl seriously for about a year. Then she broke the relationship off. Now that I'm married, I am sold-out to Allison and I wouldn't think twice about going back to that girl. Why? Because *my relation to her is broken.* This is how I see my relation to the sin of pornography—it is broken. I'm sold-out to my Savior! I'm alive and free in Him!

"So we praise God for the glorious grace he has poured out on us who belong to his dear Son. He is so rich in kindness and grace that *he purchased our freedom* with the blood of his Son and forgave our sins. He has showered his kindness on us, along with all wisdom and understanding" (Ephesians 1:6-8 NLT). In the chapters ahead, we'll talk more about the importance of God's Word and prayer, and how to war against the enemy. For now, know and believe that your freedom has been paid for by Jesus Christ, God's Son, and "if the Son sets you free, you will be free indeed" (John 8:36 NIV). Believe it. Speak it. Live it!

Encouragement from the Heart of a Woman

Man of God, your entire walk with Him is a walk of faith! And this part is no exception. It takes faith to see yourself as dead to sin and free from porn. It may seem foolish to speak things over your life that don't presently exist, but do it anyway. I have learned that it is better to **feel** *foolish and* **be** *free than be foolish and remain trapped in sin.*

Years ago, I needed a deeper revelation of how much God loves me. At that time, I was listening to a teaching by Joyce Meyer in which she shared about how she received a deeper revelation of God's love by speaking His promises out loud over her life. It was evident that she had a real, heartfelt revelation of His love, and I wanted what she had. So I did what she encouraged us to do—I began proclaiming, "God loves me. God loves me. God loves **me***!" While I initially felt awkward saying it, eventually this truth became a reality in my heart, creating a powerful paradigm shift that has affected my entire life.*

Speaking the truth of God's Word out of your mouth speeds up the process of freedom. It prepares your mind, will, emotions, and body to experience freedom. Your words out of your mouth cement in place what Christ has already paid for. Like God, begin to speak and call the things that presently don't exist as though they do (see Romans 4:17). See yourself free, totally at peace, and able to enjoy sex the way God intended. Begin to say, "I am dead to sin. I no longer want to look and lust after other women. I have eyes for my wife only, and I bless her, in Jesus' name!"

I believe in you, Man of God. God is good and His plan for you is amazing! He does not show favoritism. What He did for Vincent and me in our marriage, He will do for you and your wife in your marriage. Believe Him for it! Speak it out! Fight with all your might! All of heaven is on your side.

Sum It:

Your freedom over porn and every other sin known to man has been purchased by Jesus Christ. Sin's power over you is broken; you are *not* doomed to keep repeating the same sins. But you must believe it in order to receive it. What you believe and say about yourself, both out loud and internally (self-talk), will define who you are and determine what you become. Get your words lined up with God's Word. Think, say, and believe what He says about you. See yourself dead to sin, but alive to God in Christ!

Study It:

Proverbs 18:21; 23:7; John 8:31-32, 36; Romans 6; 10:9-10; 4:17; 2 Corinthians 5:17, 21; Galatians 3:13; Ephesians 1:3-8; Colossians 1:13-14; Titus 2:11-14

Apply It:

1 Describe how you see yourself. In your mind, are you a sinner who's always falling into sin or God's righteous son who is growing in His grace?

_____

_____

_____

_____

_____

2 What kind of things do you normally *think* and *say* to yourself about you— how is your *self-talk*? What words and phrases regularly come out of your mouth about yourself?

_____

_____

_____

_____

Replace negative words and phrases with positive proclamations from Scripture. You can use the verses presented in this chapter or your Bible concordance or an online search engine (like biblegateway.com) to look up key words and their synonyms and antonyms.

3 Carefully reread and meditate on Romans 6:2-6 in the chapter above. What is the Holy Spirit speaking to you from this passage? Using these verses, write a personalized declaration of your freedom from sin's power and the demands of your flesh.

_____

_____

_____

_____

_____

4 What is your greatest takeaway from this chapter? What scriptures, principles, or ideas exploded in your heart? How are you challenged? What action(s) is God prompting you to take?

_____

_____

_____

_____

_____

Things I Want to Remember:

Pray It:

"Father, thank You for paying for my freedom. Jesus, thank You for selflessly laying down Your life and taking the punishment for all my sins. Thank You for not only forgiving me but also setting me free from the power of sin itself. Through You I am not doomed to keep repeating the same sins! Make these truths heart revelations, not just head knowledge. Help me to think of myself and see myself as dead to sin and alive in You, and let the words of my mind (my self-talk) and mouth reflect it. In Jesus' name, Amen!"

PART 2
THE GREAT ESCAPE
21 Steps to Freedom

Break Free
From Past Sin Patterns

ONE BROTHER TO ANOTHER

"To fall in love with God is the greatest of all romances; to seek Him, the greatest adventure; to find Him, the greatest human achievement."

— Augustine[1]

Step 1

ABIDE IN RELATIONSHIP WITH JESUS

I am the Vine, you are the branches. When you're joined with me and I with you, the relation intimate and organic, the harvest is sure to be abundant. Separated, you can't produce a thing.

John 15:5 The Message

Jesus is all about relationships. Everywhere He went, He built them. He befriended Mary, Martha, and Lazarus. He connected with Zacchaeus, Nicodemus, and the woman at the well. From the children He blessed to the Twelve He prayerfully handpicked, He gave all who received Him the right to become sons and daughters of God (see John 1:12).

You too are created to be in *relationship* with Him—a union of communion and friendship. For God so loved *you*—yes you—that He gave His Son, and if you believe in Him, you will not perish but have everlasting life. And that life starts now! If you have never entered into a relationship with Jesus, there's no time like the present! Just surrender yourself to Him and invite His Spirit to come live in your heart. (Check out pages 260-262.)

Please know that freedom from porn will *not* come from following a bunch of rules. It will come as you abide in relationship with Jesus. Yes, there are principles you need to apply, and we will clearly outline them in the remainder of this book. But they are powerless to produce freedom and change apart from Christ. Abiding in relationship with Jesus is your first and most important step to freedom.

Relationship Produces Oneness

Jesus was in relationship with the Father while here on earth, and They were inseparable. Again and again, He said, "I am *in* the Father and the Father is *in* me."[2] They were One then and They are One now. Oneness was Jesus' source of success. The same kind of relationship He had with the Father, He wants to have with you—you living in Him and Him living in you. Oneness is what you were created for.

He says, "Live in me, and I will live in you. A branch cannot produce any fruit by itself. It has to stay attached to the vine. In the same way, you cannot produce fruit unless you live in me" (John 15:4 GW). Did you catch that? You cannot produce fruit unless you *live in Jesus*—this includes the fruit of living porn-free. Jesus continues, "I am the Vine, you are the branches. When you're joined with me and I with you, the relation intimate and organic, the harvest is sure to be abundant. Separated, you can't produce a thing" (John 15:5 The Message). Wow! What a mouthful.

Living in relationship with Jesus empowers you to produce and enjoy the fruit of His Spirit. In addition to love, joy, and peace, your life will also yield the righteous fruit of sexual purity and self-control. Jesus' words in John 15:5, along with the principle of Philippians 4:13, have become my motto for daily living: "Apart from Jesus I can do nothing. But in Him—as one with Him—I can do all things!"

In Christ, You Have Everything You Need

As Jesus lived in oneness with the Father, everything the Father had was available to Him.[3] And as we live in oneness with Jesus, everything He has is available to us. Ephesians 1:3 (GW) says, "Praise the God and Father of our Lord Jesus Christ! *Through Christ*, God has blessed us with *every spiritual blessing* that heaven has to offer." And in 2 Peter 1:3 (NLT) we learn that "by his divine power, God has given us *everything* we need for living a godly life. We have received all of this by coming to know him...."

Take a moment and reread those verses. Everything, yes *everything*, you'll ever need is generously available to you through Christ. In the chapters ahead, we are going to explore many proven steps to freedom—things like starving your flesh, feeding your spirit, avoiding the scenes of temptation, and living on guard. The desire and power to do all these is available to you as you live in relationship with Jesus. How do you receive it? By asking for it in prayer.

Jesus said, "I will do anything you ask the Father in my name so that the Father will be given glory because of the Son. If you ask me to do something, I will do it" (John 14:13-14 GW). As a man, you need self-control and victory over sexual temptation. This is God's will and your inheritance through Christ. Whenever you are struggling with temptation or in trouble, He is always ready to help.

God declares, "Because He Himself [in His humanity] has suffered in being tempted (tested and tried), He is able [*immediately*] to run to the cry of...those who are being tempted and tested and tried.... Jesus understands every weakness of ours, because he was tempted in every way that we are. But he did not sin!" (Hebrews 2:18 AMP; 4:15 CEV).

Jesus walked where you have walked and was tempted sexually as you have been tempted. Yet He did not sin! He overcame the world, the flesh, and the devil, and His strength to overcome and walk in purity is available to you through relationship with Him. He has what you need! The desire and power to submit to God, resist the devil, and control your thoughts—*everything* is yours for the asking as you abide in relationship with Jesus.

When Relationship Is Weak, Temptation Is Strong

I have discovered that temptation is strongest and I feel most like giving in when I have neglected my relationship with Jesus. Lack of time with the One who loves me most spells disaster. Little by little, I become blinded by pride, and instead of focusing my attention on Him as my source of strength, I begin to focus on me as my source of strength.

When I try to remain pure in my own power, I struggle. When I make prayer my last resort instead of my first response, I struggle. And when I don't feed my spirit God's Word or fail to speak it over my life, my situations, and against the enemy, I struggle. When my relationship with Him is weak, temptation is strong. But when my relationship is strong, temptation is weakened.

Always remember, it's Christ living in you that empowers you to walk in victory over temptation. The healthier your relationship is with Him, the stronger your resistance will be to temptation. Walking in freedom from porn and every other sin is a direct result.

The Key to a Strong Relationship

How can you strengthen your relationship with Jesus? Two key ingredients—*time and attention*. This is what God yearns to have with you. Scripture says, "...The Spirit Whom He has caused to dwell in us yearns over us and He yearns for the Spirit [to be welcome] with a jealous love" (James 4:5 AMP). God doesn't just want to spend time with you on Sunday morning. He craves to be welcome in your life every day.

Now you may be thinking, *How do I spend time with God? I can't see Him?* Well, how did Jesus spend time with Him? He regularly pulled away for private moments in His presence. Deserts, seasides, mountains, and gardens were all places He frequented.[4] What did Jesus do in these places? He prayed and communed with the Father. He openly talked, shared His heart, and carefully listened. He meditated on Scripture and was empowered by the Holy Spirit to walk in purity and stability. All these are benefits of being in relationship with Jesus.

"But Vincent, I thought God is always with us. Didn't He say He would never leave us or forsake us?[5] Why is pulling away necessary?" Yes, God is always with us, and in Him we live, move, and have our being (see Acts 17:28). But you can be in the same room with someone and be totally oblivious to their presence. We've all done it, and at times we have done it to God.

Times of undivided attention are needed to build a strong relationship. Think about it. How do you feel when someone you love purposely comes to see you and gives you their undivided attention? That's right, you feel loved, valued, and important. How do you feel when they humbly thank you and praise you for things you've done? How about when they ask for your advice with their decisions? You're drawn to them, right? You want to do whatever you can to help them. Well, how do you think God feels when you purposely pull away to give Him your undivided attention—when you thank Him and praise Him for the things He's done? I'll tell you—He's thrilled!

Your love and attention magnetically draw Him to you. Scripture promises if you "come close to God... God will come close to you..." (James 4:8 NLT). I love what David says in Psalm 25:14 (CEV): "Our Lord, you are the friend of your worshipers...." Friend, you have never tasted true friendship until you have experienced the friendship of God! There is no one like Him. I love my wife greatly and she loves me. But God's friendship is greater. He can go where no man or woman can go—inside of us! Like a master mechanic who can fine tune an engine, Jesus knows just what to do inside of you to make things right. As you make time for Him, you will never be the same.

As You Spend Time with Jesus, You Become Like Jesus

Enoch, the seventh son from Adam, had a strong relationship with God. Scripture says, "After the birth of Methuselah, Enoch lived in close fellowship with God for another 300 years...Then one day he disappeared, because God took him" (Genesis 5:22, 24 NLT). Moses spent time in God's presence...a lot of time. When he would return, his face glowed with God's glory—a glow so powerful he covered it! (See Exodus 34:28-35.) Peter was also tightly connected with God, fellowshipping regularly with His Holy Spirit. What was the result?

People were miraculously healed just by his shadow! (See Acts 5:14-16.) That's the power of God's presence. And fellowship with Him is not reserved for a select few—it's available to *you* through His Holy Spirit!

The disciples spent three years in constant fellowship with Christ. When He ascended into Heaven, the Father sent the promised gift of His Holy Spirit. Empowered by the Spirit, these men who once ran in fear for their lives now boldly proclaimed the gospel. "The members of the council were amazed when they saw the boldness of Peter and John, for they could see that they were *ordinary* men with no special training in the Scriptures. They also recognized them as *men who had been with Jesus*" (Acts 4:13 NLT). Being with Jesus turns ordinary men into extraordinary men! When you're abiding in relationship with Him, people can see the difference.

Make no mistake, the people you hang around rub off on you. How they think, talk, and act influence how you think, talk, and act. The more time you spend with them, the more you become like them. The same is true with your relationship with Jesus. When you actively include Him in your daily activities, His character rubs off on you. As you regularly spend time in His Word and in His presence, you will begin to think, talk, and act like Him. Indeed, we "...are being transformed into his likeness with ever-increasing glory, which comes from the Lord, who is the Spirit" (2 Corinthians 3:18 NIV).

Has Your Affection Been Misplaced?

Years ago, when I first began earnestly seeking God for freedom from porn, He impressed upon me an unexpected reason for the addiction. He said, "One of the reasons you're struggling is because your *affection is misplaced*. You're seeking satisfaction in My creation, but what you're really craving is Me, your Creator. Nothing can fill that void except Me."

John Eldredge explains this misplaced affection quite eloquently saying, "Aching for we know not what, we meet Eve's daughters and we are history. She is the closest thing we've ever encountered, the pinnacle of creation, the very embodiment of God's beauty and mystery and tenderness and allure. And what goes out to her is not just our longing for Eve, but our *longing for God* as well. A man without his true love, his life, **his God**, will find another. What better substitute than Eve's daughters? Nothing else in creation even comes close."[6]

Friend, Jesus longs for relationship with you. And you long for relationship with Him...whether you realize it or not. There is a "God hole" in you that only He can fill. This is not something that happens once at an altar or in a weekly church service. The God hole in you can only be satisfied by living in relationship with Jesus. As C.S. Lewis so aptly said, "A car is made to run on gasoline, and it would not run properly on anything else. Now God designed the human machine to run on Himself. He Himself is the fuel our spirits were designed to burn, or the food our spirits were designed to feed on. There is no other."[7]

Will You Accept His Invitation?

Right now Jesus is standing at the door of your heart knocking. Can you hear Him? He is saying, "Look! I have been standing at the door, and I am constantly knocking. If anyone hears me calling him and opens the door, I will come in and fellowship with him and he with me" (Revelation 3:20 TLB).

He says, "Come to me, all of you who are weary and carry heavy burdens, and I will give you rest" (Matthew 11:28 NLT). Are you weary from carrying a heavy load of guilt and condemnation? Are you tired of trying to break free from porn's prison in your own power? Jesus says, "Come to Me, and I will give you rest." He then says, "Take my yoke upon you. Let me teach you…" (vs. 29). In other words, "Spend time in fellowship with Me, and I will show you how to live porn-free." My brother, accept His invitation. True freedom is found in relationship with Him!

Encouragement from the Heart of a Woman

Jesus is the reason I'm alive today. Without Him, I wouldn't be here. If it wasn't for Jesus, there would be a gravestone with my name on it somewhere. Jesus is my life! Man of God, I encourage you to make time to spend with Him. He is the only One who can satisfy your every need, desire, and dream. He knit you together in your mother's womb and knows everything about you (see Psalm 139). He completely understands you and longs to be your closest friend.

In relationship with Him, you don't have to be the "covering." Instead, you get to be covered by Him. Just as your wife and children get to relax and look to you for direction, protection, and provision, He wants you to relax and look to Him for the same. He is ultimately responsible for you and your household. He wants to be the One you run to in your times of need. And no what matter the need is, He longs to meet it.

In His presence, you can remove all the different "hats" you wear. There are no quotas to meet and no performances required. Just be yourself. In the beginning, it may be a challenge to carve out time to spend with Him, so start small...perhaps 10-15 minutes a day. God will honor the steps you take toward Him. He will not look upon your efforts as too small or insignificant. He is kind, merciful, and gracious.

Remember, God saved you because He loves you. If He wanted to condemn you, He never would have sent Jesus to die in your place. Unlike people, He is able to separate the sin from the sinner and genuinely love and accept us just as we are. He is patient and knows that where you are presently is not where you will always be. He approves of you, Man of God. He sees greatness in you and longs to love you. Keep on keeping on! You're becoming more like Him each day. I call you blessed and highly favored!

Walk It:

You are created to be in *relationship* with Jesus. There's a "God hole" in you that only He can fill. Freedom from porn will not come from following a bunch of rules. It will come as you abide in relationship with Him. Oneness is your source of success. In Him, you have everything you need to live godly. When your relationship is strong, temptation is weakened. You keep it strong by spending time with Him. Being with Jesus changes you from an ordinary man into an extraordinary man! Accept His invitation. Apart from Jesus, you can do nothing. But in Him, you can do all things!

Study It:

Abiding in Christ: Matthew 11:28-30; John 1:12; 15:1-17; Acts 4:13; 2 Corinthians 3:18; Philippians 4:13; James 4:5, 8; Hebrews 2:18; 4:15-16; Psalm 25:14; 34:5; Revelation 3:20 **Everything:** Ephesians 1:3; 2 Peter 1:3; Psalm 34:8-10; 84:11

Apply It:

1 Carefully read Jesus' words in John 15:1-17. What is the Holy Spirit showing you in these verses?

_____

_____

_____

_____

_____

2 Pause and pray, "Holy Spirit, what's hindering me from developing a daily relationship with You? What kind of thinking or activity is stopping me?" Be still and listen. Write what He reveals.

_____

_____

_____

_____

_____

3 You can't get back yesterday, but you can certainly seize today! Again, pray, "Holy Spirit, You know my schedule. When can I commit to spending focused time with You? Where is a good, quiet place to meet, and how much time should I set aside?" Be still and listen. Write what He reveals.

_____

_____

_____

_____

_____

4 What's your greatest takeaway from this chapter? What scriptures, principles, or ideas touched your heart most? How are you challenged? What action(s) is God prompting you to take?

_____

_____

_____

_____

_____

Things I Want to Remember:

Pray It:

"Father, thank You for wanting to be in relationship with me. Forgive me for not making more time to spend with You and for misplacing my affection. Help me to know—really know in my heart—that freedom comes from abiding in relationship with You, not from following rules. Your Spirit living in me and through me is the power to produce change. Teach me how to be one with You. Remind me, Holy Spirit, that everything I need to live a pure life is available through You. All I have to do is ask. Help me to do my part to keep our relationship strong—to regularly give You my time and attention. Show me specific times I can pull away and be with You. I love You, Father! In Jesus' name, Amen!"

ONE BROTHER TO ANOTHER

"The Bible never says that God resists a drunkard, a thief, or even a murderer, but he does resist the proud. Every kind of sin can be cleansed and forgiven if we humble ourselves and confess it to the Lord."

— **Jim Cymbala**[1]

Step **2**

ADMIT IT. CONFESS IT. REPENT.

If we refuse to admit that we are sinners, then we live in a world of illusion and truth becomes a stranger to us. But if we freely admit that we have sinned, we find God utterly reliable and straightforward—he forgives our sins and makes us thoroughly clean from all that is evil.

1 John 1:8-9 Phillips

Admitting you have a problem, *confessing* it as sin, and *repenting* is where freedom begins. As you abide in relationship with Jesus, these three actions are inseparable. Like a tightly woven braid, it is often hard to tell where one begins and another ends. Admitting, confessing, and repenting is a humble way of life that puts you in position to receive a steady flow of God's grace.

Admit You Have a Problem

What keeps so many men from admitting they have a problem with porn and lust? For some it's fear, but for many it's *pride*. Pride separates us from God and is essentially the root of all sin. Pride says things like, "*I* don't have a problem. *I* am just as normal as the next guy. *I* can stop looking at this stuff anytime *I* want." That's pride—the big "I" is right at the middle of everything.

The truth is, if you could stop looking at porn on your own, you would have done it already. You are powerless in your own ability to defeat sin. But when you humble yourself before God and say, "Lord, I have a problem with sexual impurity. I can't kick it on my own. Please help me," you open yourself up to God's forgiveness and freedom. It's the humble that get the help! "For God sets Himself against the proud...[and He opposes, frustrates, and defeats them], but gives **grace** (favor, blessing) to the humble" (1 Peter 5:5 AMP).

What is *grace*? It is not a "license to sin" or sin's "big cover-up." Grace is God's power not to sin. It is given to us by His Holy Spirit of grace (see Hebrews 10:29). Yes, grace is God's undeserved favor, but it is also His **supernatural strength and ability** to live like Jesus!

Confess It to God

Once you humble yourself and admit you have a problem, *confess* it to God. By definition, the word *confess* in Scripture literally means "to speak the same thing." When you confess your sins to God, you agree with Him—you say, "What I'm doing is wrong. Lusting after women on the computer, in print, and in person is sin." When you confess sin, you bring it into the Light of God's presence. And in His presence we find love, mercy, forgiveness, and the power (grace) to change!

God promises that "if we [freely] admit that we have sinned and confess our sins, He is faithful and just (true to His own nature and promises) and will forgive our sins [dismiss our lawlessness] and [continuously] cleanse us from all unrighteousness [everything not in conformity to His will in purpose, thought, and action]" (1 John 1:9 AMP). Wow! What an incredible promise. Admitting and confessing our sin puts us in position to genuinely repent.

Repent of Your Sin

The word *repent* is the Greek term *metanoeo*, which basically means "to change one's mind and heart."[2] Real, heartfelt repentance signifies you have turned your mind and heart **away from sin** and **toward God**. You actually think differently. Repentance is like an alignment for your car. Whenever you hit potholes, you need a realignment to get your car going straight again. Repentance is the realignment of the soul that keeps you straight with God. While sin separates, repentance reunites. It is His gift that keeps on giving. His mercy never runs out!

Repentance is also like taking a *spiritual bath*. When I work outside all day, I get dirty and smelly. Similarly, when we're dirty spiritually, we give off an odor—a smell that repels the Lord and attracts the enemy. Just as flies are drawn to dirty, rotten garbage in a landfill, Satan—aka "Lord of the Flies"—is drawn to us when we've not cleansed ourselves spiritually. Think about it. A person who hasn't taken a bath in days stinks. Likewise, when we fail to admit, confess, and repent of our sins, we stink spiritually. Many Christians are living stinkin' lives because they haven't taken a spiritual bath in a long time.

What does a spiritual bath look like? It starts by uncovering yourself—you must remove everything on the surface and be real and honest with God. Next, wet yourself with the "water" of the Word. This means prayerfully entering His presence by speaking His promises.[3] Now lather up your sponge with soap. Spiritually, our soap is the precious blood of Jesus that takes sin away.[4] Our sponge is the Person of the Holy Spirit who sanctifies us and makes us like Jesus.[5] Once you verbally apply the blood of Christ to your life and ask the Holy Spirit to do the internal cleaning that only He can do, use the water of the Word again to "rinse off." Speaking scriptures like Romans 8:1-2 and John 3:17-18 removes the residue of condemnation and guilt that the enemy often tries to make cling to us. Once you've rinsed, you are ready to "put on Christ," your incredible robe of righteousness![6]

Do you want to walk in that fresh, clean feeling of freedom? Then you need to regularly come *clean* with God: Admit your problems, confess them as sin, and repent.

What Happens If You Deny God's Conviction?

As you've been reading, you've probably felt the conviction of God's Spirit—an uneasiness or inner knowing that you've sinned. What happens if you ignore it? Look at King David. He had a problem with lust. He not only committed adultery, but also had the woman's husband murdered in order to cover up his sin. A careful study of Scripture reveals that David "pretended" everything was fine for awhile. All the while something was eating at him inside. Look at what he said:

> "When I refused to confess my sin, my body wasted away, and I groaned all day long. Day and night your hand of discipline was heavy on me. My strength evaporated like water in the summer heat. Finally, I confessed all my sins to you and stopped trying to hide my guilt. I said to myself, 'I will confess my rebellion to the Lord.' And you forgave me! All my guilt is gone" (Psalm 32:3-5 NLT).

Denial keeps the sin of sexual impurity hidden in the dark. Satan is the ruler of darkness (see Ephesians 6:12). Anything you keep in the dark, Satan can rule over. "But if we [really] are living and walking in the Light, as He [Himself] is in the Light, we have [true, unbroken] fellowship with one another, and the blood of Jesus Christ His Son cleanses (removes) us from all sin and guilt [keeps us cleansed from sin in all its forms and manifestations]" (1 John 1:7 AMP). Admitting the problem, along with confessing it and repenting of it as sin, is stepping out of the dark and into the Light of God's grace. It's only in the Light that lust loses its power and cleansing and forgiveness are received.

Friend, get in agreement with God. Call your sin, *sin*. Admit it, confess it, and repent. "Well, I've done that already," you say, "and I fell into the same mess again." Do it again! Remember, admitting, confessing, and repenting is a way of life, not a one-time event or an annual activity. This practice keeps you on the same page with God, receiving a steady flow of His supernatural strength (grace).

Don't wait till you feel you've punished yourself enough to ask for forgiveness. Humble yourself, ask Him for forgiveness, receive it, and go on! Respond to the godly sorrow He is allowing. "For God sometimes uses sorrow in our lives to help us turn away from sin and seek eternal life. We should never regret his sending it..." (2 Corinthians 7:10 TLB).

Encouragement from the Heart of a Woman

Are you tired of the rollercoaster of emotions...desire, false fulfillment, guilt, and condemnation, only for this horrific ride to repeat itself? Sure, your flesh enjoys the pleasure that porn provides, but that pleasure is a fleeting counterfeit. The aftertaste of pain and the problems it produces are real and often lasting.

Proverbs 28:13 (TLB) says, "A man who refuses to admit his mistakes can never be successful. But if he confesses and forsakes them, he gets another chance." Man of God, don't wait another day to admit you have a problem. Confess your sin—call it what God calls it, and repent. You have been bound far too long. Jesus yearns to bring you freedom. Allow His love to penetrate your heart and His blood to wash you clean. You are safe in His care, and He is longing to grant you the strength you need to overcome.

*Know that this is just a season, and God has not brought this area of your life into the Light to walk away from you or point a finger of fault. He has revealed it because He intends to walk with you **through** it. Rare and beautiful gems are waiting—gems like peace, purity, and sexual fulfillment that are absent of guilt and condemnation. Repent and break free, mighty Man of God! Abundant life is waiting!*

Walk It:

Admitting you have a problem, confessing it as sin, and repenting is where freedom begins. To confess means to get in agreement with God and call sin, sin. To repent means to turn your mind and heart away from sin and toward God. Don't let fear, pride, condemnation, or guilt keep you from coming clean with Him. Make admitting, confessing, and repenting of sin your humble way of life. It will put you in position to receive a steady flow of God's grace—His supernatural strength and ability to live like Jesus.

Study It:

1 John 1:7-10; Psalm 32:3-5; 51; 2 Corinthians 7:10; Proverbs 28:13-14; Revelation 3:19-20. Also check out the scripture references in the endnotes.

Apply It:

1 Carefully meditate on 1 John 1:7-10. Why is it important to see *admitting* you have a problem and *confessing* and *repenting* of your sin as a *way of life*, not a one-time event?

_____

_____

_____

_____

2 Have you ever specifically defined the sin issue you're battling? If so, describe what it is. Pause and pray, "Lord, please give me grace—the power of Your Spirit—to see my situation for what it really is." Write what He reveals.

_____

_____

_____

_____

3 Sin is like yeast placed in a ball of dough; a little bit eventually spreads throughout and affects every part of us. Again, pause and pray, "Holy Spirit, what areas of my life are being affected by this sin? What areas have I been unable to see? How can I change this?" Listen and write what He reveals.

_____

_____

_____

_____

4 What is your greatest takeaway from this chapter? What scriptures, principles, or ideas exploded in your heart? How do they challenge you? What action(s) is God's Spirit prompting you to take?

_____

_____

_____

Pray It:

"Father, I admit I have a problem with lust and looking at porn. You call it sin, so I confess it as sin. I repent for looking at and lusting over all the impure images I have seen. Please forgive me. I will no longer keep this hidden in the dark for Satan to rule over me. And I will no longer punish myself; I will receive Your forgiveness. Wash me clean of all guilt and shame. 'Create in me a new, clean heart, O God, filled with clean thoughts and right desires. Restore to me again the joy of your salvation, and make me willing to obey you' (Psalm 51:10, 12 TLB). Thank You, Father. In Jesus' name, Amen."

ONE BROTHER TO ANOTHER

"God wants to share with you the secret of his life-giving, soul-freeing covenant. He wants you to lay hold of a truth that will cut off all your chains. So—are you still hooked by a secret sin? Is your mind riddled with lustful thoughts? Are you gripped by a besetting sin you know is defiling God's temple, your body? ...The Lord says his covenant is your passport to victory—to gaining dominion over your sin. ...He decrees that all of {these} blessings are tied directly to seeking him."

—David Wilkerson[1]
The New Covenant Unveiled

Step **3**

DESTROY THE STRONGHOLDS

...The battle we are fighting is on the spiritual level. The very weapons we use are not those of human warfare but powerful in God's warfare for the destruction of the enemy's strongholds. Our battle is to bring down every deceptive fantasy and every imposing defense that men erect against the true knowledge of God.

2 Corinthians 10:3-5 Phillips

Once you have admitted you have a problem and confessed and repented of it, you are ready to work with God to *destroy the strongholds* of sexual impurity. The fight you are in is *not* physical. It is a spiritual war with spiritual weapons, and they are powerful! Second Corinthians 10:5 in The Message makes this clear: "We use our powerful God-tools for smashing warped philosophies, tearing down barriers erected against the truth of God." The strongholds we're after are the warped philosophies and the deceptive fantasies about sex that are contrary to the truth of God. But first...

What Is a Stronghold?

Good question. The word *stronghold* in this verse is the Greek word *ochuroma*. It's a term that was used to describe a **castle** or **fortress**. Ancient fortresses had very thick, high and immovable walls. They were built to keep intruders *out*. Interestingly, this same Greek word in New Testament times was also used to describe a **prison**. Prisons are places of punishment and captivity.[2] While a fortress is made to keep people *out*, a prison is made to lock people *in*. Are you seeing the connection between the word stronghold and porn?

Within the context of this passage, the word *stronghold* is "a fortress or prison of wrong thoughts." In our case, it's a fortress or prison of lies about sex. This thinking is contrary to the truth of God's Word. It has become so ingrained in our brains that we naturally fall into it like a *rut* in the road. As a *fortress*, strongholds of sexual impurity *stop the truth* from getting in. As a *prison*, strongholds of sexual impurity *hold you captive* to the devil's deceptions. Either way you look at it, it is bondage.

How Are Strongholds Built?

Strongholds are built one thought at a time in the invisible area of the soul. Each thought is like a brick in the walls of your thinking. In between the layers of brick is the "mortar" of your emotions (feelings). A quick study of the brain's major functions reveals that our thinking and feelings are positioned together in the frontal lobe. These invisible impulses are so tightly woven together they are often hard to tell apart. And as we learned earlier, there is nothing stronger than a thought cemented in place with a strong feeling.

Satan's aim is to get you to *accept* his lies as truth. When you accept a thought, you believe it to be true. The thoughts you accept become your beliefs—they are like bricks in the walls of your understanding. Right thoughts based on the truth of God's Word become strongholds of righteousness. Wrong thoughts based on the warped philosophies of the world and the lies of the enemy become strongholds of unrighteousness that need to be destroyed.

Like a master mason, the enemy ingeniously attempts to build strongholds in our lives when we are children. Initially, strongholds of sexual impurity are built out of ignorance. For example, I did not purposely seek the porn I saw at age nine or the neighbor girls who exposed their genitals. I also had no control over the fears and false feelings about sex passed on to me through my bloodline. Eventually, however, I had to own my actions—I had to take responsibility for my choices and behavior. The same is true for you.

Please realize, when you don't reject impure, ungodly thoughts, you accept them by default. By not choosing to reject these thoughts, you're actually making a decision to accept them. Every time I accepted the enemy's invitation to look at porn, I accepted another brick for the stronghold of sexual impurity. Every time I chose to look at a woman on paper, on the computer, or in person and lust after her in my heart, another brick of wrong belief was cemented in place. Every time I heard a song laced with lyrics of lust and didn't turn it off but allowed it to entertain me, the fortress of lies about sex was fortified. The same is true for you. A lie believed makes us deceived.

How Are Strongholds Destroyed?

Ultimately, God is the One who destroys strongholds, and we work with Him to do it. Amos 5:8-9 (GW) declares, "...His name is the Lord. *He destroys strongholds and ruins fortresses.*" We're powerless on our own, but in Christ, we are victorious. Yes, even against porn.

What's your part? It starts with consistently seeking God through *prayer*. Prayer is essentially talking and listening to God. It's ongoing communication with your heavenly Father that releases His power to destroy ungodly strongholds and build strongholds of righteousness. Prayer starts with *admitting and confessing* to God you have a stronghold. This is followed by *repentance*—turning your mind and heart away from sin and toward God. Next, ask God to destroy the stronghold of sexual impurity and take back the "ground" in your soul from the enemy. Then, *speak His Word* over your life and against the enemy. This is a crucial step we will discuss in detail in the coming chapters. God's Word coming out of your mouth and empowered by His Spirit is invincible!

Remember, "We use our powerful God-tools for smashing warped philosophies, tearing down barriers {strongholds} erected against the truth of God" (2 Corinthians 10:5 The Message). Our powerful God-tools include prayer, God's Word, and the blood and name of Jesus. As you abide in relationship with Jesus and submit yourself to His Spirit, victory is certain. And, while ungodly strongholds are being destroyed, you are also working with God to build strongholds of righteousness. How? By meditating on and speaking His Word, praying, and feeding your spirit good things. We'll talk more about these in the chapters ahead. Stay tuned...

Encouragement from the Heart of a Woman

I always thought that the stronghold in my life was my vulgar mouth. However, through years of walking with the Lord, He revealed to me that my mouth was only the fruit of a deeper root. That root was actually fear.

A spirit of fear began building a stronghold in my life when my parents got divorced. Not only did my dad move out, but he also took all of his guns and ammunition. For many years my dad and siblings and I not only shot guns together but also reloaded our ammunition. Now, I'm not saying he was wrong for not leaving a gun for his 12-year-old daughter. However, in my little mind, when he left and took the guns and ammunition with him, I felt unprotected. This left a void in my life...a void that opened the door to fear.

Ironically, the way fear displayed itself in my life was through my mouth. My words became my weapon of protection. I was very angry and spouted off many negative, angry, and hurtful things. This method of defense became a stronghold. It was only through abiding in relationship with Jesus that this stronghold was destroyed. God's amazing love for me and His patience with me demolished the fortress of fear. Little by little, He rebuilt a stronghold of His peace in my life. To this day, He continues to reaffirm His real love and protection through His presence that is always with me.

Man of God, I encourage you to continue to work with the Holy Spirit's promptings to destroy the strongholds of wrong thinking and build new strongholds—strongholds of righteousness. Lean on, trust in, and rely on God to construct a fortress of truth. As you walk in repentance, submit yourself to God, and resist the devil, you will walk in true freedom!

Walk It:

A *stronghold* is a fortress or prison of thoughts and feelings that is built in our soul. In this case, it is a fortress or prison of lies about sex. Strongholds are built one thought at a time. When you accept the enemy's lies, you place another brick of false belief in the wall of your understanding. Ungodly strongholds are destroyed by God as we seek and work with Him, using our powerful spiritual weapons. These include prayer, the Word, and the blood and name of Jesus. As you work with God to destroy ungodly strongholds, you are also working with Him to build strongholds of righteousness.

Study It:

Amos 5:8-9; Romans 8:37; 1 Corinthians 15:57; 2 Corinthians 2:14; 10:3-6; Ephesians 6:10-18; Hebrews 4:12; Revelation 12:11

Apply It:

1 In your own words, briefly describe how a stronghold of sexual impurity is built in your life.

_____

_____

_____

_____

2 According to God's Word, how is an ungodly stronghold destroyed? What are your weapons?

_____

_____

_____

_____

_____

3 Along with destroying ungodly strongholds, it's vitally important to build strongholds of righteousness. How can you work with God's Spirit to see this happen in your life?

_____

_____

_____

_____

4 What is your greatest takeaway from this chapter? What scriptures, principles, or ideas exploded in your heart? How are you challenged? What action(s) is God's Spirit prompting you to take?

_____

_____

_____

_____

Pray It:

"Father, I have a stronghold of sexual impurity in my life. I have accepted countless thoughts and feelings about sex that are contrary to the truth of Your Word. Please forgive me. Wash me clean of the perversity I have accepted as truth. Tear down the enemy's stronghold of lies. Take back the ground in my soul and help me build strongholds of righteousness in its place. Thank You, Father. In Jesus' name, Amen."

ONE BROTHER TO ANOTHER

"Temptation always comes by way of a thought, and the key to resisting temptation is to take that initial thought captive to the obedience of Christ. ...If you don't take captive the initial thought, you will probably lose the battle to temptation. We all have to learn how to practice threshold thinking. We need to take the way of escape the moment our thoughts are contrary to the truth and righteousness."

—Neil T. Anderson[1]
Victory over the Darkness

Step **4**

TAKE CONTROL OF YOUR THOUGHTS

Casting down arguments and every high thing that exalts itself against the knowledge of God, bringing every thought into captivity to the obedience of Christ.

2 Corinthians 10:5 NKJV

Your mind is the control center of your life. Consequently, it is the battlefield upon which you wage war. Your flesh, the world, and the enemy are constantly vying for your attention—presenting you with one ungodly, deceptive thought after another. Where your attention goes, the power flows. The war for sexual purity will be won or lost by what you entertain in your brain. What's the key to preventing strongholds of sexual impurity from forming? How can you keep yourself from falling into the pit of porn? The answer is to *cast down and take captive wrong thoughts.*

What Does "Cast Down and Take Captive" Mean?

Second Corinthians 10:5 explains how we are to maintain control over our thoughts. It says we are to *cast down* "arguments and every high thing that exalts itself against the knowledge of God" (NKJV). The words *cast down* in the Greek mean "to pull down, demolish, destroy, or refute."[2] What are we to pull down, demolish, destroy, and refute? *Arguments* and any *thought, idea,* or *feeling* that exalts itself above the truth of God's Word.

An *argument* is a reason or set of reasons used to persuade you to believe and ultimately act a certain way. (Some Bible versions use the words imaginations, theories, or reasonings here.) Another word to understand in this verse is the word *exalts*. It is the Greek word *epairo,* which means "to rise above in pride."[3] In pride, the enemy and your flesh constantly bring arguments, thoughts, ideas, and feelings to you to persuade you to believe and behave contrary to God's Word.

Satan has used this method since the Garden of Eden, and our flesh is vulnerable to it. He tries to get us to *doubt* the Word: "Did God really say that?" Next, he *twists* the Word: "You're not going to die…" And then he *perverts the character of God*: "God is withholding something good from you. You're missing out. He knows if you do this, you'll come to your senses and see that you don't need Him."[4] Are you getting a picture of how the enemy operates?

God says to cast down any thought, idea, or feeling that comes to your mind that is contrary to the truth of His Word. At the same time, you are to *take it captive and make it obey Christ* (see 2 Corinthians 10:5). To me, what God is speaking through Paul in this verse is that you and I are like spiritual policemen. We have authority in Christ, and we are to exercise it.[5] When wrong thoughts or feelings bombard our brain, we are to recognize them and say, "Hold it right there! You are a lie against the truth of God's Word, and I refuse to accept you or let you into my thinking, in Jesus' name." With the sword of the Spirit pressed against the enemy (and our flesh), we can recognize and reject wrong thinking and keep our focus on right thinking.

What's the Best Time to Deal with Wrong Thoughts?

Temptation, whether it's from your flesh or the enemy, always comes to you in the form of a thought. The best time to tackle it is *immediately*. That's when you're strongest and it is weakest. Wrong thoughts are most easily removed before they have a chance to get rooted. With every temptation, there is a *way of escape*! Scripture says, "God is faithful; he will not let you be tempted beyond what you can bear. But when you are tempted, he will also provide a way out so that you can stand up under it" (1 Corinthians 10:13 NIV).

Dr. Neil T. Anderson, founder of *Freedom in Christ Ministries*, talks about winning the battle for your mind and the necessity of tackling temptation when it first hits. He states:

> "If you don't take captive the initial thought, you will probably lose the battle to temptation. We all have to learn how to practice **threshold thinking**. We need to take the *way of escape* the moment our thoughts are contrary to the truth and righteousness."[6]

Imagine this: You're helping a good friend do some remodeling work on an old vacant house. As you're cleaning up debris, you stumble upon an X-rated DVD in the top of a closet. It was left behind by the previous tenants. Immediately, thoughts and ideas flood your brain. *Wonder what's on this? Maybe you ought to check it out. It's yours* now. *Take it. Slip it in your pocket. You can have some real fun later.* Along with these thoughts, past feelings connected with viewing porn attempt to rise up and capture your emotions. In that moment, you have a choice: obey the thoughts, ideas, and feelings rising up against God's Word, which says to flee sexual immorality,[7] or cast them down. What would you do?

Interestingly, this scenario happened to me this past year. Although it was unexpected, it didn't catch me totally off guard. I have stumbled onto smut at other people's houses many times through the years—usually magazines. In years past, I often fell into the trap and looked at it. Thankfully, God has done a work in my life and changed me. This time, instead of doing what my flesh and the enemy wanted, I did what God wanted.

I immediately picked up the DVD, and while the thoughts were bombarding my brain, I violently began to bend it back and forth until it broke in half. I then repeated the action with the two halves. As I did it, I said in a low but commanding voice, "Satan, I will not go back into that prison! I refuse your temptation. Flesh, you are dead to this! I will honor my Lord and my Lady!" I then picked up my cell phone and texted my wife and briefly informed her of what had just happened. Together, we shared a major victory!

What did I do? I casted down the arguments, thoughts, and ideas of porn's counterfeit sexual fulfillment. I refused to let the enemy's lies join forces with my flesh and direct my behavior. I made them obedient to Jesus. What would happen if I as a man in this position were to hesitate? Dr. Anderson says:

"If he hesitates *at the threshold,* stares at the picture and begins to fantasize about it, he will trigger an emotional landslide, producing a physical response that will be difficult to stop. He must *capture the initial tempting thought* or it will probably capture him."[8]

Friend, practice threshold thinking—tackle temptation immediately, and you'll avoid it most assuredly.

Think About What You're Thinking

First John 4:1 (NIV) says, "Dear friends, do not believe every spirit, but *test the spirits* to see whether they are from God...." In context, John was talking about the spirits in people, but this principle also applies to our thoughts and feelings. That is, we are not to receive every thought and feeling that drops in our heads. Instead, we are to *test the spirits* behind them to determine who they're from and if they're worth our attention.

Thoughts and feelings that are good or godly are going to reflect the fruit of God's Spirit. Galatians 5:22-23 (NLT) says, "...The Holy Spirit produces this kind of fruit in our lives: love, joy, peace, patience, kindness, goodness, faithfulness, gentleness, and self-control...." Good, godly thoughts and feelings will create these life-giving qualities in you. They will also motivate you to these kinds of actions toward others. Any thought or feeling that produces the opposite qualities is not from God and should be thrown out.

I love what veteran ministers John and Paula Sanford shared about dealing with thoughts. John said the Lord "impressed on Paula and me that we were to check every *thought* before we accepted it, every *feeling* before we embraced it (and gave it life within us), every *action* before we did it, by some simple questions."[9] What are these simple questions?

As questionable **thoughts** form in your mind, develop a habit of asking…

"Is this the way Jesus would *think*?"

As questionable **emotions** are rising within, ask…

"Is this what Jesus would *feel*?"

As questionable **actions** seem to be prompted, ask…

"Is this what Jesus would *do*?"

What are these questions doing? They are testing the spirits to see if the thoughts and feelings we are receiving and the actions we are considering are godly and worth our attention. The answer is always, "If Jesus would not *think* it or *feel* it or *do* it, neither will I." In other words, "I will think and feel and do only what Jesus would."[10]

Friend, take time to think about what you're thinking. Use the Philippians 4:8 filter: "...**Fix your thoughts** on what is true, and honorable, and right, and pure, and lovely, and admirable. Think about things that are excellent and worthy of praise" (NLT). There are eight specific standards given in this verse. Each acts as a filter through which you can pour every thought. If a thought doesn't line up with one of these standards, throw it out.

Bottom Line: Renew Your Mind!

In order to recognize and reject wrong thinking, you must renew your mind. I cannot stress to you more emphatically your need to feed on truth. The Word of God is a life-giving read worthy of your time and attention. I am who I am because of God's Word. There is nothing more transforming and invigorating than time spent in the Scriptures with the Holy Spirit as your Teacher.

Satan is a liar, your flesh is a liar, and so is the world. The only defense against lies is **truth**. Think about it. What's the first piece of spiritual armor? The belt of *truth*. What's the sixth piece of spiritual armor? The sword of the Spirit, which is the *Word of God* (see Ephesians 6:14, 17). Jesus said, "…If you abide in My word, you are My disciples indeed. And you shall know the truth, and the truth shall make you free" (John 8:31-32 NKJV). Friend, take control of your thoughts. Do what you need to do to get the Word of God in you! Renew your mind with truth, and God will set you free!

Encouragement from the Heart of a Woman

Man of God, as I was reading this chapter, praying and preparing to write to you, two things came to mind. First, the Holy Spirit, our totally cool Teacher, showed me something special about Philippians 4:8 (worth reading in the Message Bible). It says to fix our thoughts on that which is true, honorable, right, pure, lovely, and admirable. The Spirit showed me that this is a description of Jesus! Jesus is true, honorable, right, pure, lovely and admirable! If we remain focused on Him, we will achieve victory in our battles. Again, it is all about our relationship with Him.

The Holy Spirit then gave me an example of a tightrope or high wire walker—a funambulist. Not only does a funambulist have to maintain his balance, he also has to maintain his focus. If he gets distracted and starts to watch the circus below while walking the high wire, he will lose his balance and fall. He has to keep his eyes, mind, and body focused on the task at hand in order to achieve success. If he does not remain focused, he could lose his life.

Your walk with Christ is no different. If you become distracted by the thoughts or images that battle for your attention, you will lose your focus and fall. Satan is like a child who is desperately trying to get his parents' attention so they'll give him what he wants. That's what the enemy desperately wants from you—attention. He will create quite an impressive side show to get you to look. I urge you not to be impressed by him or the thoughts he brings. Likewise, don't focus on past failures or minor setbacks. If he succeeds at distracting you, he will stop your forward progress and you will lose the battle at hand. This is a universal truth that applies to all areas of life, not just porn.

Man of God, make it your aim to remain focused and faithful to your goal—sexual purity. My prayer for you is that you will become passionate about purity, being both diligent and careful to guard your eyes, mind, and heart against the side show the enemy puts on. He is a big liar and seriously wants to take you out. The good news is that Jesus already overcame him, so you are victorious in Him. You are loved and cherished, Man of God! I call you blessed! I declare you are an overcomer in Jesus' name!

Walk It:

Your mind is the control center of your life. It's where the war for sexual purity will be won or lost. To maintain control over your thinking, cast down any thought, idea, or feeling contrary to God's Word immediately. This is the way of escape. Think about what you're thinking. Use the Philippians 4:8 filter and the standard of the fruit of the Spirit to determine what to keep and cast down. If Jesus wouldn't think it, feel it, or do it, neither should you. The bottom line: Renew your mind with truth, and God will set you free!

Study It:

Filter Your Thoughts: Psalm 19:14; 2 Corinthians 10:3-5; 1 Corinthians 6:18; 10:13; Galatians 5:22-23; Philippians 4:8; 1 Thessalonians 4:3-8; 1 John 4:1 **Use the Word:** Psalm 119:9; John 8:31-32; 17:17 Ephesians 6:14, 17 **Renew Your Mind:** Romans 12:2; Ephesians 4:22-24; Joshua 1:8

Apply It:

1 Explain what it means to *cast down and take captive wrong thoughts*. Why is it vital to do this immediately? What will happen if you hesitate?

_____

_____

_____

_____

_____

2 Thoughts, ideas, and feelings that are contrary to God's Word must be recognized and rejected. List some examples of wrong thinking that you commonly face. What scriptures can you speak to refute these lies?

_____

_____

_____

_____

You can find related scriptures to your topic by inserting key words in the search bar at www.biblegateway.com.

3 Carefully read Galatians 5:22-23 and Philippians 4:8. How do these passages help you test the spirits behind the thoughts and feelings coming into your mind and filter out the wrong ones?

_____

_____

_____

_____

_____

Pray It:

"Father, I don't want the mind of my flesh, the mind of the world, or the mind of the enemy. I want Your mind. You said in 1 Corinthians 2:16 that I have the mind of Christ and hold the thoughts, feelings, and purposes of His heart (AMP). Please let Your mind rule all my thoughts, feelings, and desires. Teach me how to recognize and reject wrong thoughts immediately. By Your grace, I will only think, feel, and do what Jesus would. Please give me a desire for and understanding of Your Word. As You did with the two disciples on the road to Emmaus,[11] open the Scriptures to me and renew my mind daily. Thank You, Father. In Jesus' name, Amen!"

ONE BROTHER TO ANOTHER

"Stop looking. And stop putting yourself in the position to look! ...We must stay away from people, places, and contexts that make sin more likely. If it's certain bookstores, hangouts, or old friends from high school, stay away from them. If cable or satellite TV or network TV, the Internet, or computers are your problem, get rid of them. Just say no to whatever is pulling you away from Jesus. Remember, if you want a different outcome, you must make different choices."

— Randy Alcorn[1]
The Purity Principle

Step 5

DON'T GIVE THE ENEMY AN INCH

Neither give place to the devil.

Ephesians 4:27 KJV

Six small words, but what a powerful message! *Don't give the enemy an inch* means don't give him **place** in your life. Within the context of this passage, the words *neither give place to the devil* refer to dealing with anger promptly, before the day ends. But this principle applies to all areas of our lives, including walking in freedom over porn. How do you avoid giving place to the devil? By recognizing and avoiding the scenes of temptation and by starving your flesh. These are principles we will examine more closely in the coming chapters. But first...

Understand What "Give Place" Means

The original Greek word for place is *topos*. It describes a specific, geographical location. It's the word from which we get the term *topographical map.*[2] Literally, the word *place* means "opportunity, power, or occasion for acting."[3] Giving place to Satan is giving him opportunity and power to influence and bring destruction into your life and the lives of others. It's like renting him a room in your soul. From this position in your mind and emotions, he establishes his strongholds.

Every time you accept his ungodly thoughts and don't reject them, you give him *place*, and another brick is added to his fortress. You can give place to the enemy in areas of anger and unforgiveness, doubt and fear, lust and porn, and a whole host of other things. God does not want you to give place to Satan anywhere. He wants you to learn to recognize and reject the enemy's lies and give place to the truth of His Word.

As a husband and father, you are the spiritual covering for your family. Imagine yourself as a huge golf umbrella and your wife and kids are huddled under you. When you are spiritually healthy and pursuing God, the panels of your umbrella effectively keep the weathering, worldly influences from affecting them. However, if you are giving place to Satan by feeding on porn or anything else ungodly, you're creating "holes" in your umbrella. What you allow to "reign" in your life, you allow to "rain" on theirs. They become more vulnerable to any sin you choose not to stand against. Is it really worth it?

Understand Your Enemy

Another interesting word in Ephesians 4:27 is *devil*. It is the Greek word *diablos*. It's really more of Satan's job description than his name. Author, pastor, and Greek scholar Rick Renner explains:

> "The word 'devil' is a compound of the words *dia* and *balos*. The word *dia*…in this particular case…means *through*, as to pierce something from one side all the way through to the other side. The word *balos* means to *throw*, as when a person throws a ball, a rock, or some other object. When these two words are joined, it means to repetitiously throw something—striking again and again and again until the object being struck has finally been completely penetrated."[4]

Sound familiar? That's the way Satan and his forces operate. They attack your mind again and again and again, bombarding your brain with one filthy thought and image after another. Like the rapid fire of a machine gun, he strikes over and over and over again, trying to wear down your resistance. As soon as you let your guard down, he gives one final punch, penetrating and gaining place in your soul. Like an unwanted guest in your home, he brings in as much baggage as you will allow. What can you do?

Get Rid of Him and His Stuff

If you've given place to diablos, you need to serve him an eviction notice. Go to God in prayer. Admit it, confess it, and repent. Submit yourself to God anew and ask Him to tear down any stronghold of sexual impurity Satan has tried to build (see steps 1 thru 3). These steps to freedom are to be repeated as often as needed. You are not less of a person for repeating a step, and God is not disappointed in you. You are working out your salvation—fighting the good fight of faith to live free.[5] God is on your side, cheering you on and empowering you to make right choices.

Oh, one more thing. *Get rid of the enemy's stuff.* You know, the magazines, DVDs and any other porn-related trappings you've hidden under the dresser, in the trunk of your car, beneath your mattress, under the insulation in the attic, or in a computer file. Yes, this includes swimsuit magazines, lingerie catalogs, and those muscle magazines with their "soft" porn images. Remember, *don't give the enemy an inch*! If you give him an inch, he'll take ten miles. It's time to make a clean break and get rid of all the things that cause you to fall back into old sin patterns. Wherever the trash is stashed, find it and dispose of it.

My heart's cry is to be able to say what Jesus said just before going to the cross. He declared, "…The prince (evil genius, ruler) of the world is coming. And he has no claim on Me. *[He has nothing in common with Me; there is nothing in Me that belongs to him, and he has no power over Me]*" (John 14:30 AMP). The more you and I rid our lives of the things that belong to Satan—both the material and immaterial attitudes of the heart—the less power he has over us.

Don't be ignorant of the enemy's devices (see 2 Corinthians 2:11). Make it your aim to give him no claim on you or your family. **Don't give the enemy an inch!**

Encouragement from the Heart of a Woman

Man of God, the enemy's not only after you, but he's after your children and your children's children. Like it or not, you have been placed in authority over your family by God. He has given you to your wife and children as their covering. You are their first line of defense here on earth—you are their protector! Whatever you allow in your life, you give the enemy permission to try to bring into their lives. Where Satan defeats and enslaves you, he has strong opportunity to defeat and enslave them. It's kind of like a 2 for 1 deal—a deal he really likes. He knows what he's doing, and he's playing for keeps. He's a PIG!

First Corinthians 6:18 (NLT) says, "Run from sexual sin! No other sin so clearly affects the body as this one does. For sexual immorality is a sin against your own body." This sin weakens you like no other sin. It makes you vulnerable and easier to defeat in every other area. By imprisoning you in porn, the enemy has blockaded an avenue God created to make you stronger. When you enjoy God-created, God-approved sex within the safety of your marriage, you actually strengthen your union. And when you and your wife are strong, you are both more of a threat to the kingdom of darkness.

Thankfully, the enemy's actions and your struggle with sin are not catching God by surprise. Just as He walked with Vincent and me through our journey to freedom, He will be faithful to walk with you. He is more than able! According to Jeremiah 29:11, He has a good plan and a good future for you! And that future doesn't include addiction to pornography. It includes the good things that God has prepared for you, your wife, and your children even before the foundations of the earth were laid.

*Like Vincent, I urge you to get rid of anything connected with your previous lifestyle of lust. With the same urgency and diligence you would rid yourself of cancer cells, rid yourself of porn's trappings! Don't give the enemy an inch! You are covered in prayer, Man of God. You **are** going to make it!*

Walk It:

"Don't give the enemy an inch" means *don't give him **place***. Giving Satan place means giving him power and opportunity to bring destruction into your life and the lives of your wife and kids. Don't listen to the lies he hammers against your head. Recognize and resist him. Pull the plug on his operation. Protect yourself and your family—get rid of him and his stuff. Instead, give place to God's Word and Spirit!

Study It:

John 14:30; 1 Corinthians 10:6-9; 2 Corinthians 2:11; Ephesians 4:26-27; 5:2-8; 6:10-18; Colossians 3:1-8; 1 Peter 5:8-9; 2 Peter 1:5-10

Apply It:

1 Describe what it means to give place to the enemy. How does the meaning of *diablos* help you recognize the enemy's strategy/attack more clearly.

_____

_____

_____

_____

2 Pause and pray, "Holy Spirit, where am I *giving place* to the enemy—how am I empowering him? Do I have any of his stuff? If so, what do I have and where is it?" Get quiet before the Lord and listen as He speaks to you. Write what He reveals and take any action He prompts.

_____

_____

_____

_____

3 How will your wife and kids be affected by you giving place to porn and other ungodly thinking and behavior? Can you see any effects manifesting in their lives now? How does this motivate you to live clean, pure, and free?

_____

_____

_____

_____

4 What's your greatest takeaway from this chapter? What scriptures, principles, or ideas spoke to your heart most? How are you challenged? What action(s) is God prompting you to take?

_____

_____

_____

_____

Pray It:

"Father, forgive me for giving place to the enemy. I have given him opportunity and power to bring problems into my life and my family's life. Tear down any stronghold he has built in my life or the lives of my wife and children. Take back the ground I surrendered. Today is a new day and I want to go in a new direction. Show me anything I have that belongs to Satan—books, magazines, movies…any of his stuff. I am getting rid of it. Help me and my family replace his trash with Your treasures. Thank You, Father, for always leading me in victory in Christ (see 2 Corinthians 2:14). In Jesus' name, amen."

ONE BROTHER TO ANOTHER

"We can win over jealousy, a bad temper, greed, and even pride. We can train our consciences to avoid theft, bad mouthing, and lying. But who do you know who could avoid a peek at pornography if convinced no one would find out?

…What is the solution when temptation rages? If we are weak and have not taken precautions, if we have not applied preventive medicine, we have already failed. The only answer is to plan, to anticipate danger, to plot the way of escape. The time to build hedges is before the enemy attacks."
— Jerry B. Jenkins[1]
Hedges

Step **6**

AVOID THE VERY SCENES OF TEMPTATION

Let your way in life be far from her, and come not near the door of her house [avoid the very scenes of temptation].

Proverbs 5:8 AMP

Avoid the very scenes of temptation. When I read this verse in the Amplified Bible, the Lord made it explode in my heart and gave me a new perspective. Immediately, I pictured the scene of a crime roped off by yellow police tape so no one could enter. That's the way you need to see the places you have frequently fallen into sin—as the scene of a crime against God, your wife, and your children that you never want to enter again.

Proverbs 5 is all about the adulteress—aka the loose, immoral, seductive woman. Remember, *pornography* is prostitution on paper, the computer, etc. God says to "let your way in life be far from her, and come not near the door of her house [avoid the very scenes of temptation]." Slow down and let those six words sink deep into your heart: "Avoid the very scenes of temptation." Regularly doing this one thing is a major step toward freedom.

Take a Different Route

Imagine this: You just started a new job and you're on your way home from work. It's your first day and you're driving a new route. About ten minutes into your journey, you turn a corner and fall into the deepest pothole you've seen in your life. It's so deep and wide your front end bottoms out and drags the ground for what seems like an eternity. Upon arriving home, you discover your shocks are shot, your tire has a bubble in its sidewall, and your car frame is bent. The question is: Do you take the same route home again? Hopefully not.

The same is true with porn. Porn is a pothole to your soul. God says, "A whore is a bottomless pit; a loose woman can get you in deep trouble fast. She'll take you for all you've got; she's worse than a pack of thieves" (Proverbs 23:27-28 The Message). Porn in any form is a deep pit—a pit we must learn to recognize and avoid.

When I was a young teenager, there was an exercise show on a local TV station that came on every day at three o'clock. Often, no one was home at that time, so I'd sit and watch. My eyes, which are the windows of my soul, absorbed image after image of legs in leotards and all the curves that came with them. After releasing myself sexually, deep shame and guilt filled my heart. God's Spirit living in me was grieved. I would repent, feel better, but be right back in the same seat doing the same thing within days.

Sickened by my pattern of sin, I cried out, "God, I'm sorry. I don't want to keep doing this. Please help me." Faintly, I heard in my heart, *Since you know the time and place the sin keeps happening, avoid it. Don't turn on the TV at three. Do something different—somewhere else.* "Avoid the very scenes of temptation"—that's what He was telling me. Instead of falling into the same pothole, I needed to take a different route. I did it, and it helped tremendously.

Slowly but surely, I learned to apply this principle to many of the "scenes" of temptation I faced. This included the porn magazines near the lockers at the seafood dock where I worked, the magazine racks in the mall bookstores, and certain gas stations that displayed smut in clear view. Yes, porn's availability has increased since then, but this principle still works. God promises you that "though sin is shown to be wide and deep, thank God his grace is wider and deeper still!" (Romans 5:20 Phillips).

Repeated Principles Are Important

Avoiding the scenes of temptation is a principle found throughout Scripture. Look at what God says: "Turn from all known sin and spend your time in doing good..." (Psalm 34:14 TLB). "Avoid evil and walk straight ahead. Don't go one step off the right way" (Proverbs 4:27 GNT). "The wise watch their steps and avoid evil; fools are headstrong and reckless" (Proverbs 14:16 The Message). "Avoid every kind of evil" (1 Thessalonians 5:22 GNT). Why does God repeat this principle again and again? Because it is extremely important.

I believe avoiding the scenes of temptation is the heart of what Jesus is saying in Matthew 5:29-30 (AMP). Talking about overcoming lust, He says, "If your right eye serves as a trap to ensnare you or is an occasion for you to stumble and sin, pluck it out and throw it away. ...And if your right hand serves as a trap to ensnare you or is an occasion for you to stumble and sin, cut it off and cast it from you. It is better that you lose one of your members than that your entire body should be cast into hell (Gehenna)."

As we learned earlier, Jesus is *not* telling you to literally gouge out your eye or cut off your hand if it is causing you to sin. He is saying to cut off or avoid any thing that "serves as a trap to ensnare you or is an occasion for you to stumble and sin." He is telling you to plan ahead and **avoid the very scenes of temptation**.

Being Tempted Is Not a Sin

One thing is clear: You and I will face temptation. Jesus said, "There will always be temptations to sin..." (Luke 17:1 NLT). Even Jesus was tempted. Scripture says, "We have a chief priest {Jesus} who is able to sympathize with our weaknesses. *He was tempted* in every way that we are, but he didn't sin" (Hebrews 4:15 GW).

Don't just quickly read over that verse. Slowly read it again and let its truth sink in. Jesus was tempted in *every* way that we are, but He did *not* sin. This means temptation in and of itself is not a sin; it's giving in to temptation that is sin. Also, if Jesus was tempted in *every* way, He had to be tempted to lust after women and masturbate. Yes, He was fully God, but He was also fully man—a man who had hormones and a sex drive like you and me. In order for Him to fully understand what we go through, He had to be tempted in this area. This is why He is able to "...understand and sympathize and have a shared feeling with our weaknesses..." (Hebrews 4:15 AMP).

Why should the fact that Jesus was tempted encourage us? I believe the answer is found in the next verse: "Let us therefore approach the throne of grace with fullest confidence, that we may receive *mercy* for our failures and grace to help in the hour of need" (v. 16 Phillips). Praise God for His mercy! Because of His mercy, which He freshly supplies each day, we are not thrown out of His presence (see Lamentations 3:22-23). And thank God for His grace! It is the supernatural power of His Holy Spirit not to sin and to avoid the very scenes of temptation.

Friend, don't let the devil dupe you into believing you have sinned just because he tempts you. He is a liar. When you're tempted, run to Jesus and ask Him for grace not to sin. Scripture says, "He gives us more and more grace (*power of the Holy Spirit*, to meet this evil tendency and all others fully)..." (James 4:6 AMP). "For because He Himself [in His humanity] has suffered in being tempted (tested and tried), He is able [immediately] to run to the cry of...those who are being tempted and tested and tried…" (Hebrews 2:18 AMP). If you do fall into temptation and sin, run to Him for mercy. He offers it freely! Confess and repent of your sin, receive His forgiveness with a humble heart, and go on. His love for you will never change—even if you are disobedient. How great is our God!

Encouragement from the Heart of a Woman

Your purity matters! If it didn't matter, the battle wouldn't be so intense. Yes, you are up against a cunning, formidable foe. But as I shared with Vincent many times throughout our journey, don't be impressed by his temptations or stop to admire his work. It only makes you lose momentum in moving forward into the freedom Christ has paid for you to have.

To help Vincent avoid the scenes of temptation, I chose to put a stop on receiving any catalogs by mail that could cause him to fall. At his request, I blocked the Internet access in his office, leaving the only opportunity for him to go online in the family room where the computer was in full view. I also helped him by quickly changing the channel when sleazy commercials came on. Stop and think. What are some ways you can allow your wife to help you avoid the scenes of temptation you face?

Man of God, I urge you to reveal and deal with every scene of temptation. Don't hide or withhold one tool the enemy has been using in your life—don't keep your deepest, darkest, favorite places of sin covered. Expose and repent of every outlet of perversion. This is crucial to your freedom. You must be honest about where you are and what you have been allowing in your life. You cannot be totally free until you are totally honest.

You were meant to live in peace and victory in Christ. Right now He is standing at the door of your heart knocking. He wants to come in and walk with you through this. In Matthew 11:28-30, He says, "Are you tired? Worn out? Burned out on religion? Come to me. Get away with me and you'll recover your life. I'll show you how to take a real rest. Walk with me and work with me—watch how I do it. Learn the unforced rhythms of grace. I won't lay anything heavy or ill-fitting on you. Keep company with me and you'll learn to live freely and lightly" (The Message).

Can you hear Him calling you, Man of God? Accept His invitation! Ask Him to help you find new paths that lead to purity. He will faithfully show you how to form healthy habits and avoid the very scenes of temptation. Yes, it's going to be a battle at times, but your purity is well worth fighting for! I challenge you to set aside a specific time every day to get away and learn from Jesus. It doesn't have to be all day—just a part of your day. Lean on Him and rely on His strength. He loves you and longs to help and heal you. You and your journey are covered in prayer.

Walk It:

Avoiding the very scenes of temptation is a major step toward freedom. Porn is a pothole to your soul. Instead of falling in the same places of sin again and again, take a different route. Plan ahead. Cut off anything in your life that easily ensnares you or causes you to stumble into sin. Ask the Lord to help you develop some new, healthy habits that lead to righteousness. When you're tempted, run to Him for grace to escape it. And if you fall into sin, ask Him for mercy. He will willingly grant it!

Study It:

Avoid Temptation: Psalm 34:14; Proverbs 4:25-27; 5:1-23; 7:1-27; 23:27-28; Matthew 5:27-30; 18:8-9; Mark 9:43-47; 1 Thessalonians 5:22; 1 Peter 3:10-12 **Run to Jesus:** Matthew 11:28-30; Romans 5:20; Hebrews 2:14 - 3:1; 4:14-16

Apply It:

1 Stop and think: What specific *scenes of temptation* is God showing you to avoid?

_____

_____

_____

_____

_____

_____

2 Pray and ask the Holy Spirit to give you a practical plan of action to avoid the "scenes" you listed above. Say, "Lord, what new 'routes' can I take to avoid each of these scenes of temptation? Please help me form new habits and put them into practice." Listen and write what He reveals.

_____

_____

_____

_____

_____

_____

3 It is vital to know what Jesus experienced while here on earth. Carefully read Hebrews 2:14 - 3:1 and 4:14-16. What is the Holy Spirit speaking to you in these passages and how do they encourage you?

_____

_____

_____

_____

_____

4 What is your greatest takeaway from this chapter? What scriptures, principles, or ideas exploded in your heart? How do they challenge you? What action(s) is God's Spirit prompting you to take?

_____

_____

_____

_____

_____

Things I Want to Remember:

Pray It:

"Father, thank You for showing me this powerful principle. Please help me put it into practice starting today. Show me the scenes of temptation where I'm frequently falling into sin. Help me to see them as the scene of a crime that I don't want to reenter. Give me Your grace and a practical plan of action to avoid every one of them. I don't want to be spiritually lazy. From this day forward, I want to take a different route far from the potholes of porn. In Jesus' name, Amen."

ONE BROTHER TO ANOTHER

"To put it bluntly, your flesh is a weasel, a poser, and a selfish pig. And your flesh is not you. Did you know that? Your flesh is not the real you. ...And the only way to deal with it is to crucify it."

— John Eldredge[1]

Wild at Heart

Step 7

STARVE YOUR FLESH

*Let us be Christ's men from head to foot, and give
no chances to the flesh to have its fling.*

Romans 13:14 Phillips

To *starve your flesh* means to not give your old, ungodly nature any chance to have its way. Taking control of your thoughts, not giving the enemy an inch, and avoiding the very scenes of temptation are all ways to starve your flesh. This practice is one of the most important steps you can take to break free from past patterns of sin. To starve your flesh is to stop feeding it—to cut off its source of fuel. Whatever you feed is going to live. What you starve is going to die.

What Is the Flesh?

For years I had this question. Then I learned that the flesh is basically all we are *apart from God*. It is our "old nature"—the combined ungodly cravings of our body and soul that must be put to death daily. This includes excessive, ungodly cravings to be sexually stimulated by porn and find release through masturbation. Romans 8:6 (AMP) reveals that "the mind of the flesh [which is *sense and reason without the Holy Spirit*] is death...."

Interestingly, our physical bodies are made of the same elements found in dirt. And dirt is what Satan feeds on. No kidding. When God judged Satan for tempting Adam and Eve, He told him he was cursed to "...eat dirt all {his} life" (Genesis 3:14 The Message). When you feed your flesh, you feed the enemy. The more dirty thoughts, movies, music, and images you take in, the more he has to "eat." Yes, this is figurative, but it is an undeniable principle with far-reaching effects.

Don't Dine with Demons

Did you know that you can "dine" with demons? God, through the apostle Paul, said, "...I do not want you to *fellowship* and be *partners* with diabolical spirits..." (1 Corinthians 10:20 AMP). In 2 Corinthians

6:14-15 (The Message), He adds, "…How can you make a partnership out of right and wrong? That's not partnership; that's war. Is *light* best friends with *dark*? Does Christ go strolling with the Devil? Do trust and mistrust hold hands?" Clearly, hanging out and being friends with the enemy is *not* what God wants.

As a believer, you're part of Christ's body (see 1 Corinthians 12:27). He lives in you; you are the house of His Spirit (see 1 Corinthians 6:19). When you willingly choose to feed your flesh porn or watch and listen to ungodly movies, music, TV, Internet, etc., you open the door of your soul for unclean and evil spirits to fellowship with you. You *give place* to the enemy. God would *not* say "don't fellowship or be partners with diabolical spirits" if it was not possible. It is possible, and that's why He warns us to separate ourselves from such things. To break free, you must break fellowship—you must starve your flesh.

What Fuels the Fire of Impure Desire?

To starve your flesh is to cut off its fuel supply. Picture this: You light a small candle and set it on a table. You then take a clear drinking glass, turn it upside down, and cover the candle. What eventually happens to the flame? That's right; it goes out. You cut off its fuel supply of oxygen. The same thing will happen to the fire of impure desire when you cut off the fuel supply of filth you have been feeding on.

Take an inventory of what you're feeding your soul and spirit. What Internet sites are you surfing? What video games are you playing? What books and magazines are you reading? What TV shows and movies are you watching? Most of us would not walk up to an attractive couple at the mall and say, "Excuse me. My wife and I are looking for some entertainment tonight. Would you come over to our house and have sex in our living room while we sit and watch?" Yet, that's what we do when we rent and view movies containing sexual, "adult" content. We are paying to be entertained by perversity.

How about your *relationships*? Are any of them causing you to sin? If possible, cut them off. If you can't because they are a family member or coworker, drastically limit your time with them. What about the music you're listening to? This was a huge issue in my life when I was a teen. Messages in music become embedded in your brain. Think about it. What kind of effects do you think songs like "I Want Your Sex," "Pour Some Sugar on Me," and "Hungry Like a Wolf" have on us? A steady diet of this type of music will only serve to cement the sin of sexual impurity in your life. This is the enemy's stuff that Jesus is urging you to get rid of.

Whatever is fueling the fire of impure desire needs to be cut off. This is what it means to starve your flesh. What you feed will live. What you starve will die. If the World Wide Web is entangling you in sin, get rid of it till you are stronger. Some will say, "Oh, but Vincent, that sounds so extreme!" It may be, but extreme problems require extreme solutions. *How badly do you want to be free?* When your desire to be free is greater than your desire for sexual release from porn, you will do whatever it takes to be free. Let me say that again: When your desire to be free is greater than your desire for sexual release from porn, you will do whatever it takes to be free.

What's the Answer?

There is only one door to freedom, and that door is a relationship with Jesus Christ! He is not a way—He is THE way (see John 14:6). So, "clothe yourself with the Lord Jesus Christ (the Messiah), and **make no provision for [indulging] the flesh** [put a stop to thinking about the evil cravings of your physical nature] to [gratify its] desires (lusts)" (Romans 13:14 AMP). Jesus said, "...The flesh conveys no benefit whatever [there is no profit in it]..." (John 6:63 AMP). "So I say, let the Holy Spirit guide your lives. Then you won't be doing what your sinful nature craves" (Galatians 5:16 NLT). Starve your flesh and feed your spirit!

Encouragement from the Heart of a Woman

Starving the flesh is crucifying the flesh. To me, this means saying no to it every time it wants something outside of God's will and timing. Looking at porn, exploding in anger, cursing somebody out, eating too much, etc., are all things your flesh may want or feel like doing, but you can learn to tell it no by the power of the Holy Spirit. Crucifying your flesh is not a one-time event, but a process—a process that requires both prayer and fasting (see Matthew 17:14-21).

Fasting applies to more than just food. It also includes the things we feed our mind, will, and emotions (our soul). It's true that media is a huge part of our daily lives. However, sometimes it is necessary to pull away from our natural, normal way of doing things so that we can hear from God and experience a new, more powerful way of living.

Vincent and I are blessed with four incredible children who enjoy media just as much as anyone else. However, there are times when we choose to restrict their media consumption. When we do, our home is a much different place. Instead of watching movies or playing video games, they invest in their relationships with each other and those around them. We often find them reading together, writing a story together, making a movie, or learning a new craft. Overall, we have less strife and more peace. Fasting from media recalibrates our focus on what's most important—our relationships with Jesus and each other.

So, as I mentioned before, consider doing a total media fast for 21 days (or at least a partial fast). During the times you would normally be surfing the Internet or watching movies, feed your spirit the truth of God's Word and time in His presence. God will take note of every effort you put forth to grow spiritually. As you cry out to Him for help, He will empower you to walk out of the prison of porn and into freedom.

Man of God, smother the flame of perversity in your life—starve your flesh. And as you do, remember to feed your spirit. Train yourself to say NO every time your flesh wants its way. Push past the momentary discomfort and focus your mind on the blessings God has given you. The feelings of pressure to go look at something will pass. As you draw closer to Jesus and allow Him to live through you, He will empower you to live the pure life He lived and reap the harvest it brings.

Walk It:

To starve your flesh means to stop feeding it—to cut off its fuel source. It means to not give your old, ungodly nature any chance to have its way. With God's strength, you can cut off any entertainment, relationships, etc., that are fueling the fire of impure desire. What you feed will live. What you starve will die. Feed your spirit God's Word and let the Holy Spirit guide your life. Then you won't be doing what your sinful nature craves.

Study It:

Flesh vs. Spirit: Proverbs 27:20; John 6:63; Romans 8:5-13; 7:18; Galatians 5:16-18 **Starve the Flesh:** Matthew 5:27-30; 18:8-9; Mark 9:43-47; Romans 6:1-14; 13:12-14; 1 Corinthians 6:12-20; 10:20-23; 12:27; Galatians 2:20; Ephesians 5:11-18; Colossians 3:1-10; 1 Peter 2:11 **The Power of Friends:** Psalm 1; Proverbs 13:20; 1 Corinthians 5:11; 15:33; 2 Corinthians 6:14-15; 2 Thessalonians 3:14

Apply It:

1 Ask yourself: *Am I starving my flesh or feeding it? Am I dining with demons or have I put out the fire of impure desire? What evidence in my life backs up my answer?* Get quiet before the Lord and ask Him to show you your heart. Write what He reveals.

_____

_____

_____

_____

2 What practical steps can you take to starve your flesh? Again, pray and ask God for His input.

_____

_____

_____

_____

3 What would a media fast look like for you? Pause and pray, "Lord, what media should I fast from? How long should my fast be? What scriptures should I feed my spirit?" Quietly listen for the plan He reveals. Write it and ask Him for grace to carry it out.

_____

_____

_____

_____

4 What is your greatest takeaway from this chapter? What scriptures, principles, or ideas exploded in your heart? How are you challenged? What action(s) is God's Spirit prompting you to take?

_____

_____

_____

_____

Pray It:

"Father, please forgive me for feeding my flesh. I did not know I was fellowshipping with the enemy. Show me any place I am fueling the fire of impure desire, including any movies, music, magazines, Internet sites, video games, or relationships I need to cut off. Give me the power and desire to effectively starve my flesh and feed my spirit every day. I want You to guide my life, Holy Spirit. Please purify my heart and mind with the blood of Jesus. Thank You, Father. In Jesus' name, Amen."

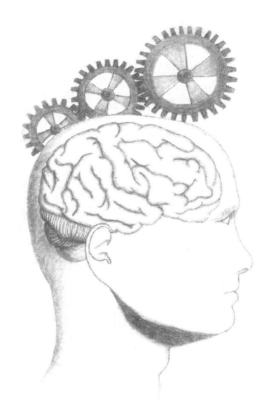

Establish New Habits
That Help You Live Pure

ONE BROTHER TO ANOTHER

"The most holy and necessary practice in our spiritual life is the presence of God. That means finding constant pleasure in His divine company, speaking humbly and lovingly with Him in all seasons, at every moment, without limiting the conversation in any way. ...The presence of God is, then, the life and nourishment of the soul, which can be acquired with the grace of God."

— Brother Lawrence[1]
The Practice of the Presence of the Lord

Step 8

FEED YOUR SPIRIT

*I am the Bread—living Bread!—who came down out of heaven.
Anyone who eats this Bread will live—and forever! The Bread that
I present to the world so that it can eat and live
is myself, this flesh-and-blood self.*

John 6:51 The Message

Next to starving your flesh, the most important thing for you to do is *feed your spirit*. What you starve is going to die. What you feed is going to live. Feeding your spirit is spending time with God—it's your devotional relationship with Jesus. How this specifically looks for you will likely be different than it looks for me, and that's okay. Each of us is unique, and our devotional time with the Lord will have its own unique flavor. That being said, there are two universal aspects of feeding our spirit, and they are spending time in God's written Word and spending time with Jesus, who is the Word made flesh.

God's Word Is Spiritual Food

The Bible, which is the written Word, is God wrapped in print. Why has it been given? God says, "Like newborn babies, you must crave pure spiritual milk so that you will grow into a full experience of salvation. Cry out for this nourishment" (1 Peter 2:2 NLT). As you feed your spirit the Word, you will receive life-giving sustenance that can be found in no other place.

David loved God's Word. He said, "How sweet your words taste to me; they are sweeter than honey" (Psalm 119:103 NLT). Jeremiah greatly prized the Word too. He proclaimed, "Your words are what sustain me; they are food to my hungry soul. They bring joy to my sorrowing heart and delight me. How proud I am to bear your name, O Lord" (Jeremiah 15:16 TLB).

I cannot put into words how radically the Word of God has transformed my life. I am who I am because of it. Reading, studying, meditating on, and memorizing Scripture continues to shape my thoughts, words, and actions. This intangible substance produces tangible results when consumed regularly. Without God's Word, I'd be dead. We'll focus on the Word's importance and power in the coming chapters. For now I'll say, do what you need to do to get God's Word in you.

Fellowshipping with Christ Is Spiritual Food

Jesus Christ, who is the Living Word, is God wrapped in flesh. Scripture declares, "In the beginning [before all time] was the Word (Christ), and the Word was with God, and the Word was God Himself. And the Word became flesh and dwelt among us…" (John 1:1 AMP; v. 14 NKJV). Jesus Christ who stepped out of eternity and into time "…is the sole expression of the glory of God…the perfect imprint and very image of [God's] nature…" (Hebrews 1:3 AMP).

Feeding your spirit is all about maintaining a healthy relationship with Jesus. He is your food. Three times in John 6 Christ identifies Himself as the *Bread of Life*, saying, "…Whoever comes to me will never be hungry again. Whoever believes in me will never be thirsty" (v. 35 NLT). When you are spiritually *full* of the Living Bread, you don't have an appetite for spiritual junk food like porn. King David says that in the Lord's presence are *fullness* of joy and pleasures forevermore (see Psalm 16:11).

Hopefully it is becoming clear that your greatest remedy against pornography is intimacy with Jesus. It's all about *relationship*. And your relationship with Him is nurtured by developing a lifestyle of prayer, letting His Word dwell in you richly, and allowing His Spirit to empower you to walk in freedom.

My father, Frank Newfield Sr., is an anointed counselor of over thirty years. He's worked with many Christian men, including ministers, who have fallen into the pit of porn. One day I asked him, "Dad, what is the greatest common denominator among all these men who have given place to the enemy in the area of porn?" Without hesitation he answered, "They lost their personal devotional time with God; it was the first thing to go."

This is what happened with a couple of ministers I know and have ministered to personally. In their journey to freedom, they have learned that their level of victory over porn is directly linked to their level of intimacy with Jesus. When they spend daily, quality time with Him, the desire to give in to porn diminishes and they're stronger spiritually to quickly say no to temptation. If their personal time with

Christ becomes "hit and miss," temptation wins. The more they miss, the more vulnerable they become.

Fellowship with the Father through His Son, Jesus, is the greatest defense against sin. Please don't miss this point—it's the most important point of all. Nothing—absolutely nothing—is a substitute for time spent with Jesus. Remember, He is LIFE,[2] and fellowship with Him releases LIFE into every part of you—spirit, soul, and body.

Don't Let Anything or Anyone Keep You from Jesus!

Now, if you haven't already discovered, there is nothing that the enemy will fight you harder on than spending time with God. He will use anything he can to prevent you from feeding your spirit because he knows that when you spend time in God's Word and His presence, you become like Him. Time spent with Jesus = a strong spirit that is able to resist temptation. Therefore, you can't allow anything or anyone to keep you from Jesus!

Remember the story of blind Bartimaeus? He was sitting on the side of the road near Jericho begging for money to survive. "When Bartimaeus heard that Jesus of Nazareth was nearby, he began to shout, 'Jesus, Son of David, have mercy on me!'" (Mark 10:47 NLT). At that point, many yelled at him and told him to be quiet. But that didn't stop Bartimaeus. He shouted all the louder, desperately attempting to connect with Jesus. What happened? Jesus heard him, stopped what He was doing, and took time to heal him.[3]

How about the woman who had the issue of blood for twelve years? She had suffered a great deal from many doctors who attempted to help her, and she had spent all her money in the process. She had heard about Jesus and knew He was passing by. In desperation, she pressed through the massive crowd that swarmed around Him, attempting just to touch the tassel of His robe. "For she kept saying, If I only touch His garments, I shall be restored to health" (Mark 5:28 AMP). What happened? She touched the edge of Jesus' robe and immediately she was healed.[4]

Can you hear what God's Spirit is saying? He's saying, *Don't let anything or anyone keep you from Jesus!* Like Bartimaeus, call upon the Name of the Lord and tell Him what you need. Like the woman with the issue of blood, press in to His presence and receive the healing and freedom that only He can provide. These people were desperate for Jesus, and they didn't let anything stand in the way of getting to Him.

"But, I feel so *guilty*," you say. "I feel bad because I've fallen into the same sin again and again." Or, "I feel guilty because it's been so long since I spent time with God. I just can't ask Him to forgive me for the same sin *again*." I understand. I've felt that way too. But you've got to move beyond feelings of guilt and believe God's Word.

"But I'm *afraid*," you say. "I'm afraid He is upset with me because I haven't spent time with Him." Or, "I'm afraid that God is mad at me because I've sinned again. I'm afraid I've done so much wrong that I can't be forgiven." Again, I understand feeling afraid. But you have to push past feelings of fear and believe God's Word.

God says **nothing** can separate you from His love—*nothing* (see Romans 8:38-39). You cannot be good enough to enter His presence, so don't try. Just come as you are on the merits of Christ's finished work. It's His mercy, grace, and shed blood that gives you the right to fellowship with Him.[5] Remember: "…While we were still sinners, Christ died for us" (Romans 5:8 NIV). Neither your unfaithfulness nor disobedience can stop His love. He loves you—period. And His love never changes. It's not based on your good behavior, how much of the Bible you read, or how many hours you pray. His love is based on Him. God is love (see 1 John 4:8). It's not something He does; it's who He is.

So don't let anything or anyone keep you from Jesus! Don't follow your feelings or listen to the lies of the enemy. Jesus is your life, your breath, your wisdom, your peace, your healing, your protection, your joy, your acceptance, your purity, your freedom, your **everything**! Live your life like you are desperate for Him, and you will have everything you need to thrive!

How Can You Effectively Feed Your Spirit?

There are many ways to feed your spirit, but as I said before, each of us is unique. Therefore, our devotional time with the Lord will also be unique. Some proven ways to feed your spirit include: reading, studying, and meditating on God's Word; listening to the Bible on CD or MP3; listening to Christian teachings on CD, podcasts, TV, radio, etc.; listening to Christian music; and reading devotional and topical books on Christian living. Another way of feeding your spirit is through *prayer*—talking and listening to God. This includes thanking, praising, and worshipping Him, as well as simply sitting quietly in His presence.

When Allison and I first got married, someone hit me from behind and totaled my car. This left us with one vehicle and me riding the bus to work for several months. Initially, I was aggravated and frustrated because I had to get to work about 45 minutes early. But God turned this into one of the most rewarding devotional times in my life. Instead of sitting around sulking, I began reading the one-year Living Bible. To this day I am amazed at how the Holy Spirit made the Word come alive as I sat by myself and read. It was life-giving! I actually looked forward to my time with God.

Time passed and that season of our life changed. With the change of seasons came a change in how I spent time with the Lord. This is natural and normal. The bottom line: Spend time with God any way you know that works. Do some research and experiment with different things. This is part of "working out your salvation" (see Philippians 2:12). Pause and pray, "Lord, at this season of my life with the commitments I have, how can I feed my spirit? In what ways can I spend time with You and feed on Your Word?" Get quiet and expect Him to respond. It may not be immediately, but He will lead you and show you what to do.

Encouragement from the Heart of a Woman

Life is undeniably about seasons. As a wife and mother of four amazing daughters, one of my biggest challenges is finding time alone. Every day is extremely busy and I'm pulled in many directions, much like you, I'm sure. While I do wear an apron, I'm nothing like Susanna Wesley; I can't just pull it over my head and spend time with Jesus.

Prior to becoming a mother, my time with Jesus was rich and regular. Usually the first hour of my day (or longer) was spent in prayer, Bible reading and study. Each day brought new revelations about God, myself, and the world around me. It was a great time of life indeed.

Then the blessings of our children came. With each additional blessing, my time became more and more divided. Consequently, my life took on a completely new look. As the demands increased, I learned that I was a very impatient person. This was not a good character trait to have while being responsible to teach and train little people!

Lack of patience caused me to cry out to God for help. He answered by directing me to His Word, specifically 1 Corinthians 13 in the Amplified Bible. Over time, I committed the chapter to memory and would quote it three times a day—morning, noon, and night. I felt as if God, my Great Physician, had prescribed it to me like spiritual antibiotics. His Word molded and shaped me into a more patient person. Oh, I still have moments of impatience. When it happens, I begin quoting 1 Corinthians 13. Immediately, I experience His love and strength. I'm so grateful for Him directing me to His Word and encouraging me to memorize it. He truly is my ever-present help in time of need!

Man of God, don't be robbed of this blessing! Feed your spirit. Spend time in God's Word memorizing specific scriptures He shows you. By investing this time, you will have His truth within you to draw strength from whenever you need it. There's nothing sweeter than receiving help from God in your moment of need. It solidifies your relationship with Him, infusing you with His rich, undeniable love. I call you blessed and highly favored among men. You are an overcomer in Christ!

Walk It:

Feeding your spirit is spending time with God—it's your devotional life with Christ. It includes spending time in the written Word and with the Living Word, Jesus. Your greatest remedy against pornography is intimacy with Jesus. It's all about relationship. Time spent with Jesus = a strong spirit that is able to resist temptation. Nothing— absolutely nothing—is a substitute for spending time with Him, and nothing can separate you from His love. So don't let anything keep you from Him. He is your everything!

Study It:

The Written Word: Deuteronomy 8:3 (Matthew 4:4); Joshua 1:8; Psalm 1:1-3; 119:103; Jeremiah 15:16; 1 Peter 2:2 **Jesus, the Living Word:** John 1:1-14; 6:25-35; 48-63; Hebrews 1:3; **His Presence:** Psalm 16:11; Matthew 11:28-30; Revelation 3:20 **His Love:** Romans 5:8; 8:31-39

Apply It:

1   Look back over your life. In what ways have you effectively fed your spirit? Jot down anything that has energized and empowered you to live clean and experience the fruit of God's Spirit.

_____

_____

_____

_____

Check out Galatians 5:22-23 and also and Romans 14:17.

2   Pray and ask the Lord, "What obstacles are keeping me from spending regular time with You, feeding on Your Word, praying and sitting in Your presence? How can I overcome them?"

_____

_____

_____

_____

3   Again, pray. Say, "Lord, at this season of my life with the commitments I have, how can I feed my spirit? In what specific ways can I spend time with You and feed on Your Word?" Get quiet and expect Him to respond.

_____

_____

_____

_____

The Lord will speak and show you what to do (see Psalm 25:12; 32:8).

4   What is your greatest takeaway from this chapter? What scriptures, principles or ideas spoke to your hear most? How do they challenge you? What action(s) is God prompting you to take?

_____

_____

_____

Pray It:

"Father, thank You for the spiritual food of Your Word and fellowship with Your Son, Jesus! Forgive me for not feeding my spirit like I should; thank You for Your patience and love. Please give me a desire to feed my spirit daily, just as I feed my physical body. And give me a practical plan I can follow. If there is something I need to cut out, show me what it is. Jesus, I want to become one with You and Your Word. Holy Spirit, this is a work that only You can do; please help me to do my part and trust You to do Yours. In Jesus' name, Amen!"

ONE BROTHER TO ANOTHER

"Rest precedes rule. Peace precedes power. Do not seek to rule over the devil until you are submitting to God's rule over you. The focal point of all victory comes from seeking God until you find Him, and having found Him, allowing His Presence to fill your spirit with His peace. From full assurance at His right hand, as we rest in His victory, let us rule in the midst of our enemies."

—Francis Frangipane[1]

Step **9**

SUBMIT TO GOD...RESIST THE DEVIL

*Submit to God. Resist the devil and he
will flee from you.*

James 4:7 NKJV

Submit to God. A phrase that releases great power when obeyed. You cannot resist the devil or starve your flesh without first submitting to God. You need His strength, and His strength comes through living in submission. Again, it is all about relationship with Jesus. To *submit* means "to bring oneself under the control (or authority) of someone and obey."[2] In essence, submitting to God is surrendering your will to His will, without murmuring or complaining. Submission is a character trait of Christ that shined through His life and empowered Him to walk in victory.

Jesus Submitted to God

I believe the essence of Jesus' existence on earth can be summed up in seven words: *To do the will of the Father*. This is what it means to submit to God. Over and over, He made this statement throughout His ministry, a statement most commonly found in John's Gospel. Jesus said, "For I have come down from heaven, not to do My own will, but the will of Him who sent Me. I can of Myself do nothing. As I hear, I judge; and My judgment is righteous, because **I do not seek My own will but the will of the Father who sent Me**" (John 6:38; 5:30 NKJV).

The most difficult temptation Jesus faced was in the Garden of Gethsemane. It was there He had to make a decision: follow the will of His flesh and avoid the cross, *or* submit to His Father's will and embrace the cross. The battle He faced was so intense that He sweat drops of blood (see Luke 22:44). Through intense prayer and the power of the Holy Spirit, Christ fought against His flesh and won. He submitted to the Father—He came under His Father's authority. He died to His flesh's will and obeyed the Father's will.

Three times Jesus prayed, "Not My will, Father, but *Your will* be done." This is submission in a nutshell. A life submitted to God is a life seeking after and centered in God's will. Self is dead. It is crucified daily. Your flesh doesn't get a vote. The big "I" is crucified with Christ, and "I" no longer lives; Christ lives through you (see Galatians 2:20). This is not just on Sundays, but *every* day. As Paul proclaimed, we must proclaim: "…I die *daily* [I face death every day and die to self]" (1 Corinthians 15:31 AMP).

Submission Is a Way of Life

Submitting to God is a *learned lifestyle* of surrender. It is trusting Him daily and not relying on your own understanding, but following His lead in all things (see Proverbs 3:5-7). It's giving up what you want, what you think, and how you feel in exchange for what God wants, thinks, and feels. That's what Jesus did. The ability to submit to God is not something you can receive through prayer alone. It is an attitude of the heart developed by the Holy Spirit as you live in relationship with Him and cooperate with His promptings.

Remember what Jesus said about following Him? He said we need to deny ourselves and take up our cross daily. Denying ourselves and taking up our cross means dying to self—starving the flesh. Jesus said, "Anyone who intends to come with me has to let me lead. You're not in the driver's seat—I am. Don't run from suffering; embrace it. Follow me and I'll show you how. Self-help is no help at all. Self-sacrifice is the way, *my* way, to finding yourself, your true self. What good would it do to get everything you want and lose you, the real you?" (Luke 9:23-25 The Message) Are you seeing a common trend?

Dying to self = living victoriously in Christ!

"So here's what I want you to do, God helping you: Take your everyday, ordinary life—your sleeping, eating, going-to-work, and walking-around life—and place it before God as an offering. Embracing what God does for you is the best thing you can do for him. Don't become so well-adjusted to your culture that you fit into it without even thinking. Instead, *fix your attention on God*. You'll be changed from the inside out…" (Romans 12:1-2 The Message).

Resist the Devil at His Onset!

In a position of submission to God, you are ready and able to resist the devil. And the best time to resist him is at his *onset*. God says, "Keep your mind clear, and be alert. Your opponent the devil is prowling around like a roaring lion as he looks for someone to devour.

Be firm in the faith and resist him…" (1 Peter 5:8-9 GW). The Amplified Bible says, "Withstand him; be firm in faith [**against his onset**—rooted, established, strong, immovable, and determined].…"

God wants you to say "no" at the get-go. Your point of greatest strength against temptation is when it first comes. When the enemy or your flesh brings thoughts of evil against your mind, declare your allegiance to God and your unwillingness to yield to temptation. What does this look like? Let's say you've had a horrible day. You get home from work only to face unexpected bills, sick kids, a broken-down car, and an exhausted wife. Alone in your bedroom, the enemy seizes a prime opportunity to tempt you to view porn. He whispers, *You haven't enjoyed time with your wife in days. And you know nothing's going to happen with her tonight. No one's around. Go ahead and look. You deserve it. No one's going to know.*

At Satan's onset—when he *first* brings his temptation—declare your allegiance to God and resist him. Say, "Lord, You see where I am, how I feel, and what the enemy is tempting me to do. I submit myself to You and ask for Your grace (power) not to give in to temptation, in Jesus' name." Now stand and pray against the enemy! Say, "Satan, I stand against you in the name of Jesus Christ. I will not look at your trash—I will not give you an inch to operate in my life or my family's life. Porn is poison, and I will not drink it again. God will supply all my needs, and my sexual fulfillment will be experienced with my wife. I put the blood of Jesus over my life, my wife, our marriage, and against you! No weapon formed against us will prosper! Be gone, in Jesus' name!"

Friend, this is prayer—spiritual warfare prayer that connects you with Christ and defeats the devil. We will talk more about this and how to use Scripture, the sword of the Spirit, in the chapters ahead. For now, know that the time to defeat the enemy is when he first comes. Your point of greatest strength against temptation is at his onset. Declare your allegiance to God and **say no at the get-go**. If your resistance to temptation is low, feed your spirit! Get alone with God and spend time in His presence and His Word. If you need to confess and repent of sin, do so. These things will boost your "spiritual immune system," increase your resistance to the enemy, and reposition you in submission to God.

Overcome Evil with Good!

As we wrap up this chapter, I want to share one more thing, and that's the power of overcoming evil with good. Once you have submitted yourself to God and resisted the devil, you can land him a knockout punch by doing something good for someone else. Through the apostle Paul, God says, "Don't let evil conquer you, but conquer evil by doing good" (Romans 12:21 NLT).

Many men become mesmerized by the temptations the enemy brings. Like a deer in the headlights, we can become paralyzed by the fear of falling into sin. I have experienced this firsthand. One of the best ways to escape this trap is by shifting our focus off the enemy and his temptation and onto God and the good works He has called us to do.

Doing good includes many things, like thanking and praising God. Psalm 92:1 (NKJV) says, "It is *good* to give thanks to the Lord, and to sing praises to Your name, O Most High." King David knew this and declared, "O magnify the Lord with me, and let us exalt His name together" (Psalm 34:3 AMP). With his next breath he informs us that the Lord delivered him from all his fears (v. 4). King Jehoshaphat experienced the delivering power of praise and worship when the Ammonites and Moabites came against the nation of Judah. Scripture says, "When they began to sing and to praise, the Lord set ambushments against the men of Ammon, Moab, and Mount Seir who had come against Judah, and they were [self-] slaughtered" (2 Chronicles 20:22 AMP). Indeed, it is good to praise and thank God! It delivers us from fear and destroys the enemy.

Another good thing you can do to overcome evil is to begin praying for others—starting with your precious wife. Ask God to continue to heal her within and bless her with everything good you can think of. Bless your marriage, your children, your pastor, and anyone else the Lord brings to mind. Praying for others will cause Satan to flee because he hates it. Doing good is a proven way to put the enemy on the run!

So, submit yourself to God, resist the devil and he *will* flee. Submission puts you in position to win. As you stay submitted to God, you stay plugged in to the power of His grace. You are ready and able to resist the enemy and win against every temptation that comes your way—even the temptation of porn.

Encouragement from the Heart of a Woman

As I have mentioned, one thing I have struggled with is impatience—a character trait I sincerely dislike in myself because it is so contrary to Jesus. While I have grown tremendously in this area, I still have ample room for growth. One thing I have noticed is that when the Holy Spirit shows me I am being impatient and I quickly agree with Him and submit to His leadership, it doesn't take long for me to overcome it. It's kind of like stopping a boulder from rolling downhill; it is much easier not to let it begin rolling than to try and stop it once it starts.

Take vanilla wafers, for example. Yes, I said vanilla wafers. Personally, I love them! However, I am just not self-disciplined enough to have them in my house. Really, if I open the box, I will eat ALL of them. It's just a reality in my life, and my family knows it. So you know what? I don't bring them into my house. Yes, my children are deprived of vanilla wafers. However, my hope is that one day they will realize that some things are just not worth the struggle. The Bible says to be mastered by **nothing** (see 1 Corinthians 6:12-13). For me, this includes vanilla wafers.

Man of God, I encourage you to agree with the Holy Spirit. The moment He prompts you that you are heading into trouble, submit to Him and resist the devil. Do this **before** you search the Internet, make the phone call, or open the magazine. As Vincent pointed out, God instructs us to resist the devil and "be firm in faith [**against his onset**...]" (1 Peter 5:8 AMP). Victory is won when you resist temptation as soon as it appears. It is much easier to cast down and take captive wrong thoughts and avoid sin before you see ungodly images!

Once your eyes, mind, and body are engaged, the enemy has you in his grip, and his influence is much stronger. At that point, he's calling the shots and you've become his puppet. Therefore, as soon as you feel the urge to fall back into old habits, pray. Calling out to God for help before your eyes and mind are involved is the best plan of action. "As the scripture says, 'Everyone who calls out to the Lord for help will be saved'" (Romans 10:13 GNT).

Again, don't be impressed by Satan's schemes, and don't magnify the temptation, making it bigger than it really is. What you magnify in your mind and with your mouth grows. Instead, "Let us keep our eyes fixed on Jesus, on whom our faith depends from beginning to end..." (Hebrews 12:2 GNT). With your eyes fixed on Jesus, you will become God-conscious, not sin-conscious! In this position of submission, you'll have all the power you need to resist the enemy. IN CHRIST, you are the victor!

Walk It:

Submitting to God is surrendering your will to His will. It is a learned lifestyle developed in you by the Holy Spirit. You cannot resist the devil or starve your flesh without first submitting to God. You need His strength, and His strength comes through submission. In a position of submission, you are ready and able to resist the devil at his onset—to say NO at the get-go. This is your point of greatest strength against temptation. Don't let evil conquer you, but conquer evil by doing good!

Study It:

Submit to God: Psalm 62:5-8; John 5:19-30; 6:38-40; Romans 6:12-19; James 4:7-10
Resist the Devil: Matthew 4:1-11 (Luke 4:1-13); Ephesians 4:26-27; 6:10-18; 1 Peter 5:8-9

Pray It:

"Father, I submit myself to You anew. Please forgive me for making what I want, think, and feel more important than Your will. In my heart, I don't want to look and lust at women in porn. Please change my desires. Rewire my mind, will, and emotions to crave my wife only. I want to want only what You want…please help me. Holy Spirit, remind me daily to surrender my will to You. Reveal the enemy's temptations and attacks at his onset, and empower me to open my mouth and stand against him with Your Word. Where I am right now is not where I will always be. You are changing me, and I praise You for the mighty man of God You are making me. In Jesus' name, Amen!"

Apply It:

1 In your own words, briefly explain what it means to *submit yourself to God*. Are you doing this? If not, why? In what area of your life do you find it hardest to submit to God? Pray and ask Him to show you why.

_____

_____

_____

_____

2 Jesus lived submitted to the Father. From your knowledge of His life, how did this daily choice positively impact His life? How did it positively impact those around Him? (What was the fruit?)

_____

_____

_____

_____

3 Carefully reread Jesus' words in Luke 9:23-25 and God's words through Paul in Romans 12:1-2 in the chapter. What is the Holy Spirit speaking to you in each of these passages?

_____

_____

_____

_____

4 Pause and write a prayer declaring your allegiance (submission) to God and resisting the devil.

_____

_____

_____

_____

5 What is your greatest takeaway from this chapter? What scriptures, principles, or ideas exploded in your heart? How are you challenged? What action(s) is God's Spirit prompting you to take?

_____

_____

_____

_____

ONE BROTHER TO ANOTHER

"Interestingly, the Bible says little about success, but a lot about heart, the place where true success originates. ...Watch it carefully. Protect it. Pay attention to it. Keep it clean. Clear away the debris. ...It is there that character is formed. It alone holds the secrets of true success. Its treasures are priceless—but they can be stolen. Are you guarding it?"

—Charles R. Swindoll[1]
The Quest for Character

Step 10

"ON GUARD!"

Be on guard. Stand firm in the faith.
Be courageous. Be strong.
1 Corinthians 16:13 NLT

Have you ever heard the French phrase "En garde!"? It's been tossed between fencers for centuries. It means to be **on guard**—"to adopt a defensive stance in readiness for an attack."[2] A swordsman whose guard is down is vulnerable and will be stabbed or fatally wounded by his opponent. In the same way, you will be stabbed or fatally wounded if you fail to adopt a defensive stance and be ready for Satan's attacks. With God's strength, you can learn to guard your eyes and ears, as well as your mind and heart.

Guard Your Eyes and Ears

Guarding your eyes and ears is your first line of defense. Everything you see and hear influences who you are and what you do. We talked about this in Chapter 7. Again, what you think is what you will become (see Proverbs 23:7). Since our eyes lead the way in all we do, let's take a few moments and focus there.

In chapter 8 we learned that God has wired men to be sensitive to visual, sexual signals. These signals trigger biological reactions that are the source of the sexual rush. Visual stimulation is sexual foreplay for men. Remember, *the look is the hook*. Therefore, you must learn to guard your eyes and stop the internal porn flick before it starts.

It's no coincidence that God's instruction to *guard our heart and listen carefully to His Word* is located right next to His command to *keep our eyes off prostitutes*. The Living Bible makes this passage in Proverbs 4 very clear, saying, "Spurn the careless kiss of a prostitute {the definition of porn}. Stay far from her. Look straight ahead; don't even turn your head to look. Watch your step. Stick to the path and be safe. Don't sidetrack; pull back your foot from danger" (vv. 24-27).

What's the heart of this passage? Stay far from porn—avoid the scenes of temptation. The moment it appears, get away from it—don't give it a second look. Here's a perfect example. This morning I decided to check the news on-line. There on the home page were three or more sexually arousing stories complete with teaser photos. Immediately, my flesh wanted a closer look. At the same time, a little voice within me said, *Get off the site. There's nothing here you need to see. Don't wait. Get off now.* In that moment, I had a choice: starve my flesh or feed it. I chose to starve it. I obeyed the Spirit's voice and refused to give the enemy an inch. This is a picture of living **on guard**.

Again and again, you will face situations like these. In those moments, you must choose to starve your flesh by starving your eyes. You cannot avoid every impure sexually stimulating image, but you can learn to reject them. You haven't sinned just because they pop up in front of you. It's what you do with them that can bring you into sin. If you choose to look, lust, and feed your flesh, porn's stronghold will be strengthened. But if you choose to starve your flesh and run from evil, you will strengthen God's stronghold of righteousness in your life.

Jesus said, "Your *eyes* light up your inward being. A pure eye lets sunshine into your soul. A lustful eye shuts out the light and plunges you into darkness. So watch out that the sunshine isn't blotted out" (Luke 11:34-35 TLB). Friend, stay away from places that you know you have fallen in the past. And learn to **bounce your eyes** off impure sexually-stimulating images. The moment they appear, bounce your eyes onto something else—preferably your wife. This is a healthy habit learned by practice. You can develop it by praying and drawing on the strength of God's Spirit, which we'll talk about in the coming chapters.

Guard Your Mind

Guarding your mind is your second line of defense. Inevitably, what you allow your eyes to dwell on, you allow your mind to dwell on. And what you allow your mind to dwell on eventually fills your heart and directs the course of your life. As Joyce Meyer so aptly says, "Where the mind goes, the man follows."

Guarding your mind starts with knowing "the big picture." In other words, what is your mind set on? What is your overall main focus? God says, "Those who live according to the flesh *set their minds* on the things of the flesh, but those who live according to the Spirit, {set their minds on} the things of the Spirit" (Romans 8:5 NKJV). Stop and ask yourself and the Holy Spirit, "On what is my mind set—what is my overall main focus?" In most cases, the answer is right under your nose.

The words of your mouth reveal not only what is filling your heart, but also what is filling your mind.

God says, "*Set your minds* and keep them set on what is above (the higher things), not on the things that are on the earth. For [as far as this world is concerned] you have died, and your [new, real] life is hidden with Christ in God" (Colossians 3:2-3 AMP). This is the same principle Jesus talked about in Matthew 6:33: Seek *first* the kingdom of God and His righteousness. It's also the principle found in Proverbs 3:5-6: Trust in the Lord with all your heart, acknowledge Him in all your ways, and don't lean on your own understanding.

From Genesis to Revelation, we're instructed again and again to have a God-focused mind-set. What's the result of a God-focused mind-set? "{God} will **guard** him and keep him in perfect and constant peace whose mind...is stayed on You {God}, because he commits himself to You, leans on You, and hopes confidently in You" (Isaiah 26:3 AMP). This promise is echoed by God in Philippians 4:7.

Now, you may say, "Well, I start out with my mind set on God. But something always happens that gets my mind on the wrong thing." I understand. I've experienced that too more times than I can count. When this happens, you must learn to "press the reset button." Remember the last time a storm came and there was a power failure at your house? When the power returned, the clock on your microwave started blinking 12:00 a.m. What did you do? You stopped and reset it. Similarly, when you have a spiritual power failure and your mind goes on the blink, you need to stop and reset your mind on the Lord.

Pressing the reset button is submitting yourself to God and resisting the devil so that he will flee. It is praying, speaking the Word, and taking control of your thoughts. Regardless of how you feel or what the enemy says, you "...have the mind of Christ (the Messiah) and do hold the thoughts (feelings and purposes) of His heart" (1 Corinthians 2:16 AMP). So take time throughout each day to think about what you're thinking about and "...fix your thoughts on what is true and good and right. Think about things that are pure and lovely, and dwell on the fine, good things in others. Think about all you can praise God for and be glad about" (Philippians 4:8 TLB).

Guard Your Heart

As you guard your eyes, ears, and mind, you are also guarding your heart, which is ultimately the most vital part of who you are. God says, "Above all else, guard your heart, for it is the wellspring of life"

(Proverbs 4:23 NIV). Your heart is the core of who you are, and if your core is rotten, the fruit of your life will be rotten. Your heart is also like a well or spring of water. If your spring becomes polluted, you and everyone who drinks the "water" of your life will become sick or even die, depending on the intensity of the toxins it contains.

How do you guard your heart? The answer is found in the same chapter of Proverbs. In the three previous verses, God says, "My child, pay attention to what I say. *Listen* carefully to my words. Don't lose *sight* of them. Let them penetrate deep into your *heart*, for they bring life to those who find them, and healing to their whole body" (Proverbs 4:20-22 NLT). Now don't rush. Go back and read the passage again, this time more slowly.

Did you catch the connection? God says, "Listen carefully." That means "open your *ears*." He then says, "Don't lose sight." In other words, "open your *eyes*...stay focused." What does God want you to open your eyes and ears to and stay focused on? **His Word**. What's the payoff? His life-giving truth will penetrate deep into your heart, bringing life and healing to your whole body! "How can a young person live a clean life? By carefully reading the map of your Word" (Psalm 119:9 The Message).

All through Scripture, God's recipe for a *healthy heart* is repeated: Stay connected with the Word. Proverbs 7:1-3 (NIV) says, "My son, keep my *words* and store up my commands within you. Keep my commands and you will live; guard my teachings as the apple of your eye. Bind them on your fingers; write them on the tablet of your *heart*." The way to guard your heart is to fill your ears with and focus your eyes on God's Word *regularly*. Remember, the Bible is the Word wrapped in print, and Jesus is the Word wrapped in flesh. As you spend time with the written Word and the Living Word, living on guard will become second-nature!

God Is Your Guardian!

Hopefully it's becoming clear. The ability to live *on guard* flows naturally out of living in relationship with Jesus. Feeding your spirit His Word and spending time in His presence is *your* part. From this position of submission, God Himself, through the Person of His Spirit, will guard you and empower you to stand against temptation. That is His part. As you do your part, God will faithfully do His.

"God's your Guardian, right at your side to protect you...God guards you from every evil, he guards your very life. He guards you when you leave and when you return, he guards you now, he guards you always" (Psalm 121:5-8 The Message). "God can guard you so that you don't fall and so that you can be full of joy as you stand in his glorious presence without fault" (Jude 1:24 GW).

Friend, get to know your Guardian! He longs to fill every part of your heart. As you hang out with Him, He'll give you a tender heart that is sensitive and responsive to His touch.[3] As you saturate yourself in His Word, He will renew your mind to think the way He thinks.[4] As you pray and invite His involvement in your life and situations, He will give you peace that passes all understanding and guard your heart and mind.[5]

Encouragement from the Heart of a Woman

Over the last few years I have had a deep inner cry for God to do two specific things in me. First, the closer I have come to know Jesus, the more I have longed to be changed and more like Him. Second, I have had an intense desire to have "eyes that see, ears that hear, and a heart that responds" to God's will and His ways. Because of His faithfulness, He is answering both of these prayers. I am becoming more like Jesus, and He is opening my eyes and ears to see and hear the way He does.

In the process, something unexpected has happened. As my eyes and ears have become more sensitive to the unseen things of the Spirit, I've noticed that irritations, temptations, and other things in the natural have become less vibrant and impressive. Why am I saying this? Because I want to encourage you to pray for God to open your spiritual eyes and ears and align your heart with His. As you allow Him to do this, the things of earth—including the lustful attraction of porn—will diminish, and the struggle you now face will become less intense.

*Man of God, there is safety and healing for you and your family as you begin to see, hear, think, and feel the way God does. Having His vision, hearing, mind, and heart guards you because you are seeing and understanding things as they **really are**. As you begin to see porn for what it really is and the enemy's ultimate goal of enslavement, I believe that a holy indignation will rise up in you, and you will begin to hate the very thing that has had you bound. Allow the Holy Spirit to do this work in you. You are one step closer to freedom. I call you blessed!*

Walk It:

To be *on guard* is to adopt a defensive stance and be ready for the enemy's attacks. With God's strength, you can learn to guard your eyes and ears, as well as your mind and heart. Your eyes and ears are your first line of defense; your mind is the second. Guard your eyes by *bouncing them* away from impure images. Guard your mind by keeping it set on God and good things, taking captive every thought that doesn't agree with His Word. Guard your heart by feeding your spirit the Word and spending time with Jesus. As you do your part, your Guardian God will faithfully do His!

Study It:

Heart: Proverbs 2; 4:20-27; 7:1-5; Psalm 119:9-16; 2 Peter 3:17-18; Deuteronomy 4:9 **Eyes:** Job 31:1; Psalm 119:37; Luke 11:34-35; Hebrews 12:2 **Mind:** Romans 8:5-6; 12:2; Colossians 3:2-3; Isaiah 26:3 **Avoid Immorality:** Malachi 2:14-16; 1 Thessalonians 4:3-8 **God's Your Guardian:** Psalm 121; Jude 1:24; Philippians 4:6-8

Pray It:

"Father, please forgive me for allowing my eyes, mind, and heart to roam into areas of ungodliness. Help me live on guard—help me establish a sure defense against lust and porn in all its forms and be ready to stand against the enemy. Teach me how to guard my eyes and ears, as well as my mind and heart. Help me to develop the habit of bouncing my eyes off impure images and setting my mind and keep it set on good, godly things. Give me a growing desire to spend time in fellowship with You and Your Word. Be my Guardian God! In Jesus' name, Amen!"

Apply It:

1 List the top 5 weaknesses (types of images/situations) you must learn to guard your eyes against.

_____

_____

_____

_____

Example: lingerie ads in the newspaper, beer commercials on TV, etc.

2 Which of these can be avoided altogether? How can you avoid them?

_____

_____

_____

Get God involved. Ask Him for wisdom on how to avoid the avoidable. Write what He reveals.

3 For things that can't be avoided, pray and ask God for a practical plan to guard yourself from each.

_____

_____

_____

_____

Be still and listen for the voice of God's Spirit. Write what He reveals and put it into practice.

4 Pause and pray, "Holy Spirit, what is my mind set *on*—what is my main focus? What topics make up most of my conversations and prayers? What do I think about most often?" Get quiet and listen. Write down what He reveals.

_____

_____

_____

5 What is your greatest takeaway from this chapter? What scriptures, principles, or ideas exploded in your heart? How do they challenge you? What action(s) is God's Spirit prompting you to take?

_____

_____

_____

_____

ONE BROTHER TO ANOTHER

"The intensity of a man's ability to notice women was given to him so his wife would be attractive to him all the days of his life. This characteristic of men has been vastly exploited over the years. ...The modern media has turned his concentration into a commodity. As a result, any man who wants to have a lifelong relationship of pleasure with his wife must discipline his eyes to stay focused on her. To accomplish this, and to protect all areas of a man's sexuality, a man must put Jesus in charge...."

—Bill and Pam Farrel[1]
*Men Are Like Waffles—
Women Are Like Spaghetti*

Step 11

EAT WHAT'S ON YOUR PLATE

Drink water from your own well—share your love only with your wife. Why spill the water of your springs in the streets, having sex with just anyone? You should reserve it for yourselves. Never share it with strangers.

Proverbs 5:15-17 NLT

How many times did you hear, "Don't eat that! It will spoil your appetite"? I heard it more times than I can count. The fact is it's true. If I snacked on potato chips, candy, and cookies from the time I got home from school until the time my mom served dinner, I wasn't hungry anymore. I was full. But what I had eaten was nutrient-depleted, and I missed enjoying the real meal that was made with love for me.

There is a powerful principle here that applies to our quest for sexual purity. I call it "Eat What's on Your Plate." God says, "Drink waters out of *your own* cistern [of a pure marriage relationship], and fresh running waters out of your own well. [Confine yourself to *your own* wife]..." (Proverbs 5:15, 17 AMP). This is sexual satisfaction to the max! It is sex that's God-created, God-approved, and God-blessed! The question is...

Are You Hungry for Your Wife?

Be honest. Do you have a *take it or leave it* attitude when it comes to making love to your wife? If so, you are not hungry for her. Your appetite has been spoiled either by the sexual "junk food" of porn or the food from other "dishes" you have been feasting your eyes on. I experienced this years ago, and it is a miserable place to be.

Remember, as a man, sex starts with your eyes. Visual stimulation is sexual foreplay. It's a powerful part of your sexual fulfillment, and when you're feasting your eyes on your wife, it's wonderful. However, when you look and lust at the women in porn or elsewhere, you steal something that is rightfully hers. If the tables were turned, would you like your wife receiving part of her sexual fulfillment from another man? I know I wouldn't.

Friend, "…you will always harvest what you plant. Those who live only to satisfy their own sinful nature will harvest decay and death from that sinful nature. But those who live to please the Spirit will harvest everlasting life from the Spirit" (Galatians 6:7-8 NLT). So why not begin planting healthy seeds of self-control, faithfulness, and pure love? By confining your visual gratification to your wife only, you *will* become hungry for her. Trust me—*your* dish will become "delish" as you redirect your sex drive.

Redirect Your Sex Drive

Amazing things begin to happen as you confine where you dine. Whenever your eyes or thoughts are drawn to another woman, **bounce them away** and put them back on your bride. As you train your eyes and your mind to only receive visual stimulation and gratification from your wife, a fresh fire of pure desire is rekindled. Oh, hear what I am saying, Friend! Your wife's shape will begin to take on an electrifying new look. Every part of her will become exciting new territory to explore!

God will honor your efforts to starve your flesh and avoid the scenes of temptation. He will bless your marriage of fidelity with the most fulfilling sexual adventures you've ever experienced. Yes, it may take time, but anything worth having takes time. I have experienced this phenomenon firsthand and so have many others. My wife and I are now in our third decade of marriage, and I can wholeheartedly say the sexual intimacy we share now is exponentially better than when we first got married—it's off the charts!

Does this mean I'm never tempted to look at porn on the Internet or lust after another woman? No. But I have learned to redirect my attention and affection to my wife. I've learned to tell myself, *Don't go there, Vincent. Porn is a pothole to your soul. Don't go back into that prison. That's not your plate. Yeah, the women in porn may "look" good, but they're poison and will bring you to poverty. The pleasure is fleeting, but it bites bitterly in the end. Treasure the rich love of your bride! She is real, life-giving, and guilt-free!*

In my life, freedom is now the norm, and the constant struggle is gone because of the power of God's grace and His Word. By confining my eyes to the precious prize God has given me, I have opened the door for His blessings on my marriage. You can do the same!

Create a Fresh Craving

In addition to prayer and investing in your relationship with God, there's something else you can do to create a fresh craving for your bride and promote healing in your marriage. In the past, you've probably made and played mental tapes of other women, right? Well, why not use your God-given imagination in a positive way? Pray, and ask the Holy Spirit to bring back to your memory the enjoyable encounters you've shared with your bride. Think of each exciting time of exploration and ecstasy you've experienced together. Let your mind's eye feast on each passionate portrait of her you can remember. This is godly. This is sex that is God-created, God-approved, and God-blessed!

As you mentally savor the flavor of those moments, you are rechanneling your sexual energy and excitement toward your spouse. This will create a fresh craving for her in your heart and soul that will begin to connect you closer together. I also encourage you to take time to thank God for your bride and the blessing she is. Get a journal or notebook and begin to purposely write down the good qualities she has. This is the principle of Philippians 4:8. And by all means, express your appreciation to her with words and continue to pray for God to heal her within. Actions like these, practiced on a regular basis, will cultivate a genuine love and desire for her that will bless you both in amazing ways.

Bless Your Fountain of Life!

There's one more thing I want to share. Not long ago, the Lord impressed on my heart that one of the reasons men are struggling with porn and sexual temptation is because they're not sexually fulfilled in their marriage. One of the keys to overcoming this and experiencing greater satisfaction is to begin to *bless your marriage*—including speaking a blessing on your sexual intimacy. This is God's will and He confirms it clearly in Scripture.

God wants you to bless your wife's body, including her God-created sexual anatomy. He says, "Let your fountain [of human life] *be blessed* [with the rewards of fidelity], and rejoice in the wife of your youth" (Proverbs 5:18 AMP). This verse in The Message says, *"Bless your fresh-flowing fountain! Enjoy the wife you married as a young man!"* And in the next verse God says, "She is a loving deer, a graceful doe. Let her breasts satisfy you always. May you always be captivated by her love" (v. 19 NLT).

Could this be any clearer? God wants you to fully enjoy your wife's body, and your wife to enjoy yours—without guilt or shame. I encourage you to read through Song of Songs. As you do, I believe this will become undeniably evident.

Remember, God created sex, and it's awesome within the safety of marriage! So, *eat what's on your plate*. Become enamored with your wife, and let your love and attention be for her *only*!

Encouragement from the Heart of a Woman

Man of God, I cannot encourage you enough to follow the words of wisdom Vincent is sharing. This step is crucial to your freedom as well as the healing of your marriage. You have no idea what your undivided love and attention will do for your wife and ultimately your marriage bed. When your wife knows that she alone is the object of your attention and attraction, she will come alive to you in ways you have never dreamed. She will open up to you like a beautiful rose. Believe it or not, she really does want to connect with you on an intimate level. However, knowing you are having a porn issue makes it painfully difficult for her.

I said it before, but I believe it bears repeating. Just as your wife does not understand your porn problem, you do not understand the damage this issue has caused her. She truly is in deep pain, and this painful state does not foster a desire to be intimate with you. In fact, it puts her in an angry defense mode—a mode I have personally experienced. Think about it. How hard would it be to make love to a person you are trying to protect yourself from? The truth is, it would be very hard. Making love puts both of you in a vulnerable position. And the reality is, she doesn't want to put herself in that position. I know I sure didn't. But as Vincent began to change the way he looked at me and treated me, I have been able to be more intimate with him, and this has been very good for our marriage.

Realize that becoming enamored with your wife is a process that will take time. It will not happen simply because you want it to. But as you confine your time and attention to your wife alone, your appetite will indeed increase. Consequently, she will become more attracted to you. She will know that she alone is the object of your attraction and affection. It will be very obvious to her, just as your subtle lack of attention was clearly seen and felt. Thankfully, it works both ways.

As you become truly in awe of the gift your wife is, she will sense the change and respond accordingly. I cannot stress to you enough how important your prayers are for her during this time. They will make all the difference in the world. You are her covering. God put you there. No, He didn't make a mistake. He knows you are on a journey, and He is already at the finish line, cheering you on to victory. I call you blessed!

Walk It:

God wants you to be hungry for your wife and *only* your wife. He wants you to "Eat What's on *Your* Plate." He wants you to confine your sexual appetite visually and physically to the wife He blessed you with, enjoying every aspect of her body always. This is sexual satisfaction to the max! It is sex that is God-created, God-approved, and God-blessed! Create a fresh craving for her continually. Thank God for her, pray for her, and bless her with all God's best!

Study It:

Proverbs 5, 6, and 7; Galatians 6:7-9; Ephesians 5:25-33; Philippians 4:8

Apply It:

1 Are you hungry for your wife? If not, what is spoiling your appetite?

_____

_____

_____

_____

_____

Pray and ask the Holy Spirit to show you what's going on in your heart. Write what He reveals.

2 Carefully read Proverbs 5:15-19. What is the Holy Spirit revealing in this passage?

_____

_____

_____

_____

_____

Try reading this passage in two or three Bible versions. What additional insights are you seeing?

3 Want to create a fresh craving for your wife? Take a trip down memory lane and purposely focus on the good times spent together. Write a list of desirable, stimulating, and enjoyable qualities she has. Thank God for her and pray blessings on her.

_____

_____

_____

_____

_____

In your daily prayer time, pray blessings over your wife—speak anything and everything good you can think of, especially if it is promised in Scripture. Try doing this for 21 days and watch what happens in you and in her. Journal your experience. You'll likely be amazed!

4 What is your greatest takeaway from this chapter? What scriptures, principles, or ideas exploded in your heart? How do they challenge you? What action(s) is God's Spirit prompting you to take?

_____

_____

_____

_____

_____

Things I Want to Remember:

Pray It:

"Father, please forgive me for spoiling my sexual appetite with the junk food of porn and hurting my wife in the process. You have prepared an awesome dish for me, and I want to enjoy her fully. Please help me cultivate a fresh craving for my wife and discipline my eyes and thoughts to only eat what's on my plate. Teach me how to bounce my eyes and mind away from other women and onto my wife. Continue to heal her, Lord, everywhere she hurts. I bless every part of her—body, soul, and spirit. In Jesus' name, Amen."

ONE BROTHER TO ANOTHER

"The first lesson to be learned in the renewal of the mind is not to believe old carnal feelings and thoughts when they come back after prayers for healing. ...You have the heart and mind of Christ. When the old returns, it is only an echo of the old self, only an old, practiced habitual way, sounding off again with no real intention or life behind it. It is not what you really feel or think—unless you believe it and give it life and power."

—John and R. Loren Sanford[1]

The Renewal of the Mind

LIVE FREE FROM FEELINGS

*And because we belong to Christ Jesus, we have killed
our selfish feelings and desires. God's Spirit has given
us life, and so we should follow the Spirit.*

Galatians 5:24-25 CEV

Feelings are fickle and they cannot be trusted. They can change faster than you can blink. At times they can guide us in the right direction, and other times they lead us into temptation. Our feelings, or emotions, are a part of our flesh, and along with our mind and will, they too must be made new by God's Word and Spirit.

To live free from feelings, you must crucify (starve) your flesh, resist the devil, and follow the Holy Spirit. Make no mistake: Your unrenewed flesh has a mind of its own and it is used to getting its way. Satan will seize every opportunity your flesh gives him to tag-team you right into his hands. To break free from patterns of inaccurate and ungodly feelings, you must learn to say *no* to your flesh and the devil and *yes* to God.

As you walk out your newfound freedom in Christ, you will encounter a variety of wrong feelings, including false pleasure, condemnation, guilt, and shame. Let's take a few minutes to recognize and deal with these common feelings connected with escaping the prison of porn.

Resist the Wrappings of False Pleasure

The most obvious feeling connected with porn that we must address is the feeling of *false pleasure*. It is like beautiful wrappings on a gift box filled with anthrax, arsenic, or cyanide. The wrappings seem so inviting and so exciting, but they are false advertisements. Once they are removed and the substance of what's inside is revealed, we wish we would have never opened it. The wrappings are the trappings.

"Sell the sizzle"—that's the enemy's MO. He whispers, "Oh, it feels so good looking at all the ladies. They're all yours, just waiting to be taken. They want you and will not refuse. No commitment required.

Look, enjoy, and feel that sweet release." Again and again he promises true fulfillment but fails to deliver.

Don't get me wrong. The sin of viewing porn while masturbating feels pleasurable—but only temporarily. For most men, the aftertaste of giving in to this temptation is extremely bitter. For me, feelings of guilt, condemnation, and shame hung over my head like a dark cloud. With each impure act, my sexual satisfaction decreased and the distance between me and God and me and my wife increased. Anger, self-hatred, and even depression grew. Why was I experiencing these? *God's Spirit living in me was grieved.* I was breaking a spiritual law—the law of God-created, God-approved sex between one man and one woman for life.

How do you deal with feelings of false pleasure? Treat them as the lies they are. The enemy and your flesh are trying to sell you a bill of goods that isn't real. The only way to combat their craziness is by calling Satan a liar and telling him and your flesh the truth of God's Word. When feelings of false pleasure come, say, "Satan, you're a liar, and there's no truth in you. Flesh, you're crazy; I'm not listening to you. Yeah, it may feel good, but the feelings are fleeting, and the effects are long-lasting. I don't want anymore distance between me and God or me and my wife. I don't want anymore feelings of guilt, shame, or condemnation hanging over my head, nor do I want anger and rage building in me like a ticking time bomb. I say *no to your temptation! Die flesh.* I submit myself to You, God. I resist you Satan, and you must flee! I'm not going back into that prison, in the name of Jesus!"

Overcome Condemnation

Another feeling many of us deal with is *condemnation.* I have battled this brute countless times in my pursuit of purity. It's the "you're no good" baseball bat that the enemy and your flesh love to beat you with whenever you give them the chance. They will try and make you feel condemned over past sins, present sins, and even sins you haven't committed.

Basically, to *condemn* means "to pass sentence or judgment on" with the idea of punishment to follow.[2] Scripture says, "Adam's one sin brings condemnation for everyone, but Christ's one act of righteousness brings a right relationship with God and new life for everyone" (Romans 5:18 NLT). So condemnation, along with guilt and shame, are all side effects of man's original sin. But thank God, through Jesus Christ we are set free from *all* these!

When you sin, God's Spirit living in your spirit will convict you. His conviction, though strong at times, is always gentle and accompanied by a reassuring sense that He is going to help you overcome it. He never brings pressure or condemnation. The godly sorrow He allows you to feel is meant to soften your heart and move you to repent and make things right (see 2 Corinthians 7:10-11). Exactly how God convicts you will be unique to you, but His aim is always the same—restoration of His relationship with you.

Satan, on the other hand, is the accuser of the brethren who constantly finds fault with you, God, and everyone else.[3] Your unrenewed flesh will often partner in his harassment. Through feelings of condemnation, guilt, and shame, they try to make you feel like a worthless pile of trash. But don't believe their lies!

God declares, "There is therefore now **no condemnation** to those who are in Christ Jesus, who do not walk according to the flesh, but according to the Spirit. For the law of the Spirit of life in Christ Jesus has made me free from the law of sin and death" (Romans 8:1-2 NKJV). Jesus Himself said, "For God did not send His Son into the world to condemn the world, but that the world through Him might be saved. He who believes in Him is not condemned..." (John 3:17-18 NKJV).

Friend, slowly reread those verses and let them soak into your spirit. If you have confessed your sin to God and asked Him to forgive you, you are forgiven (see 1 John 1:9). If you feel condemned after you've repented, it is *not* from God; it's from the enemy or your flesh. Settle this truth in your heart once and for all.

Scripture says, "Who dares accuse us whom God has chosen for his own? Will God? No! He is the one who has forgiven us and given us right standing with himself. Who then will condemn us? Will Christ? No! For he is the one who died for us and came back to life again for us and is sitting at the place of highest honor next to God, pleading for us there in heaven" (Romans 8:33-34 TLB). Even "if our heart condemns us, God is greater than our heart, and knows all things" (1 John 3:20 NKJV).

I encourage you to meditate on these verses and keep them close by, and the next time you feel condemned, run to God. If you need to repent of sin, humble yourself and repent. Then stand against the enemy and your flesh and speak the truth. Take God's promises and *personalize* them. That's what we've done with Romans 8:33-34 and John 3:20. Simply insert your name in the blanks and read these verses aloud over your life and against the enemy:

"There is therefore now no condemnation to me, _____, who is in Christ Jesus. I do not walk according to the flesh, but according to the Spirit. For the law of the Spirit of life in Christ Jesus has made me, _____, free from the law of sin and death. For God did not send His Son into me (_____) to condemn _____, but that _____through Him might be saved. _____who believes in Jesus is *not* condemned..."

Wow! Can you sense the freedom God's Word brings! That's the power of personalizing His promises. Verses like these declare who you are in Christ. You are not condemned. You are forgiven and free!

"But what about when I disobey?" you ask. "Isn't God mad at me?" No. God hates sin, not the sinner. He loves you, and nothing—not even your disobedience—can separate you from His love (see Romans 8:31-39). Why? Because God's love for you is not based on what you do—it's based on what Jesus *did*. Praise His holy Name!

Get Rid of Guilt and Shame

When condemnation comes, guilt and shame are often along for the ride. The enemy uses these feelings to oppress you in your soul and to try to stop you from walking with God. To *oppress* means "to exercise harsh control over."[4] Thank God He has a remedy! It is the matchless power of His Spirit. Scripture says "that God anointed Jesus of Nazareth with the Holy Spirit and with power. Then Jesus went around doing good and *healing all who were oppressed by the devil*, for God was with him" (Acts 10:38 NLT). God is the same yesterday, today, and forever. What He did through Jesus then, He does through His Spirit now—He heals those who are oppressed by the devil.

Friend, Jesus not only paid for your sin, He also paid for your guilt and shame! Under the Old Covenant, there was a sacrifice made for guilt (see Leviticus 7:1-5). Under the New Covenant, Jesus became the sacrifice to end *all* sacrifices (see Hebrews 9:11-15). Isaiah prophesied, "But He was wounded for our transgressions, He was bruised for our **guilt** and iniquities; the chastisement [needful to obtain] peace and well-being for us was upon Him, and with the stripes [that wounded] Him we are healed and made whole" (Isaiah 53:5 AMP). The price for your guilt has already been paid. Jesus, the not-guilty One, became the guilty one, so that we could be guilt-free.

God has also taken away your shame. In Joshua 5:9 (NLT), "the Lord said to Joshua, 'Today I have rolled away the shame of your slavery in Egypt....'" To you living under the New Covenant in Christ, God says, "…The one who trusts in him {Jesus} will never be put to shame" (Romans 9:33 NIV). Get a hold of that! Through your faith in Jesus, God has cancelled condemnation, gotten rid of guilt, and stripped shame of its power. How? It's through the shed blood of Jesus! God declares, "…The blood of Christ will **purify our consciences** from sinful deeds so that we can worship the living God…" (Hebrews 9:14 NLT).

"But what if I still feel guilty, even if I haven't sinned?" Amazingly, "even if we feel guilty, **God is greater than our feelings,** and he knows everything" (1 John 3:20 NLT). You are not guilty, not condemned, and shame-free in Christ Jesus!

Live Free from Feelings!

Friend, don't follow your feelings—live free from them. "A sound mind makes for a robust body, but runaway emotions corrode the bones" (Proverbs 14:30 The Message). As Joyce Meyer powerfully puts it, "Stop bowing down to your feelings—stop depending on and placing more value in how you feel than on the Word of God. Exalt the Word over your feelings—believe what the Bible says over how you feel…. Every time feelings come up to try and steal your righteousness, peace, and joy, find out what the Word of God says, and then open your mouth and speak the Word. Eventually the Truth will override and change your feelings."[5]

While you can't *feel* your way into a right action, you can *act* your way into a right feeling. As an act of your will, choose daily to agree with God's Word and think, speak, and act right, by His grace. Eventually right feelings will follow right actions.

Encouragement from the Heart of a Woman

Years ago, worry and negativity were a big part of my life. When I was twelve years old, my life changed dramatically due to much upheaval in my family. Consequently, I began to worry perpetually about my mother's safety and stability. Then three years later, my beautiful thirteen-month-old niece passed away. This devastated me and caused me to become very negative and cynical about life. Feelings of fear, anger, and depression were constant companions. I surrendered to the belief that life was not worth living, and eventually, I ended up a miserable, suicidal mess!

Then at age eighteen, while on a retreat, I encountered the real love of Jesus, and my life has never been the same! Through my relationship with Him, He has changed the way I see, think, and feel. Today, as I remember and write about who I was, it seems like I am writing about someone else, and I guess I am. You see, I'm dead to the old Allison and all those debilitating feelings, and I'm ALIVE in Christ!

Man of God, the enemy will continually try to convince you that you are guilty, condemned, and alone. If he succeeds, then you are just that. When you believe and receive his false feelings of guilt and condemnation, you surrender your place of innocence and freedom in Christ and become his slave. Don't believe him. Jesus said that Satan is a liar and the father of lies and there is no truth in him (see John 8:44).

If you're in Christ, you are not guilty. You are righteousness! You are more than a conqueror! You are powerful! Not because you have earned this status by good behavior, but because you have received it as a gift from Jesus! He took you and me just as we were—condemned, guilty, defeated sinners. He cleaned us up and gave us new clothes—a robe of His righteousness that He purchased with His blood.[6] He also gave us a permanent home in Him, making us co-heirs of not only heavenly blessings but also His very nature (see 2 Peter 1:3-4).

Realize that your feelings are not the truth. They are just feelings. I know they can be powerful at times, but don't believe them. Only the truth of God's Word points true north at all times, and there's no expiration date on truth. Have faith in Jesus and His Word. Hold on to your place of power in Him. Live free from feelings. Live by truth!

Walk It:

Feelings are a part of your flesh. They're constantly changing, and therefore shouldn't be trusted. To live free from ungodly feelings like false pleasure, condemnation, guilt, and shame, you must crucify (starve) your flesh and resist the devil. Choose to believe God's Word over ungodly feelings. Personalize His promises and speak them aloud over your life and against the enemy. While you can't feel your way into right actions, you can act your way into right feelings. Eventually right feelings will follow.

Study It:

No Condemnation: John 3:16-18; Romans 5:12-19; 8:1-4, 31-38; 2 Corinthians 7:10-11; 1 John 3:19-20 **No Guilt:** Leviticus 7:1-5; Hebrews 9:11-15; Isaiah 53:5 **No Shame:** Joshua 5:9; Romans 9:33 **Satan's MO:** Revelation 12:10; Job 1:6-12; 2:1-7 **Say No to Flesh:** Romans 6:11-14; Galatians 5:24-25; Colossians 3:1-5

Apply It:

1 Carefully read these verses about being "in Christ" and write a declaration to speak against the devil and your flesh when ungodly feelings arise. (See 2 Corinthians 2:14; 5:17, 21; Romans 3:24; 6:6, 11; 8:1-2.)

_____

_____

_____

_____

2 Briefly, describe the differences of how God _convicts_ you of sin and how your flesh and the enemy try to _condemn_ you and make you feel guilty and ashamed.

_____

_____

_____

_____

3 How powerful is the blood of Jesus? Read Hebrews 9:14; 13:12; 1 John 1:7; Revelation 1:5; 12:11. What is God's Spirit revealing to you in these verses? How are you encouraged?

_____

_____

_____

_____

Like the Israelites applied the blood of the Passover lamb to their homes, begin to symbolically apply the blood of Jesus to your mind, will, emotions, body, marriage—everything. Although you can't see it, the enemy can, and he runs from the blood!

4 What is your greatest takeaway from this chapter? What scriptures, principles, or ideas spoke to your heart most? How do they challenge you? What action(s) is God prompting you to take?

_____

_____

_____

Pray It:

"Father, please forgive me for believing and giving in to the ungodly feelings of my flesh and the enemy. I don't want to fall for the feelings of false pleasure any longer. I don't want to live under the weight of guilt and shame or cower under condemnation. Help me believe and speak Your Word to my flesh and against the enemy: 'Fleshly feelings, I'm dead to you. Satan, you're a liar! I have been crucified with Christ, and my sin-loving, condemned and guilt-ridden old nature no longer lives. But Christ lives in me! I am the righteousness of God—forgiven and free from following my feelings!' Thank You, God! In Jesus' name, Amen!"

ONE BROTHER TO ANOTHER

"...Confess your temptations and your sin to someone you can trust. Over the years it has been my experience that temptation, which flourishes in secret, somehow loses much of its mesmerizing power when it is confessed and exposed to the light of Christian love."

—Richard Exley[1]

Deliver Me

Step 13

BE ACCOUNTABLE TO OTHERS

Confess to one another therefore your faults (your slips, your false steps, your offenses, your sins) and pray [also] for one another, that you may be healed and restored [to a spiritual tone of mind and heart]....

James 5:16 AMP

Accountability is a powerful key to living free. It ranks high on the list of proven steps—right next to starving your flesh, feeding your spirit, and maintaining a healthy relationship with Jesus. James 5:16 nails this principle in place, instructing us to *confess to one another* our faults—our "slips" and "false steps" into sin. When we do, we open ourselves to God to "be healed and restored" in our mind and heart.

Over the years, I have been accountable to men who have helped me learn who I am in Christ and face the music about my thinking and behavior. They have asked the hard questions and helped me to avoid making major mistakes as well as break free from sinful habits like pornography. Indeed, there is something very powerful about being in close relationship with one or more Christian brothers.

The Power of a Friend

You've probably heard it said, "Show me your friends, and I'll show you your future," and it's true. The people you hang out with are going to make or break you. God says, "Walk with the wise and become wise; associate with fools and get in trouble" (Proverbs 13:20 NLT). Godly men who are growing in Christ will keep you sharp, focused, and on your toes.

All through Scripture, we're given snapshots of the power of good friends. David had Jonathan, Paul had Timothy, and Jesus had Peter, James, and John. Yes, even Jesus, the Son of the Living God, needed friends to confide in and share His life with. He laughed with them and celebrated special occasions, and He cried with them during times of loss. He even let them into His heart during His darkest hour. My brother, if *Jesus* needed friends, you and I need friends too.

I must admit, for years I did not see the value of godly men in my life. I experienced a lot of rejection during my junior high and high school years, so I became guarded and would only let people get so close. Over time, God healed me of many hurts and delivered me from many fears, and I have learned to let people get closer to me. There are two men in particular that I have reached out and opened up to. Both are mature Christians walking in victory over lust—qualities I highly recommend in an accountability partner.

What did I receive from being accountable? Strength, wisdom, conviction, correction, and encouragement not to quit. God says, "It's better to have a partner than go it alone. ...If one falls down, the other helps, but if there's no one to help, {it's} tough! (Ecclesiastes 4:9-10 The Message). One thing is for sure: If you keep your sin a secret and try to battle it on your own, you will lose. I and many others can confirm this. God declares, "A person standing alone can be attacked and defeated, but two can stand back-to-back and conquer. Three are even better, for a triple-braided cord is not easily broken" (Ecclesiastes 4:12 NLT). There is power in partnership! And when Jesus is invited into that partnership, victory is imminent!

Confide in Someone You Trust

Now you don't want to confess your struggles with temptation and your slip-ups to just anybody. You want to find an accountability partner who knows you, loves you, and wants the very best for you. They have no ulterior motives or personal agendas for your life. They won't condemn you if you fall, but they will also not condone your sin. They are a good listener and will speak the truth in love. The two men I confided in fit this to a tee. Stop and think, *Who in my life meets this criteria?* Pray and ask the Holy Spirit for His input.

Once you find and connect with someone, *openly share your heart.* When I first opened up, I shared briefly how I started looking at porn and how it was affecting my marriage. Initially, I would only contact my accountability partners when I had fallen into sin and was overwhelmed with guilt and condemnation. Eventually, I established a more *proactive* approach, contacting them more regularly—especially during times of temptations. They were always available when I called or came to see them. They listened to me and loved me enough to tell me where I was wrong and what I needed to do. They also prayed for me and gave me scriptures to help me overcome temptation. Many of the steps in this book have come from our conversations, including the vital need of spending time in God's Word and presence.

How Accountability Works

We are all unique, so each of us will have a unique plan of accountability. You may prefer to have mutual, one-on-one accountability. Or you may find forming an accountability group is more effective. Do what works best for you. That being said, here are some key ingredients I want to recommend.

Stay Connected: Having someone you can call day or night is suggested. Otherwise, I recommend touching base at least once a week. Usually, the deeper the addiction, the more frequent contact you will need. A face-to-face setting is best; your nonverbal communication will be visible, holding you to a higher level of honesty. A phone call is the next best thing.

Be Proactive: Instead of just contacting your partner to admit you've sinned, reach out to him in the midst of temptation. As author Randy Alcorn so aptly stated, "Honesty about our sin is good—but honesty about *temptation* is even better."[2] Some men connect daily or weekly by phone regardless of whether they were tempted. After a brief greeting and small talk, you need your accountability partner to ask you some no-nonsense questions.

Answer Key Questions Honestly:

* How is your relationship with Jesus? Are you spending time in His presence and in His Word?

* How is your relationship with your wife? Your children?

* Overall, how has your thought life been?

* What temptations have you battled since we last talked? Have you won or lost?

* Have you been honest with your answers?

* How can I pray for you specifically?

If you look at something you shouldn't and fall into sin, come clean. Confide in your accountability partner about what happened and ask him to pray for you. I don't believe it's necessary or profitable to share every minute detail of your disobedience. If you start describing all the details of the images you saw and what you did, there's a good chance it could stir up ungodly feelings in you and in him. Simply give the overall picture and answer any specific questions he asks.

Receive Prayer and Counsel: Once you've honestly answered each question, listen and receive counsel. "For by wise counsel you will wage your own war, and in a multitude of counselors there is safety" (Proverbs 24:6 NKJV). God will speak to you through your partner(s), and what He says will be life-changing if you are open. My life is living proof!

I have been privileged to serve as an accountability partner to a number of men and have discovered that there is almost always a *pattern* to falling prey to porn. As we have noted, with every man, including myself, the number one cause for relapsing into sin is failing to maintain a personal relationship with Jesus. When spending time in His presence and in His Word becomes "hit and miss," temptation tends to win. The second common cause for a sin relapse is using porn as a coping mechanism for dealing with increased stress. Your accountability partner will help you discover any patterns of thinking and behavior that are setting you up to sin. Together you can establish a plan to avoid these.

Your Ultimate Accountability Partner

It's important to have one or more godly men with whom you can share your heart and receive good counsel. In time, however, I believe your ultimate accountability partner should be your wife. The two of you are one flesh; your life overwhelmingly affects hers. No one on earth wants you to live free from porn more than she does. And no one has more to gain from you living clean and pure.

Now you may be thinking, *But Vincent, I could never tell my wife about this. I'd never hear the end of it. There's no telling what she would do. She may withhold sex from me for months. Then where would I be?* I realize being honest with your wife may be scary. It was for me when I first started. But in time you need to do it. Prayerfully seek the Lord for the right timing and ask Him to prepare her heart. She is your greatest ally in your fight for freedom, and you owe it to her to walk in truth.

Again, don't try to explain all the details of what happened. She is not going to understand it. I'm a man and I don't fully understand it. Am I saying you should lie or misrepresent the truth to your wife? Absolutely not. Share the essence of what happened, sincerely apologize for your actions, ask her to forgive you, answer any questions she has, and ask her to pray for you.

Realize that your body is not your own. It belongs to God first and your wife second. He says, "Don't you realize that your body is the temple of the Holy Spirit, who lives in you and was given to you by God? You do not belong to yourself, for God bought you with a high price. So you must honor God with your body" (1 Corinthians 6:19-20 NLT). As a follower of Christ, God's got first dibs on you, and according to 1 Corinthians 7:4 your wife has seconds: "For the wife does not have [exclusive] authority and control over her own body, but the husband [has his rights]; likewise also the husband does not have [exclusive] authority and control over his body, but the wife [has her rights]" (AMP).

So prayerfully open your heart and become accountable to your wife. As you humble yourself and confess your faults, God will honor His Word and not only heal and restore your mind and heart, but also your marriage. Trust God, my brother. Great days are ahead!

Encouragement from the Heart of a Woman

Accountability is necessary to achieving victory over bondage, regardless of the sin. The Bible says, "As iron sharpens iron, so one man sharpens another" (Proverbs 27:17 NIV). The unspoken fact here is that people, like iron, get dull at times and need to be sharpened. This scripture makes me think of an accountability partner. If you're married, the best person for this job is your spouse.

Without a doubt, being Vincent's accountability partner ranks as one of the most difficult things I have been called to do. Man of God, it's really important to realize that this will not be an easy task for your wife. If you are blessed with a wife who will walk beside you through this, consider yourself highly favored. Depending on how long you've been married, no one on earth loves you more than she. And no one on earth has more to gain or lose from your success or failure to be sexually pure.

I sincerely encourage you to answer her every question. She may have many and her questions may get on your nerves after a while. Be patient with her. More than likely, as the two of you walk through this, she will have fewer questions. She is growing and healing just as you are. This is one of the most emotionally challenging things a woman can walk through. Just as I did not understand Vincent's addiction to pornography and masturbation, he did not understand my deep, inner pain.

The only thing to do in this situation is to give each other over to Jesus in these areas because He does understand! As husbands and wives, we cannot bring the healing and freedom needed, but Jesus can. He will be the One who bridges the gap and brings healing and restoration. He is faithful to do what we cannot do. Man of God, be accountable and be healed. I call you victorious!

Walk It:

Accountability is a powerful key to living free. It allows you to be healed and restored in mind and heart by God's Spirit. An accountability partner should be a mature Christian walking in victory over lust. They should have no ulterior motives or personal agendas. They won't condemn you if you fall, but they will also not condone your sin. They are a good listener and will speak the truth in love. Your ultimate accountability partner should be your wife. Good accountability includes staying connected, being proactive, answering key questions honestly, and receiving prayer and biblical, godly counsel.

Study It:

Friends: Proverbs 11:14; 13:20; 24:6; 27:5-6, 17, 19; Ecclesiastes 4:9-12 **Accountability & Counsel:** Proverbs 11:14; 12:15; 13:10; 15:22; James 5:16; 1 Corinthians 6:10-20; 7:4

Apply It:

1 Do you have men you can confide in and be accountable to? If so, who are they and how do they help strengthen you in your Christian walk? If not, why—what has kept you from being accountable to someone?

_____

_____

_____

_____

_____

2 If you don't have an accountability partner, the Holy Spirit has probably brought someone's name or face to your mind. Who is it? What steps can you take to establish accountability with them?

_____

_____

_____

_____

_____

Is there anyone who comes to mind that you need to limit your time with or stop hanging around altogether? Ask God for wisdom and grace to avoid evil associations (see 1 Corinthians 5:11; 15:33).

3 What is your greatest takeaway from this chapter? What principles, scriptures, or ideas exploded in your heart? How do they challenge you? What action(s) is God's Spirit prompting you to take?

_____

_____

_____

_____

Pray It:

"Father, please forgive me for knowingly and unknowingly withdrawing from other men. I now know that I need accountability, but it's scary. You know all the hurts I've experienced in the past. Help me and heal me. Give me a desire to be accountable and divinely connect me with the man (or men) You know will be a good partner for me. Help me to stay connected, be proactive, answer questions honestly, and receive prayer and godly counsel. And please show me how and when to share my struggle with my wife and become accountable to her. Please prepare her heart. Give us Your grace and mercy. Reconcile us and heal our marriage. In Jesus' name, Amen!"

ONE BROTHER TO ANOTHER

"The first risings of sinful thoughts and desires, the beginnings of trifling pursuits which waste the time, trifling visits, small departures from truth, whatever would admit some conformity to the world; all these, and many more, are little foxes which must be removed. ...Whatever we find a hindrance to us in that which is good, we must put away."

—Matthew Henry[1]

Step 14

ELIMINATE THE LITTLE FOXES

Catch all the foxes, those little foxes, before they ruin the vineyard of love, for the grapevines are blossoming!
Song of Solomon 2:15 NLT

In Judea, during Solomon's day when this verse was written, there were large numbers of foxes, or little jackals. These crafty creatures, often under fifteen inches in height, would sneak into vineyards and eat the ripening grapes just before they were harvested. To prevent this, they needed to be driven out before the grapes were ripe.[2]

Symbolically, "little foxes" are the subtle, seemingly insignificant things that eat away at your relationship with God and draw you back into sin. They may seem small, but they are quite destructive and devour the priceless fruit of righteousness, love, and intimacy you share with the Lord and your wife.

Throughout my journey, I've identified some common little foxes. These include pride, unforgiveness, laziness, and plain old unconfessed sin.

Sin Separates Us

What happened to Adam and Eve when they sinned? They were separated from God. They lost the rich relationship they once had with Him and each other. God says, "Listen now! The Lord isn't too weak to save you. And he isn't getting deaf! He can hear you when you call! But the trouble is that your sins have cut you off from God. Because of sin he has turned his face away from you and will not listen anymore" (Isaiah 59:1-2 TLB). Please hear this: Sin separates you from God. Little by little, sin that is not confessed and repented of lodges in your heart and blocks the flow of God's Living Water—His life-giving Holy Spirit.[3] With Him we can do all things, but without Him we can do nothing (see John 15:5).

Does sin *totally* separate you from God? No, because nothing can separate you from His love (see Romans 8:38-39). However, unconfessed sin dulls your ears from hearing God's voice and hardens your heart from feeling His touch. The longer you are in this compromised condition, the weaker and more vulnerable you become to the enemy's attacks, the demands of your flesh, and the lure of the world. The more sin you tolerate, the weaker your resistance to it.

How are you to eliminate unconfessed sin? As soon as you mess up, fess up. Admit it, confess it, and repent (see 1 John 1:9). The best way to avoid sin is to abide in relationship with Jesus. The greatest remedy against pornography (and all sin) is intimacy with Him. Daily fellowship is not optional—it's essential. The closer you are to Jesus, the less you will want to search for porn, and the quicker you'll hear His voice and repent if you do.

Pride Blinds Us

One of the most subtle and contagious of all sins is *pride*. C.S. Lewis said, "There is one vice of which no man in the world is free; which every one in the world loathes when he sees it in someone else; and of which hardly any people, except Christians ever imagine that they are guilty themselves....The essential vice, the utmost evil, is Pride. ...It was through Pride that the devil became the devil; Pride leads to every other vice: it is the complete anti-God state of mind...."[4]

Basically, pride is the *absence or loss of humility*. It is an innate weakness in our flesh that turns our attention away from God and onto "self." This shift in focus often happens subtlety and unknowingly. When we're at our lowest point and in desperate need for God's help and we reach out to Him, humility is present and pride is absent.

Over time, as He empowers us to experience victory, we subconsciously begin to think we have achieved success on our own—that through our willpower and cleverness of mind, we have overcome temptation. *I've got this*, we unknowingly say to ourselves. *I really don't need to spend as much time in prayer and in the Word.* Consequently, we relax our guard, lessen our dependence on Jesus, and drift away from our devotional time with Him. Blinded by the light of self-exaltation, Satan sneaks in and sets us up for a fall.

Sound familiar? I've been there. God warns us, "Don't be so naive and self-confident. You're not exempt. You could fall flat on your face as easily as anyone else. Forget about self-confidence; it's useless. Cultivate God-confidence" (1 Corinthians 10:12 The Message). To me,

God-confidence is having a "nothing-everything" view of myself—I'm nothing without Jesus, but everything with Him.[5] That's humility.

Humility is the only antidote for pride. In the words of nineteenth century minister and author Andrew Murray, humility is "the place of *entire dependence on God*...the root of every virtue."[6] Humility cannot be earned at a seminary, bought at a bookstore, or put on us through prayer. It is a work of the Holy Spirit, the Spirit of Christ, and can only be received as we spend time in His presence.

I don't know about you, but I have seen who I am without Jesus, and it ain't pretty. I need Jesus every moment of every day, and so do you. Your flesh and the enemy will try to convince you otherwise, but don't listen. Stay in close fellowship with Jesus. Remember, "... God sets Himself against the proud...[and He opposes, frustrates, and defeats them], but gives grace (favor, blessing) to the humble" (1 Peter 5:5 AMP).

Unforgiveness Weakens Our Resistance

Of all the little foxes I've battled, *unforgiveness* has been the hardest. To me, nothing eats away at the love, joy, and peace between me and God and me and my wife faster. Unforgiveness is an unwillingness to let go of an *offense*, which is a hurt or mistreatment inflicted by others. Jesus said, "It is impossible that no offenses should come..." (Luke 17:1 NKJV). So you are going to be offended, and the people you're going to be offended with most are those closest to you—especially your wife. At times, you are going to say and do things to each other that are hurtful—often unintentionally. It's a part of life. The question is: Will you choose to let go of the offense and forgive?

Holding on to offense is unforgiveness, and it is sin. By doing so, you open the door for the devil, giving him place in your life to do his dirty work. I have experienced this many times, but just recently I have become more keenly aware of its connection with the temptation of porn. Allison and I are two very different people, and we don't always see eye to eye. In the heat of a disagreement, there have been times when she has said something harshly to me that really hurt, and I've done the same to her. When I hold on to the hurt, it becomes a rock of offense that lodges in my soul, cutting off the flow of God's Spirit. The longer I hold on to the hurt and choose not to forgive, the more vulnerable I become to temptation.

For example, one day while working on this book, we had a disagreement. The more we talked about it, the angrier we got.

Frustrated, I went back to my office and tried to write. Can you say "writer's block"? Not only could I not write, but I had an overwhelming urge to surf for smut on the Internet. What happened? I was offended. I had opened the door to the devil and my spiritual resistance was weakened. Using many of the steps we've talked about, I struggled to overcome the temptation, but it wouldn't go away. Frustrated, I stopped and prayed, "God, what's going on?" Instantly, in my gut I heard, "You're holding on to unforgiveness against Allison. Release it and pray a blessing over her."

Now, I was still ticked off about what had happened, but I knew from experience the grave danger of holding on to unforgiveness. It's like drinking poison and expecting it to affect the person with whom you're offended. Not wanting to experience that pain again, I asked God to forgive me for holding on to the hurt. I released Allison and the situation into His hands and prayed a blessing over her. I also prayed against the spirit of strife coming against our marriage. Immediately, I was able to resist the temptation to look at porn and begin writing. Allison and I apologized to each other shortly thereafter, and God restored our peace.

Friend, offense is going to come, so make up your mind to deal with it quickly. Just as you take out the trash so your house doesn't stink and become infested with rats, take out the spiritual trash of offense. Choose to walk in love and be willing to forgive. God will love and forgive you and give you the power to recognize and resist temptation. For a more in-depth study on dealing with offense, I highly recommend *The Bait of Satan* book and workbook by John Bevere.

Laziness Sets Us Up for Failure

One more "little fox" to watch for is *laziness*. By definition, *laziness* is "inactivity" or "an unwillingness to work." While we don't work *for* our salvation, we are to work *out* our salvation. It takes effort to starve the flesh, feed the spirit, and maintain a thriving relationship with Jesus—effort and discipline.

Like pride, laziness is a weakness of the flesh. Whenever possible, the mind of the flesh will choose comfort and convenience over effort and discipline. This seems especially true when we are experiencing an extended time of peace and success. When the enemy appears to be lying low and things are going well, we tend to coast along and become complacent, tolerating little things we would normally stand against. This is often when the enemy moves in and attempts to regain ground.

Laziness sets you up for failure. It leads to pride, spiritual malnutrition, no harvest of righteousness, slavery to sin, and ultimately God's judgment.[7] So, "never be lazy, but work hard and serve the Lord enthusiastically" (Romans 12:11 NLT). Be diligent and develop a disciplined life—a life connected in relationship with Jesus and one that obeys the promptings of His Spirit.

"Lust can only be defeated by a combination of *divine deliverance* and *daily discipline*," shares author and speaker Richard Exley. "Deliverance is fleeting at best unless it is lived out day by day. Galatians 5:16 says, 'Walk in the Spirit, and you shall not fulfill the lust of the flesh.'"[8]

When your resistance to temptation is low, stop, drop, and pray! Say, "Holy Spirit, are there any 'little foxes' I need to eliminate? Is there any unconfessed sin in my life? Am I walking in pride? Am I holding on to unforgiveness toward my wife or anyone else? Have I become lazy in my stand against sin? Please show me my heart." Then get quiet. Listen to what He says. Obey His promptings.

Encouragement from the Heart of a Woman

The enemy's plan is to steal, kill, and destroy (see John 10:10). He's not just after you, but also your marriage, your children, and your grandchildren yet to be born. He's a relentless pig! He will fight fiercely against your success and not easily give up the ground he has held in your life.

Working with your flesh, Satan will whisper thoughts like, Aw, it's just one "little" picture. This is nothing compared to the hard-core porn you used to view. Go ahead, look at it. Or in pride he'll say, Man, you can't even look at that? You're becoming a wimp, or Your wife alone will never be able to satisfy you sexually. It's just not going to happen. Statements like these are nothing but lies.

The truth is, "soft" porn isn't any better than hard-core, and just one "little" picture really does make a difference—it's the difference between your freedom and continuing in slavery! Likewise, your wife **can** *satisfy you sexually, and you're not becoming a wimp by refusing to look at and lust after other women. You are exercising self-control and resisting the devil. You're becoming a real man—a man controlled by the Spirit of God! That's a big step toward freedom and restoration.*

Choosing to live in peace, free of offense with others, is another big step—especially when it comes to your spouse. There have been times when all I could see were Vincent's flaws and the flaws of those around me. In those moments, the enemy fed me one accusation after another to widen the separation between us. Take it from me, holding on to offense makes for a miserable existence for you and everyone around you. If you take the low road and agree with the accusations, you will give up a portion of your power to live as an overcomer. Man of God, reject these negative thoughts and feelings and choose to believe the best!

I urge you to pray and ask God for strength to put 1 Peter 4:8 (AMP) into practice. It says, "Above all things have intense and unfailing love for one another, for **love covers** a multitude of sins [forgives and disregards the offenses of others]." Those two words—love covers—have revolutionized how I do life. How do you get this kind of love? Ask the Holy Spirit for it. He will pour it into your heart as you spend time in His presence.[9] Just like the love of God covers your sins, He wants you to love others and cover their sins—not expose them. He will empower you, if you ask Him. I call you blessed!

Walk It:

"Little foxes" are subtle, seemingly insignificant things that eat away at your relationship with God and draw you back into sin. They include unconfessed sin, pride, unforgiveness, and laziness. To eliminate these, learn to deal with sin quickly; allow Jesus to cultivate His heart of humility in you; let go of offense and forgive others promptly; and guard against laziness by developing a disciplined life. The closer you stay in relationship with Jesus, the quicker you'll be able to recognize and eliminate little foxes.

Study It:

Sin: Isaiah 59:1-2; 1 Corinthians 5:6-8; James 4:17; 1 John 1:7-9 **Pride/Humility:** Proverbs 11:2; 13:10; 16:18; 22:4; 29:23; Micah 6:8; 1 Corinthians 10:12; John 6:63; 15:5; Romans 7:18; 12:3, 9-18; Philippians 2:3-8; 3:3; James 4:6; 1 Peter 5:5. **Unforgiveness:** Psalm 119:165; Matthew 6:12, 14-15; Acts 24:16; Ephesians 4:26-32; 1 John 2:9-11 **Laziness**: Romans 12:11; 1 Timothy 4:7-8

Apply It:

1 Using James 4:17 and Romans 14:23, define sin. In light of these verses, is there any sin in your life that the Holy Spirit is showing you? If so, follow 1 John 1:9: Admit it, confess it, and repent.

_____

_____

_____

_____

_____

2 Carefully read Jesus' words in Mark 11:25; Matthew 6:12, 14-15; 18:21-35. What is the Holy Spirit showing you in these verses? Why is it so important to forgive others? Is there anyone you need to forgive, release, and pray a blessing over? If so, take time to pray the prayer below.

_____

_____

_____

_____

Check out Ephesians 4:32; Colossians 3:13; 1 Peter 3:7-8.

3 Pause and pray, "Holy Spirit, are there any *little foxes* I need to eliminate? Am I walking in pride? If so, where? Are there any areas in my life where I'm spiritually lazy in my stand against sin? Please show me my heart." Now get quiet and listen. Write what He says; obey His promptings.

_____

_____

_____

_____

_____

What happens when you tolerate "little foxes" in your life? Learn a lesson from the Israelites in Numbers 33:50-53, 55.

Pray It:

"Father, thank You for this revelation about the little foxes. I don't want sin, pride, unforgiveness, laziness, or anything else to draw me away from You. But I need Your discernment to recognize and eliminate these things. Please forgive me for holding on to unforgiveness toward (insert person's name). I forgive them and release them into Your hands. Bless them, Lord (pray the best blessings you can think of over that person). Show me any area where I'm being lazy or walking in pride. Forgive me and teach me what I can do differently. Cultivate a heart of humility in me. In Jesus' name, Amen!"

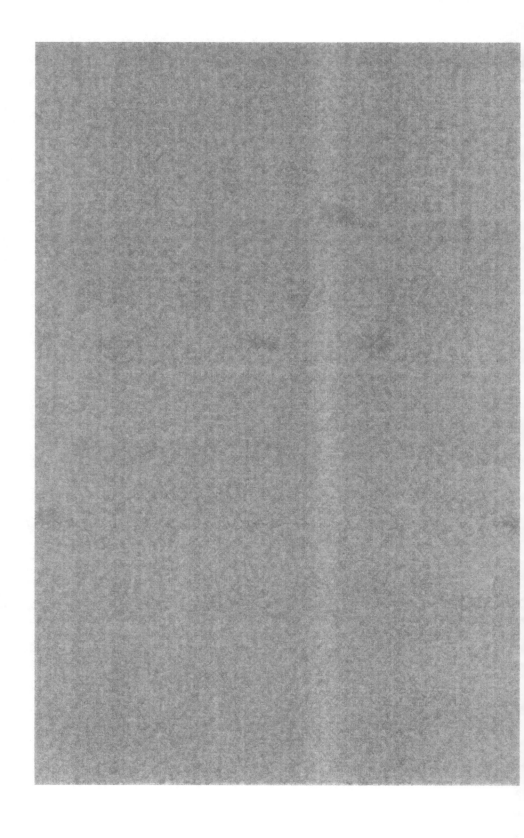

Unite with Your
Greatest Defense
of All

ONE BROTHER TO ANOTHER

"When the Friend comes, the Spirit of the Truth, he will take you by the hand and guide you into all the truth there is. He won't draw attention to himself, but will make sense out of what is about to happen and, indeed, out of all that I have done and said. He will honor me; he will take from me and deliver it to you."

—Jesus Christ
John 16:13-14 The Message

Step 15

STAY FILLED WITH THE HOLY SPIRIT

When the Holy Spirit comes upon you,
you will be filled with power....

Acts 1:8 GNT

After Jesus died and rose from the grave, He walked the earth for forty days. During that time, He revealed Himself to many of His faithful followers. Before He ascended into Heaven, with a crowd of about 500 present,[1] He gave them this strong command: "...Wait for the gift I told you about, the gift my Father promised. John baptized with water, but in a few days you will be *baptized with the Holy Spirit*. When the Holy Spirit comes upon you, you will be *filled with power*, and you will be witnesses for me..." (Acts 1:4-5, 8 GNT).

Power—that's what being filled with the Spirit is all about. He is the supernatural strength—the inner dynamo—we need to live like Jesus. Although we have talked about the Holy Spirit throughout a number of the earlier chapters, I feel it's important to devote this chapter totally to Him. He is the priceless, promised Gift of the Father, and He is worthy of our time and attention!

Who Is the Holy Spirit?

The Holy Spirit is God. He is not an "it," nor is He an optional feature to salvation. He is the third Person of the Trinity—the embodiment of God Himself—sent by the Father to represent Him on the earth. Jesus is seated in Heaven next to God the Father.[2] The Holy Spirit is presently at work on the earth bringing about God's will in and through believers. While the physical person of Jesus was limited to time and space, the Holy Spirit knows no boundaries! He can go where no one else can go—into the hearts of men, women, and children all across the earth, all at the same time!

Think about it. When you repent of your sins and invite Jesus into your life, who comes to live in you? Is it the *physical* person of Jesus? Is it God the Father? No. It is the amazing Holy Spirit! Scripture says,

"To show that you are his children, God sent *the Spirit of his Son* into our hearts, the Spirit who cries out, 'Father, my Father'" (Galatians 4:6 GNT). When you accept Jesus, your body becomes the Holy Spirit's home—His temple (see 1 Corinthians 6:18-20). The fullness of God comes to live in you in the form of His Holy Spirit.[3]

All that Jesus is and all that God the Father is, the Holy Spirit is. To put it plainly…

Jesus Christ = God the Father = the Holy Spirit

Interestingly, when you read Scripture, you will find that the Holy Spirit is the Spirit of Christ who is the Spirit of God. These titles of God's Spirit are used interchangeably throughout the New Testament. Romans 8:9-11 illustrates this clearly. What's my point? It is vital to intimately know God's Holy Spirit since He is the One living in you. *He is the One you are in relationship with.* He is the One living the life of Jesus through you as you yield to Him. He is the One changing the way you think, feel, and act to agree with the way Jesus thinks, feels, and acts. He is the One empowering you to live free from the prison of porn.

What Does the Holy Spirit Do?

The number of ways the Holy Spirit helps us is measureless. In Step 1, we learned that as we live in oneness with Jesus, everything we need is available to us. How do we receive it? Through the Person of the Holy Spirit—the Spirit of Christ. This is who you become one with—who you abide in relationship with. Jesus said, "…He [the Spirit] will take the things that are Mine and will reveal (declare, disclose, transmit) it to you" (John 16:15 AMP). Everything Jesus has—peace, joy, righteousness, self-control, a sound mind, victory over temptation, everything—is available to you through the Holy Spirit.

There are many "hats" the Holy Spirit wears, and with each one He has been given a specific name. He is your *Helper,* your *Strengthener,* and your *Advocate.* He is your *Intercessor,* the *Spirit of Truth,* and the *Spirit of Grace* who gives you the supernatural power (grace) of God to live like Jesus. He is also your *Comforter* and *Counselor.* Nothing and no one can comfort you and counsel you like the Holy Spirit. He can give you wisdom and insight not only about what to do, but also about why you feel the way you feel and react to certain situations the way you do.

I cannot count how many times the Holy Spirit has revealed to me why I was feeling and reacting a certain way. I remember one very challenging time in my life; I was battling back-to-back bouts of disappointment and trouble for months on end. Eventually, I began to experience mild depression. It was during this time I also experienced an increase in temptation to look at porn again and relieve myself sexually. Frustrated, I prayed, "Holy Spirit, what's going on? Why am I having all these thoughts and feelings again? I thought I had grown beyond this." He answered me in my spirit saying, *You have grown. You are just deeply discouraged, and your soul is longing for comfort. Your flesh, aided by the enemy, is trying to get you to comfort yourself the way you used too—through porn. Reject the thoughts and seek My comfort and the arms of your wife.* Wow! He nailed it with pinpoint accuracy. This kind of insight is priceless! And it only comes through fellowship with the Holy Spirit.

Not only is He your Comforter and Counselor, He is also the *Author of Scripture*[4] and your resident *Teacher.* Scripture says, "You have received the Holy Spirit, and he lives within you…. For the Spirit teaches you everything you need to know, and what he teaches is true—it is not a lie. So just as he has taught you, remain in fellowship with Christ" (1 John 2:27 NLT). What does the Spirit teach you? *Everything* you need to know, when you need to know it! How do you receive this incredible knowledge and wisdom? By remaining in fellowship with Christ—His Spirit.

Want to know how to specifically avoid the scenes of temptation and starve your flesh? Ask your Teacher. Want to know how to live free from ungodly feelings and eliminate the "little foxes"? Again, ask your Teacher, and He will tell you (see James 1:5). Jesus said, "When the Spirit of truth comes, he will guide you into all truth…" (John 16:13 NLT). If you ask, the Holy Spirit will reveal the truth of who Jesus is and help you understand the meaning of Scripture. He'll also show you *the truth about you,* including any specific actions you need to take in order to walk in freedom. What an incredible Gift and Friend we have in the Holy Spirit!

How Can You Be Filled with the Spirit?

Being filled with the Holy Spirit begins the moment you invite Jesus into your heart. But there is more! There is a *baptism* in the Holy Spirit that is a separate experience from salvation. Jesus spoke about this in Acts 1:5, and He wants you to receive this fullness of who He is. The word *baptize* is the Greek term *baptizo,* which means "to submerge or overwhelm." In this verse, *baptize* specifically means "to imbue—to saturate, permeate, and infuse—with the Holy Spirit." [5]

Picture yourself as a sixteen-ounce, clear drinking glass. The moment you are saved, it's like God pours the Living Water of His Spirit into you, filling you with sixteen ounces of Himself. When you are baptized in the Holy Spirit, on the other hand, it's like God installs an artesian spring inside of you that continually bubbles up with His Living Water (see John 7:37-39). Not only are you filled, but now you are a fountain overflowing with God's Spirit, pouring into and refreshing the lives of those around you! The more you are filled with the Spirit, the greater the capacity of Living Water that flows from your life.

Now I realize that there has been much controversy about the baptism in the Holy Spirit. The enemy has stirred up a lot of strife, fear, and confusion over this aspect of the Christian faith and consequently kept many of God's people from experiencing His fullness. Make no mistake. The baptism of the Holy Spirit is a gift from your Father. It's for *all* believers—including you.[6] For nearly 2,000 years, countless millions have experienced this divine empowerment and deeper level of intimacy with God, and it's phenomenal! For me, this dimension of the Holy Spirit's presence and power has been a major key to breaking free from pornography.

To be baptized in the Holy Spirit, all you need to do is *ask the Father*. Jesus said, "If your little boy asks for a serving of fish, do you scare him with a live snake on his plate? If your little girl asks for an egg, do you trick her with a spider? As bad as you are, you wouldn't think of such a thing—you're at least decent to your own children. And don't you think the Father who conceived you in love will give the Holy Spirit when you ask him?" (Luke 11:11-13 The Message). If you desire a deeper, more intimate, more powerful connection with God, ask Him to baptize you in His Holy Spirit. (For more on the Baptism in the Spirit, check out pages 261-262.)

Be Filled and Stay Filled with the Spirit!

Friend, everything that Jesus did while here on earth, He did by the power of the Holy Spirit. He was conceived by the Spirit,[7] led by the Spirit,[8] taught by the Spirit,[9] and empowered by the Spirit.[10] Scripture says, "…God anointed Jesus of Nazareth *with the Holy Spirit* and with power. Then Jesus went around doing good and healing all who were oppressed by the devil, for God was with him" (Acts 10:38 NLT). If Jesus was filled with the Spirit and relied on Him for everything, then we need to do the same!

I encourage you to open wide your heart and "**ever be filled** and stimulated with the [Holy] Spirit" (Ephesians 5:18 AMP). Let Jesus baptize you and continually fill you with His power as you pray in the Spirit's language.[11] Lean on, rely on, and trust in Him. He will infuse you with the very life of Christ to live victoriously over sexual temptation. May "the amazing grace of the Master, Jesus Christ, the extravagant love of God, the **intimate friendship of the Holy Spirit**, be with... you" (2 Corinthians 13:14 The Message). He is your very best Friend!

Encouragement from the Heart of a Woman

Words cannot express the incredible value of the Holy Spirit's friendship. His unending patience and tender compassion with me as I am becoming like Christ is the life-giving strength that enables me to grow. He sees me as a person, not as a task that needs to be completed. He is committed and faithful. He is the One who helped me see that Vincent's struggle with porn was not about me. He is the One who helped me see that I was not the first or the only person hurting in the situation. Jesus was the first to be hurt, and Vincent was hurting too. The Holy Spirit's presence in my life brought me healing and changed my whole perspective during this very difficult time.

Man of God, the Holy Spirit is all the power you need, and He's living in you! He is not only able, but also willing to help. He longs to be your closest Friend, helping you in every area of your life. He is the One who empowers you when you feel overwhelmed or like you're going to fail. He's your Source of strength and the voice of reason and encouragement that enables you to keep on keeping on.

Jesus said the Spirit is your Counselor, Comforter, Teacher, and Guide into all truth (see John 14:26; 16:13). He accomplishes these roles even on a molecular level. Because He is Spirit, He can go where no human being can go. He is able to reach the depths of who you are, bringing counsel, comfort, direction, and guidance. When you have been touched by the precious Spirit of Jesus in these ways, there's nothing man can do to change it.

Man of God, I encourage you to invite the Holy Spirit into every area of your life. Invite Him to teach you the truth about yourself and the situations you are facing. Invite Him to comfort and counsel you when you are upset or don't know how to handle something. He is truly brilliant! He has helped me and taught me more things than I can count. He will never let you down!

I pray that you will have a fresh experience with the precious Holy Spirit and that He will empower you to walk as you have been created to walk—pure and free. I call you blessed!

Walk It:

To be filled with the Holy Spirit is to be filled with *power*. He is God. All that Jesus is and all that God the Father is, the Holy Spirit is. When you accept Jesus, your body becomes the Spirit's home, and you enter relationship with Him. He is your Strengthener, Intercessor, Comforter, and Counselor. He's also your resident Teacher who guides you into all truth. Everything Jesus has is available to you through His Holy Spirit. Being filled starts at salvation and intensifies exponentially when you are baptized in the Spirit. So, open your heart…be ever-filled with the Holy Spirit! He is your best Friend.

Study It:

You Are God's Home: 1 Corinthians 6:18-20; 2 Corinthians 6:14-7:1 **The Spirit's Job:** John 7:37-39; 14:16-17, 26; 16:7-15; Acts 1:8; 2 Timothy 3:16; 2 Peter 1:20-21; 1 John 2:27 **Spirit of Jesus:** Galatians 4:6; 1 John 3:24; 4:13 **Be Filled/Stay Filled** Ephesians 6:18; 1 Timothy 4:14; 2 Timothy 1:6-7; 1 Corinthians 14:4; Jude 1:20

Pray It:

"Father, thank You for the incredible gift of Your Holy Spirit! Fill me afresh till I am overflowing with You. Holy Spirit, I acknowledge that You are God. Please forgive me for believing anything about You in error. There are many things that I don't understand, so I open myself to You fully to teach me. I want to know You intimately. Be my Helper, my Strengthener, my Intercessor, my Comforter, my Counselor, my everything! Please reveal Jesus to me. Be my Teacher and explain the Word to me as I read and study it. Guide me into all truth about God, myself, and the world around me. In Jesus' name, Amen!"

Apply It:

1 Take a moment and briefly share who the Holy Spirit is to you. What aspects of His character encourage you the most? Why?

_____

_____

_____

_____

_____

2 After hearing about the many facets of the Holy Spirit, in what area(s) of your life do you feel you can most benefit from His empowerment? How do you want Him to help you specifically?

_____

_____

_____

_____

_____

Is the Holy Spirit showing you any areas where you have not allowed Him to work? If so, take time to repent and ask Him to forgive you; invite Him to have free reign in every area of your life.

3 Carefully read 1 Timothy 4:14; 2 Timothy 1:6-7; Ephesians 6:18; 1 Corinthians 14:4; and Jude 1:20. What is the Holy Spirit revealing to you in these passages? What is your part in staying filled with the Spirit? What are the results?

_____

_____

_____

_____

_____

Have you been baptized in the Holy Spirit and filled with His empowerment? If not, you can be! Check out pages 261-262.

4 What is your greatest takeaway from this chapter? What scriptures, principles, or ideas exploded in your heart? How are you challenged? What action(s) is the Holy Spirit prompting you to take?

_____

_____

_____

_____

_____

ONE BROTHER TO ANOTHER

"...Jesus Christ did not come merely to be our helper, our divine assistant. He did not come just to take part in our lives but to take over our lives. You see, if all you want is a little help and a little boost from Jesus to get you over the top, you'll never make it. You'll never have victory. You won't find the solution to the battle within, you won't be free at last, until Jesus becomes your life. ...The answer to the infestation of sin is to exchange {your} life for Christ's life...."

—Tony Evans[1]
Free at Last

Step 16

REMEMBER...IT'S NOT IN YOUR OWN STRENGTH

...Work out the salvation that God has given you with a proper sense of awe and responsibility. [Not in your own strength] for it is God Who is all the while effectually at work in you [energizing and creating in you the power and desire], both to will and to work for His good pleasure and satisfaction and delight.

Philippians 2:12-13 *Verse 12 Phillips; verse 13 AMP*

Take a moment to slowly reread that passage again. Did you get it? You and I are to "work out" our salvation. Step by step, we are to walk out the freedom that Christ has paid for. This includes freedom from the prison of porn. How do we do it? *Not in our own strength.* Say it again, and this time, make it personal: "Not in *my* own strength." Let those words sink deep into your heart. "Not—in—my—own—strength." This is the essence of your victory as a Christian. You can only experience the fullness of salvation through the strength of the Spirit living in you.

Verse 13 continues, "for it is God Who is all the while effectually at work in you...." Once you surrender your life to Jesus and invite Him into your heart, the fullness of God—Father, Son, and Holy Spirit—comes to live inside you.[2] And God's fullness is found in His Spirit. One of the names He is given is the Spirit of Life (see Romans 8:2). What does this wonderful Spirit of do? Everything! Everything you need to become like Jesus is produced by the power of the Spirit of Life.

It's By God's Spirit

God, speaking through Paul, says, "...And as the Spirit of the Lord works within us, we become more and more like him" (2 Corinthians 3:18 TLB). It is God, in the Person of His Life-giving Spirit, who is all the while at work in you making you more and more like Jesus. He is the One who warns you to get off the computer when the temptation to surf for smut is knocking at your door. He is the One who gives you power to do what's right when that urge begins to surge within. God's Spirit living in your spirit is also the One who is grieved when you give in to temptation, resulting in feelings of inner pain and lack of peace.

Paul understood the absolute need of the Spirit. In 2 Corinthians 3:5 (TLB) he declares, "Not because we think we can do anything of lasting value by ourselves. Our only power and success comes from God." Again, in Romans 7:18 (AMP) he states, "I know that nothing good dwells within me, that is, in my flesh. I can will what is right, but I cannot perform it. [I have the intention and urge to do what is right, but no power to carry it out]." Jesus also nails this principle saying, "The Spirit alone gives eternal life. Human effort accomplishes nothing…" (John 6:63 NLT). Friend, you can't rely on your own strength to break free from wrong behavior. God says, "you will succeed, not by military might or by your own strength, but **by my spirit**" (Zechariah 4:6 GNT).

Is it sinking in? Your freedom from the prison of porn and all its lures will not come by your own strength. You will gain and maintain victory only by the power of God's Life-giving Spirit living in you. For me, it doesn't matter how many bestselling books I write or how many great sermons I preach. It doesn't matter how many hours I pray or how many scriptures I read every day. The only way for me to maintain freedom over sexual temptation and all temptation is by relying on the power of God's Life-giving Spirit living in me—period. He gives me the power and desire not to click on impure pop-ups. He gives me the power and desire not to Google a word I know is going to yield graphic images. He gives me the power and desire not to pick up a magazine filled with arousing images. And He'll do the same for you!

"What's My Part?"

Good question. Your part is twofold. First, welcome God's Spirit into your life daily through prayer, a topic we will focus on in the next chapter. Second, cooperate with the Spirit's promptings. In other words, as you abide in relationship with Him, obey what He asks you to do. He stands ready, willing, and able to help. In fact, He *craves* for you to welcome Him into every area of your life. The Scripture says, "…The Spirit Whom He has caused to dwell in us yearns over us and He yearns for the Spirit [to be welcome] with a jealous love" (James 4:5 AMP).

The word *yearn* here is the Greek word *epipotheo*. Usually it is used to describe an intense yearning for something sinful. In this case, however, it describes the Holy Spirit's craving for us—our attention, affection, and fellowship. He wants us entirely for Himself. His yearning, depicted in this verse, is as intense as a drug addict's craving for a "fix" to satisfy his addiction. That's the meaning of the word *epipotheo*.[3] Wow! Did you know God's Spirit longs to be welcome in your life that much? He does. So invite Him in! Throughout the day stop and pray,

"Holy Spirit, I welcome You to guide me in every decision. Please give me the power and desire to live a pure life, in Jesus' name."

As You Do Your Part, the Spirit Will Do His

As I mentioned before, the Holy Spirit wears many hats in your life. He is your *Helper, Counselor, Comforter,* and *Strengthener.* One way He strengthens you is by being your *Intercessor.* To intercede means to act as a mediator between you and the Father. God's Word declares, "The Holy Spirit helps us in our weakness. For example, we don't know what God wants us to pray for. But the Holy Spirit prays for us with groanings that cannot be expressed in words. And the Father who knows all hearts knows what the Spirit is saying, for the Spirit pleads for us believers in harmony with God's own will" (Romans 8:26-27 NLT).

When you don't know what to pray, the Holy Spirit prays through you. When you are confused, battered by temptation, and hurting deeply, the Spirit offers prayers through your tears and heart-wrenching groans. Other times He prays to the Father in the special heavenly language He gave you when you were baptized in Him. This is what the Scripture calls "praying in the Spirit." It is an awesome privilege and something we should practice regularly. Why? Because *praying in the Spirit releases God's power!*

Through Jude, God says, "...Carefully **build yourselves up** in this most holy faith by *praying in the Holy Spirit*" (Jude 1:20 The Message). And through Paul, God declares, "A person who speaks in tongues {the heavenly language of the Holy Spirit} is **strengthened** personally..." (1 Corinthians 14:4 NLT). If you want power to defeat the devil and crucify your flesh, you will receive it as you pray in the Spirit. This practice is the key to staying filled with the Spirit and receiving God's strength.

Friend, declare this truth out loud and let it soak deep into your heart: "It is not in my own strength that I'll find freedom. I will gain and maintain freedom from sexual temptation by relying on and receiving the power of God's Holy Spirit." As you welcome the Spirit into your life each day and pray regularly in the special language He has given you, He will faithfully prompt you to right actions. So rest in Him. He will show you how to avoid the scenes of temptation and recall to your memory the right scriptures at the right time to defeat the enemy. Remember, He loves you deeply and yearns to be welcome in your life!

Encouragement from the Heart of a Woman

In myself, apart from Christ, I have a tendency to be harsh and impatient. When I try to do things in my own strength (or my own way),

I tend to be controlling. Such was the case with Vincent as we were on our journey. In my immaturity, I tried to shame him into living a pure life. I wanted him to feel the pain he was causing me, and I foolishly expected him to heal me. This of course did NOT work. It wasn't until God's Spirit showed me how and empowered me how to love Vincent where he was that I began to actually help him experience freedom.

There are things you are presently trying to do in your own strength that are not working. Just as I could not help Vincent or experience healing without the assistance of the Holy Spirit, you too will need His assistance to walk out of the prison of porn and into freedom.

Just like you rely on the strength of your power tools to do the work you can't do on your own—rely on the strength of God's mighty Spirit. He has more horsepower than your pickup and better aim than your semi-automatic rifle. He can lead, guide, and provide you with the strength you need to walk in freedom in every area of your life.

Man of God, you were put here on this earth for great things! Allow the Life-giving Spirit of God to mature you and walk with you into them. Lean on Him for strength (grace); it's yours for the asking. All you have to do is pray. He loves and cares for you intensely. He sees you where you are today and longs to take you out of bondage into complete freedom and peace. Trust Him…HE IS ABLE!

Walk It:

Everything you need to become like Jesus is produced by the power of His Spirit—it's not in your own strength. Nothing good dwells in your flesh. As the Spirit works in you and you cooperate with Him, you are changed and experience true freedom. Welcome Him into your life every day. He yearns for your affection and fellowship!

Study It:

The Flesh Is Useless: John 6:63; 15:5; Romans 7:15-25; Philippians 3:3 **The Spirit Empowers**: Zechariah 4:6; Philippians 2:12-13; Romans 8:1-17; 2 Corinthians 3:5, 18; James 4:5-6 **Pray in the Spirit**: Ephesians 6:18; Romans 8:26-27; 1 Corinthians 14:4; Jude 1:20

Apply It:

1 In your own words, briefly describe the Holy Spirit's part and your part in the process of experiencing freedom from pornography (and all sin).

My Part: _____

_____

_____

_____

The Spirit's Part: _____

_____

_____

For help with both, check out Romans 8:1-17; 2 Corinthians 3:5, 18; James 4:5-6; Ephesians 6:18; Romans 8:26-27; 1 Corinthians 14:4; Jude 1:20.

2 Look back over James 4:5 and the original meaning of the word *yearn*. What does this speak to you about God's desire to be in relationship with you?

_____

_____

_____

_____

_____

3 What's your greatest takeaway from this chapter? What scriptures, principles, or ideas exploded in your heart? How are you challenged? What action(s) is the Holy Spirit prompting you to take?

_____

_____

_____

_____

_____

_____

Pray It:

"Father, forgive me for being proud. At times I have unknowingly thought I could kick this addiction on my own. I realize now that I cannot break free from porn or any other sinful behavior in my own strength. I need You. I welcome You, Holy Spirit of God. Invade every area of my life. Saturate me with Your power and presence. Fill me with all that You are. Give me a desire to be in relationship with You. Prompt me quickly to avoid evil. Empower me daily to say no to sin and yes to You. Thank You for Your love, mercy, and forgiveness. In Jesus' name, Amen."

ONE BROTHER TO ANOTHER

"...Prayer is to God's will as rails are to a train. The locomotive is full of power: it is capable of running a thousand miles a day. But if there are no rails, it cannot move forward a single inch. If it dares to move without them, it will soon sink into the earth. ...And such is the relation between prayer and God's work. ...Without any doubt God is almighty and He works mightily, but He will not and cannot work if you and I do not labor together with Him in prayer...."

—Watchman Nee[1]

Let Us Pray

Step 17

MAKE PRAYER YOUR FIRST RESPONSE

Pray at all times with every kind of spiritual prayer,
keeping alert and persistent as you pray....

Ephesians 6:18 Phillips

Have you ever said, "I've done everything I know to do. All I can do now is pray"? I have. This is just the opposite of what we should do. Prayer should be our *first response*, not our last resort. It is as vital to our lives as breathing.

God instructs us to devote ourselves to prayer and pray without ceasing.[2] Jesus urges us to pray, *asking*, *seeking*, and *knocking* until we receive what we need.[3] He tells us, "Don't worry about anything; instead, **pray** about everything. Tell God what you need, and thank him for all he has done. Then you will experience God's peace, which exceeds anything we can understand. His peace will guard your hearts and minds as you live in Christ Jesus" (Philippians 4:6-7 NLT).

Without question, prayer knits us together in relationship with God. It releases His victorious power in our lives to break free from the prison of pornography and every other sin we face.

What Is Prayer?

Basically, prayer is talking and listening to God. It's two-way communication and fellowship with our heavenly Father. It's not a ritual but a way of life—a natural outflow of a healthy relationship with Him.

Think about how you interact with your best friend. For me, this is my wife, Allison. Our communication includes many elements. As often as I can, I *thank* her for all she does to bring health and happiness to our relationship and home. I *praise* her for her character of boldness, determination, and selflessness. I *ask for help* when I need it and *offer help* when she needs it. When I'm upset with her or she's upset with me, we *work through disagreements*. When our passion for each other is ignited, we *express love* through words, gestures, and physical touch.

Are you getting the picture? This is a snapshot of prayer—*doing life together in relationship.* It's fully expressing yourself to God—your hopes and dreams, doubts and fears, joys and sorrows, wants and needs. It's being open, honest, and intimately connected with your Creator. It's thanking Him, praising Him, working through disappointments, asking Him for help, and doing what He asks you to do. It's receiving His love for you and expressing your love for Him. Prayer is all about relationship.

Sometimes prayer is a bold, spoken request. Other times it is sitting silently and communing with God without words. In both cases, something happens within you that cannot be put into words. An invisible exchange between you and your Maker takes place. Through prayer you open yourself to and connect with God's Holy Spirit, and He opens Himself to you. As you humbly surrender and cast your cares on Him, He downloads His life-giving energy into your being. Prayer plugs you into God's power!

Prayer Plugs You into God's Power

To break free from porn, you need God's power. Remember, it's *not in your own strength.* Prayer is the pipeline through which God's power flows. James 5:16 (AMP) declares, "…The earnest (heartfelt, continued) prayer of a righteous man **makes tremendous power available** [dynamic in its working]."

In the last chapter, we learned that victory over the magnetic pull of porn only comes through the strength and power of the Holy Spirit. The way you tap into this power is through prayer. Prayer is an act of both humility and faith. By praying to God for help, you are saying, "God I cannot do this without You; I am powerless *(this is humility).* I believe that You are real, You want to help me, and You have the power to help me *(this is faith).*"

Through prayer you stay connected with the Person of the Holy Spirit and allow Him to saturate and infuse you with all that He is. Every day, I open myself up to God's Spirit through prayer. I say, "Holy Spirit, fill every fiber of my being with You. Infuse me with inner strength. Live through me, just as You lived through Jesus, Paul, and others. I need You. Apart from You, I can do nothing, but in You and empowered by You, I can do all things."[4]

Two scripture passages motivate me to purposely pray this way. The first is Philippians 4:13 (NKJV). Maybe you have heard it. It says, "I can do all things through Christ who strengthens me." Now listen to it in the Amplified version. It says, "I have strength for all things in Christ Who empowers me [I am ready for anything and equal to anything through Him Who *infuses inner strength* into me...." Wow! Slow down and reread that verse. Christ's Spirit living in you infuses you with inner strength. All you have to do is ask Him for it and wait in His presence to receive it. This is a picture of prayer.

Which brings me to the second passage—Isaiah 40:28-31(AMP). Verse 28 proclaims, "Have you not known? Have you not heard? The everlasting God, the Lord, the Creator of the ends of the earth, does not faint or grow weary; there is no searching of His understanding." Aren't you glad God doesn't grow weary! But wait, there's more! Verse 29 says, "He gives power to the faint and weary, and to him who has no might He increases strength [causing it to multiply and making it to abound]." Oh, thank God for His promise of power! And His supply is limitless. In verse 31, He assures us that "those who wait for the Lord [who expect, look for, and hope in Him] shall **change** and **renew their strength** and power; they shall lift their wings and mount up [close to God] as eagles [mount up to the sun]; they shall run and not be weary, they shall walk and not faint or become tired."

Friend, I have prayed these verses countless times. There are days I get up and I'm exhausted mentally, emotionally, physically, and spiritually. In moments like these, I pray, "Lord, You know where I am. You said that You give power to the faint and weary, and to him who has no might, You increase strength, causing it to multiply and abound. I need You to do that today...right now. Give me Your power to live a pure life and not give in to sin. Strengthen me to guard my eyes, my mind, and my heart and avoid the scenes of temptation. Help me feed my spirit and starve my flesh, in Jesus' name."

Prayers like this touch God's heart and move Him to action. Why? They reveal a heart of humility and faith, and it's the humble that receive God's grace to walk in freedom. Remember, God "...gives us more and more grace (power of the Holy Spirit, to meet this evil tendency and all others fully). That is why He says, God sets Himself against the proud and haughty, but gives grace [continually] to the lowly (those who are humble enough to receive it)" (James 4:6 AMP).

Prayer Protects You from Temptation

Jesus knew how vital and powerful prayer is. That's why He made it a primary part of His life. He spent time in the mountains, by the sea, in the desert, and in gardens to commune with the Father and receive supernatural power.[5] Just hours before His most difficult time of testing, He pulled away to pray. It was in the Garden of Gethsemane that He won the war over His human will. He knew what was coming, and His flesh didn't want to go through it.

What was Jesus tempted to do just hours before His greatest test? He was tempted to abort God's plan of suffering and dying for the sins of mankind. Jesus' prayer—His open, honest communion with the Father —supernaturally strengthened Him not to give in to temptation. After He prayed, "Not My will but Yours, Father," Luke records that "an angel from heaven appeared and *strengthened* him" (22:43 NLT).

Notice what He told the disciples at this time: "Watch and pray so that you will *not fall into temptation*. The spirit is willing, but the body is weak" (Matthew 26:41 NIV). Did you catch that? Prayer protects you from falling into temptation. It's proactive. The real you—your born-again spirit man—wants to live free from porn, but only God's Spirit can infuse you with the power to live it out.[6] These same words of Jesus in The Message read, "Stay alert; *be in prayer* so you don't wander into temptation without even knowing you're in danger. There is a part of you that is eager, ready for anything in God. But there's another part that's as lazy as an old dog sleeping by the fire."

Friend, temptation is coming—Jesus said it would. So make the decision now to be proactive—become a man of prayer. Prayer is open, honest communion with your heavenly Father—your pipeline to His power that will strengthen you not to give in to sin. Jesus promises that "because He Himself [in His humanity] has suffered in being tempted (tested and tried), He is able [**immediately**] to run to the cry of...those who are being tempted and tested and tried..." (Hebrews 2:18 AMP). When you face temptation, *run to God in prayer*. He will immediately run to you and help. Through the power of His Spirit, He will strengthen you to say no to your flesh and the enemy and yes to His will. With man, sexual purity seems impossible, but with God, all things are possible!

Encouragement from the Heart of a Woman

As Vincent began his jailbreak from porn and we walked through that very difficult season of life, I ran to God daily to fight the temptation to pull away from him and justify divorce. According to Jesus, "Anyone who even looks at a woman with lust has already committed adultery with her in her heart" (Matthew 5:28 NLT). Vincent had done this countless times, and adultery is biblical grounds for divorce (see Matthew 5:32).

While he needed God's strength not to give in to porn's magnetic pull, I needed God's strength not to become angry, offended, and self-focused. Each time I turned to God in prayer, He was faithful to strengthen me, counsel me, and love me, restoring wholeness to my life and our marriage. Had I not prayed and received His grace (power), I would not have been healed, and total victory would have eluded us.

Man of God, I can't encourage you enough to develop your prayer life. When you face temptation, run to Jesus and pray. Not some high, lofty, fancy prayer. Just a real, simple, heartfelt cry for help. Whispering, "I need Your help," is prayer. God is faithful to turn to us when we turn to Him. Through His Spirit, He will help you and grant you grace to overcome every evil tendency. He has a wonderful plan for you. The struggle is coming to an end and you will be victorious through Christ! I call you blessed!

Walk It:

Prayer is open, honest communication and fellowship with God that knits you together in relationship. It is the pipeline through which His power flows—power to break free from porn and every other sin you face. Prayer is proactive and protects you from falling into temptation. When you face temptation, run to God in prayer. He will strengthen you by His Spirit to say no to your flesh and the enemy and yes to His will.

Study It:

Prayer Is a Way of Life: Matthew 7:7-11; 26:41; Ephesians 6:18; Philippians 4:6-7, 13; Colossians 4:2; 1 Thessalonians 5:17 **Prayer Releases Power:** James 4:6; 5:13-18; Isaiah 40:28-31; Hebrews 2:18; 4:15-16

Apply It:

1 In your own words, describe what prayer is. How does this chapter help you see prayer as a more real, relevant part of your everyday life?

_____

_____

_____

_____

2 Read Hebrews 2:18; 4:15-16; 10:19-22 and Ephesians 3:12. How should you approach God in prayer? What gives you the privilege? What else is the Holy Spirit showing you in these verses?

_____

_____

_____

_____

3 Jesus regularly invested time alone in prayer to commune with the Father and receive the Spirit's empowerment. Do you have a special time and place to be alone with God? If so, when and where? If not, ask Him to show you when and where you can meet with Him.

_____

_____

_____

_____

4 Carefully reread Isaiah 40:28-31; Philippians 4:13 and James 4:6 in the chapter. What is God speaking to you through these verses? Take a moment to write out a brief prayer using them.

_____

_____

_____

_____

Also check out Habakkuk 3:19 and David's prayers to the Lord in Psalm 18:1-3; 27:1-14; 28:1-9.

5 What is your greatest takeaway from this chapter? What scriptures, principles, or ideas exploded in your heart? How are you challenged? What action(s) is the Holy Spirit prompting you to take?

_____

_____

_____

Things I Want to Remember:

Pray It:

"Father, please forgive me for being prayerless. I have not understood its importance or power. Thank You for opening my eyes to the truth. Holy Spirit, please help me to know, really know in my heart, the vital necessity of prayer—not as something I have to do, but something I am privileged to do. Let it become second-nature, like breathing. May I pray without ceasing, effortlessly talking and listening to You throughout each day. You are my strength to live a pure life...please strengthen me! Download Your life-giving energy into me and live through me, just as You lived through Jesus. In His name, Amen!"

ONE BROTHER TO ANOTHER

"God's Word is…

1. Supernatural in origin;
2. Eternal in duration;
3. Inexpressible in valour;
4. Infinite in scope;
5. Regenerative in power;
6. Infallible in authority;
7. Universal in application;
8. Inspired in totality.

Read it through, write it down; pray it in; work it out; pass it on. The Word of God changes a man until he becomes an Epistle of God."

—Smith Wigglesworth[1]

Step **18**

LET GOD'S WORD DWELL IN YOU RICHLY

Let the word of Christ
dwell in you richly in all wisdom....
Colossians 3:16 KJV

Nothing on earth—not even all the combined knowledge of man—can surpass the life-giving brilliance and brawn of God's Word. His Word contains His thoughts, and the wisdom and power it packs is priceless! "The whole Bible was given to us by inspiration from God and is useful to teach us what is true and to make us realize what is wrong in our lives; it straightens us out and helps us do what is right" (2 Timothy 3:16 TLB).

I am convinced that one of the main reasons many Christian men struggle to live pure lives is because they don't know—I mean *really know*—God's Word. It's fun to know and talk about baseball stats, football stats, hunting stories, and the hottest fishing spots, but knowing God's Word carries far greater value. Indeed, a major key to victory is letting God's Word dwell in you richly.

What Does "Dwell" Mean?

Colossians 3:16 (KJV) says, "Let the word of Christ *dwell* in you richly...." The word *dwell* in the original Greek means "to dwell or live in a house." It's the same word used to describe someone who takes up *permanent residency*. This term depicts a person that feels so content and at home that he has chosen to live there the rest of his life.[2]

Have you ever stayed someplace where you felt very welcome? In fact, you felt so welcome and loved that you didn't want to leave? You were cared for attentively and valued highly. Whatever you needed—food, clothing, time to rest—it was provided without hesitation. You were not viewed as a bother but a *blessing*. This is exactly how we are to treat the Word of God.

Seasoned author Francis Frangipane says, "Purity of heart can be reached and maintained if we *abide in fellowship with God's Word.* ...It sets us free from the strongholds of hidden sin. It wounds but it also heals, penetrating deeply into the very core of our being. The Word of the Lord, united with the Holy Spirit, is the vehicle of our transformation into the image of Christ. Holiness comes to him whose treasure is the Word."[3]

Friend, treasure the Word and welcome it with open arms. Remember, Jesus Christ is the Word.[4] So make Him feel comfortable and at home in you. Don't treat Him, the Word, as a stranger you could care less about. Treat the Word as an honored, royal guest that you want to live in you *permanently.*

God's Word Is Your Sword

You may have heard or read about the armor of God—specifically, the *belt of truth* and the *sword of the Spirit* (see Ephesians 6:14, 17). While both of these refer to God's Word, there is a difference between them. The word *truth* in the phrase *belt of truth* is the Greek word *logos.* It refers to "the entire, written Word of God." On the other hand, the term *word* in the phrase "word of God" is the Greek word *rhema.* It is used to describe the *sword of the Spirit,* A *rhema* word, according to Greek scholar Rick Renner, is a clearly spoken, specific word from the Scriptures for a specific situation you're facing; it is placed into your heart and "hands" by the Holy Spirit to defeat the enemy.[5]

As a believer, there's nothing more powerful than God's Word in the hands of His Spirit living in you. In order to have His *rhema* Word, you must first have His *logos* Word. It is from the belt of truth (*logos*) that the sword (*rhema*) of the Spirit is drawn. As you hide God's Word in your heart, you give the Spirit ammunition to identify and destroy the enemy's lies. When Satan brings temptation, the Spirit will bring to your memory specific scriptures you need in that moment to speak and defeat Satan (see John 14:26). These are *rhema* words—the sword of the Spirit.

For example, when I'm at my desk and the enemy injects a series of sexually explicit thoughts into my mind, God's Spirit immediately takes action. He whispers, *These thoughts are not right, pure, or honorable; cast them down and take them captive. Don't let the sin of sexual immorality have dominion in your life again.*[6] Likewise, when it's late at night and all the kids are in bed, my wife is away, and I'm tempted to take a look at porn on my iPad, God's Spirit speaks to my spirit and says, *You're exhausted, Vincent. Don't give the enemy an inch. Avoid the scenes of temptation. Turn the iPad off and go to sleep.*[7] These are God's *rhema* words to me. When I speak and obey them, the enemy (and my flesh) is defeated.

Oh, how I thank God for the power of His Word and the kindness of His Spirit to bring it to mind. *Rhema* words become a deadly spiritual dagger for you to stab the enemy with when he attacks. Jesus gives us an example of this, which we'll discuss in the next chapter.

The Pen Adds Might to the Sword

Remember the old saying, "The pen is mightier than the sword"? Well, when it comes to allowing the Word to dwell in you richly, I believe *the pen **adds** might to the sword.* Again, the sword is God's Word, and one of the best ways I have found to harness its power is by writing down what it says.

Years ago I began keeping a handwritten binder of scriptures on key topics to meditate on and memorize. As I read and studied the Word and listened to teachings, certain verses would come alive. It was as if God was speaking directly to me in the situations I was facing. When these *rhema* words were illuminated by God's Spirit, I jotted them down to commit them to memory.

I wrote lists of scriptures on sleep, peace, healing, overcoming fear, developing faith, and defeating the temptation of porn. Something powerful takes place when we gaze intently at a verse and write it down. It's like the Word gets branded on our hearts and minds with a hot iron. Writing the Truth seals it deeper in our souls than reading alone. I know some who prefer to type *rhema* scriptures God gives them, and that's fine. The method matters not; it's the practice that's important. Find what works best for you and do it.

Once I had my lists of scriptures, I periodically read them out loud to commit them to memory. During one of the first readings, I read them aloud three times while recording them on a cassette tape. Yes, the days of cassettes are outdated, but the impact of hearing God's Word spoken in your voice is powerful. I encourage you to try recording Scriptures and then listening to them periodically. You'll be amazed at the effect it has on your life.

Do What You Need to Do to Get the Word in You!

Letting God's Word dwell in you richly is an inseparable part of being in relationship with Jesus. He said, "…The measure [of thought and study] you give [to the truth you hear] will be the measure [of virtue and knowledge] that comes back to you—and more [besides] will be given to you who hear" (Mark 4:24 AMP). In other words, as you let God's Word dwell in you richly, you can expect to receive a payback for your time and effort—you can expect the Spirit to recall the right scripture at the right time to defeat the enemy and your flesh.

Now, when I first started diligently reading and studying the Word, I was intimidated by people who could quickly quote Scripture, chapter and verse. At the same time, I admired them and sincerely wanted to have the same ability. I just couldn't seem to do it. Then one day when I was praying, the Holy Spirit revealed something to me. I thought, *If the enemy can cause me to remember lustful lyrics I wish I could forget and impure images I wish I could purge from my mind, certainly God can give me total recall of each scripture I chew on, chapter and verse.* So that is what I began to pray for.

I didn't ask this to be a show-off. I asked this so I could be ready to defeat the enemy and my flesh and give answers to others in need. This prayer is in accordance with God's will, and He says, "...If we ask anything according to His will, He hears us. And if we know that He hears us, whatever we ask, we know that we have the petitions that we have asked of Him" (1 John 5:14-15 NKJV). As I have stayed in His Word, God has been faithful to answer this prayer, and He'll do the same for you!

"How can a young man keep his way pure? By living according to your word" (Psalm 119:9 NIV). It's hiding God's Word in your heart that keeps you from sinning against Him.[8] It's saturating yourself in God's Word that purifies your mind, will, and emotions and washes away the residue of pornographic images and stimuli.[9] It's God's Word that packs the power to save your soul, escape the prison of porn, and live an extraordinary life for His glory![10] Friend, *let His Word dwell in you richly!*

Encouragement from the Heart of a Woman

In addition to taking control of your thoughts, you must fill your mind and heart with the truth of God's Word. This is one of the best things Vincent did. He asked God to fill his heart and mind with the Word, and as a result, he has been able to wisely and effectively fight Satan and starve his flesh.

There are many scriptures the Lord has used to radically change my thinking. As I said earlier, years ago I naturally gravitated toward the use of harsh, angry words to try and change both Vincent and my children. Somehow I had the erroneous idea that if I just got angry enough and verbalized it, they would change. Then I began to hear the wisdom of James 1:19-20 (AMP):

> "Understand [this], my beloved brethren. Let every man be quick to hear [a ready listener], slow to speak, slow to take offense and to get angry. For man's anger does not promote the righteousness God [wishes and requires]."

I put this passage on my refrigerator and dwelled on it daily. Seeing it and meditating on it again and again allowed God's truth to penetrate my mind and heart. Little by little, the Holy Spirit worked the Word into my thinking and changed me. He helped me understand that my anger would not bring about right behavior. Only God's love and patience flowing through me would. This revelation has radically changed my relationships.

Man of God, spend **time** in His Word. This is your part. The enemy wants you to believe that you don't have time. "I'm too busy" is a phrase he tries to feed you regularly, and it's a lie. You do have time. Think about it. If you found time to search for porn, look at porn, fantasize, and masturbate, then you can find time to feed your spirit God's Word. The truth is, you and I make time for what we really want to do. Time is not the issue. Lack of desire is likely the reason.

The reality is, your desire to view porn right now is probably stronger than your desire to spend time in God's Word, and this is to be expected. Go to God and acknowledge where you are. Yes, He already knows, but your humble admission is the key to moving beyond where you are to where He and you want to be. Repent of your disinterest in His Word and ask Him to forgive you and grant you a desire for Him. As you starve your flesh and feed your spirit, you will create a hunger and thirst for His Word like never before.

Remember, you are an heir of God's grace![11] Don't listen to the enemy's lies. The Word of God **can** dwell in you richly—yes you! God does not prefer one person over another.[12] He doesn't pick and choose who gets His grace and who doesn't. Grace is available to anyone who humbles himself and asks for it.[13] In other words, what He has done for Vincent, me, and others, He will do for you. Ask Him to fill your mind and heart with His Word and give you a specific, practical plan to get the Word in you. Victory is yours! Walk it out by the power of His grace.

Walk It:

A major key to victory is letting God's Word dwell in you richly. Nothing on earth can surpass its life-giving brilliance and brawn. His Word contains His thoughts, and the wisdom and power it packs is priceless! Letting the Word dwell in you richly means welcoming it as an honored, permanent guest in your life. Hiding the Word in your heart gives the Holy Spirit ammunition to identify and destroy the enemy's lies. So do what you need to do to get the Word in you!

Study It:

John 1:1-2, 14; Ephesians 6:14, 17; Colossians 3:16; Psalm 119 (especially 9-16); Proverbs 4:20-22; 6:20-24; Mark 4:24. Also, see the scriptures in question 3.

Pray It:

"Father, forgive me for not wanting to read and study Your Word. Right now, I don't have a desire to let it dwell in me richly, but I want to have it. Please change me! As I cooperate with You, Holy Spirit, and starve my flesh, create in me a craving for God's Word and presence. Give me a practical plan to feed my spirit the Scripture. As I read and hear it, reveal to me rhema words with which I can defeat the devil. If the enemy can remind me of lustful lyrics and impure images I want to forget, then You can give me total recall of Scripture. This is what I ask for. I know it's Your will, so I trust You to answer me. Thank You, Lord! In Jesus' name, Amen!"

Apply It:

1 Are you letting God's Word dwell in you richly? If so, how? If not, why—
what's stopping you?

_____

_____

_____

_____

2 In what practical ways can you plant more of the Word in your heart? Pray
and ask the Holy Spiriit for ideas.

_____

_____

_____

_____

*Feed your spirit by: listening to the Bible on CD, MP3, or a phone app; reading the Bible while on
a treadmill or stationary bike; recording key rhema words on your phone or IPod and listening to
them in the morning, in the car, or before going to sleep; listening to CD teachings or podcasts.*

3 What's so special about God's Word? Carefully read the verses below and
write what the Holy Spirit reveals to you from each group of passages.

1 Kings 8:56; Psalm 119:89; Isaiah 40:8; Matthew 5:18; Luke 21:33; 1 Peter 1:25_____

_____

_____

2 Timothy 3:16-17; 2 Peter 1:19-21_____

_____

_____

Psalm 119:9; John 15:3; 17:17; Ephesians 5:26; 1 Peter 1:22 _____

_____

_____

Jeremiah 23:29; Romans 1:16; Hebrews 4:12; James 1:21_____

_____

_____

4 What is your greatest takeaway from this chapter? What scriptures, principles,
or ideas exploded in your heart? How are you challenged? What action(s) is
the Holy Spirit prompting you to take?

_____

_____

_____

_____

ONE BROTHER TO ANOTHER

"The Bible says clearly that whosoever controls the tongue, controls the whole body. What you speak, you are going to get. ...Before you can be changed, you must change your language. ...Read the Bible from Genesis to Revelation. Acquire the Bible's language, speak the word of faith, and feed your nervous system with a vocabulary of constructive, progressive, productive and victorious words. Speak those words; keep repeating them, so that they will have control of your whole body. Then you will become victorious...."

—Dr. Paul Yonggi Cho[1]
The Fourth Dimension

Step 19

SAY WHAT YOU WANT TO SEE

...He who has My word, let him speak My word faithfully....

Jeremiah 23:28 AMP

Letting God's Word dwell in you richly is a giant step toward intimacy with Jesus and the freedom He paid for. The next step is just as important—it's speaking the Word. For years when I experienced an attack of sexual temptation, I would only *think* about scriptures. It did help, but something was missing. I was stopping just short of the manifestation of God's power, which left me frustrated and defeated.

Maybe this is where you are. If so, it's time to speak up! God says, "He who has My word, let him *speak My word* faithfully!" (Jeremiah 23:28 AMP) To experience the full flow of God's power, you must **speak His Word** faithfully, calling the things that do not exist as though they do. I call it the *say what you want to see* principle—a principle Jesus Himself lived by.

Jesus Spoke the Word

Satan knows the perfect temptation to bring and the best time to bring it. After Jesus had been fasting for 40 days, He was hungry. Scripture records that Satan came against Him with three final temptations. God gives us a snapshot of what happened in the fourth chapters of Matthew and Luke. When Satan attacked Jesus, Jesus *spoke the Word* against him and defeated him.

Satan said, "If you are the Son of God, tell this stone to become a loaf of bread" (Luke 4:3 NLT). *Jesus spoke the Word* found in Deuteronomy 8:3 and deflected the enemy's fiery dart. Satan then showed Jesus images of world powers and said, "I will give you the glory of these kingdoms and authority over them...because they are mine to give to anyone I please. I will give it all to you if you will worship me" (vv. 6-7 NLT). Again, *Jesus spoke the Word*, this time quoting Deuteronomy 6:13. A third time, Satan came against Jesus—taking

Him to the highest point of the temple. He said, "If you are the Son of God, jump off!" (v. 9 NLT) He then quoted Scripture and tried to trip Jesus up. What did Jesus do? Again, He *spoke the Word*, declaring the decree of Deuteronomy 6:16. He effectively defeated the enemy and won out over temptation.

My point is, Satan is going to come against you—especially when you are most vulnerable. This would include times when you're **H**ungry, **A**ngry, **L**onely, **T**ired, and **S**ick (or **S**tressed). Take the first letter of each of these words and you get the acronym HALTS, which is exactly what Satan seeks to do. He wants to put a HALT to your relationship with God and prevent you from influencing others. It's in these moments that you must submit yourself to God, resist the devil, and he will flee. You must open your mouth, declare your allegiance to the Lord, and speak the Word just as Jesus did. This releases God's power and puts a stop to the enemy.

Speaking God's Word Releases Power

Right after God instructs us to speak His Word faithfully, He tells us why. "Is not My word like *fire* [that consumes all that cannot endure the test]? says the Lord, and like a *hammer* that breaks in pieces the rock [of most stubborn resistance]?" (Jeremiah 23:29 AMP) Wow! Grab ahold of this truth. Speaking God's Word turns your mouth into a *flamethrower* and a *sledgehammer* in the invisible realm of the spirit.

As a flamethrower, God's Word fires forth from your mouth and incinerates everything that is contrary to the standard of Scripture. As a sledgehammer, God's Word pounds into pieces the rocks of most stubborn resistance in your life—it works to demolish *strongholds* of wrong thinking and behavior that don't line up with truth. Pause and picture this powerful imagery. God's Word spoken out of your mouth is a *flamethrower* and a *sledgehammer* against every tantalizing temptation the enemy and your flesh bring.

Let's say you're alone in the bathroom, your phone poised in your pocket. The enemy whispers, *Nobody's around. Go ahead...check out the hot new babes online. They're amazing!* With these thoughts, Satan interjects mental images of nude women from things you've seen in the past. He knows that if you accept his imaginations, your flesh will cooperate with him, creating the emotional and chemical charges that accompany sexual arousal. In an instant, thoughts, feelings, and images are bombarding your brain with the rapid fire of an Uzi. What do you do? Submit yourself to God and **speak the Word!**

Ignoring the temptation won't work—trust me, I've tried. And willpower alone won't stop him. You must submit yourself to God, resist the devil at his onset, and speak the Word. Since you're allowing the Word to dwell in you richly, God's Spirit living in your spirit will immediately pull up scriptures on the screen of your heart and mind.[2] But don't just think them—*speak them!* Say, "I will not commit adultery in my heart. I will not take the foul fire of porn in my lap and be burned. I will avoid the scenes of temptation. No weapon of sexual temptation formed against me will prosper. I resist you, Satan, and I command you to be gone from my presence in the name of Jesus!"[3]

Friend, God wants you to speak His Word diligently, especially in three specific ways: against the enemy, over your life, and over your situations. God's Word "...is alive and full of power [making it active, operative, energizing, and effective]; it is sharper than any two-edged sword..." (Hebrews 4:12 AMP). The Message paraphrase of this verse says, "His powerful Word is sharp as a surgeon's scalpel, cutting through everything, whether doubt or defense, laying us open to listen and obey. Nothing and no one is impervious to God's Word...." When you speak the Word, energy and life are released. The enemy's lies are incinerated and your flesh's stubborn cravings are crushed beneath God's sledgehammer of truth.

Say What You Want to See!

Now, you may be thinking, *Man that's a lot of work. I don't know if I can do all that or if I want to do it; it seems foolish.* Yes, it is work and you may feel silly doing it at first. But it works! And it's what we're commanded to do. In order to see freedom in your life, you have to *say* what God's Word says **first**. Get it? *Say what you want to see.* This is the faith principle of Romans 4:17 (NKJV): God "...gives life to the dead and calls those things which do not exist as though they did."

Slow down and let that really sink in. God **calls the things that do not exist as though they do exist**. He says what He wants to see! Genesis 1 paints a powerful picture of this principle. Eight times God *said* what He wanted to *see*, and it was so. He called forth plants and planets, birds and beasts, fish and the firmament. What did not exist was spoken into existence, and we are to imitate His creative nature. Ephesians 5:1 (NLT) instructs us to "imitate God, therefore, in everything you do, because you are his dear children."

When I first started standing against the temptations of porn and lust, I *saw* myself as a weakling and the temptation as all-powerful.

"Man, I'm just so weak against this," I'd say. "It's just too strong for me. I can't beat it." I was saying what I *didn't* want to see, and that's one of the reasons I kept being defeated. I was reinforcing the wrong behavior with my words. But as my relationship with Jesus deepened, His Spirit began to prompt me to say what I wanted to see manifested in my life, based on the promises of His Word. I began to call forth, or speak of, the godly behavior that did not exist as though it did.

Little by little, I began to confess scriptures *out loud* over my life, over my situations, and against the enemy. I began to say things like, "I am the righteousness of God in Christ—a new creation altogether. I am more than a conqueror through Christ, and this sin of porn will not have dominion over me. For *I* have been crucified with Christ, and *I*—my selfish, self-centered, sin-loving flesh—no longer lives, but Christ lives in me. My old evil desires were nailed to the cross with Christ; that part of me that loved to sin was crushed and fatally wounded, and sin's power over me is broken! I will not give place to you, Satan. I resist you, in Jesus' name, and command and demand you to be gone now!"[4]

Again and again, I proclaimed God's promises. Did I feel foolish? Yes, at times. Did I see immediate results? Not always. It was a process. But eventually my conduct caught up with my confession. The stubborn rocks of resistant behavior were broken, and I began to *see* what I was *saying*. The same will happen for you. Try it. Take the verses found in these chapters and begin to speak them out loud over your life, over your situations, and against the enemy. Do it for 30 days and watch what happens. You have nothing to lose…only freedom to gain!

Encouragement from the Heart of a Woman

*True, positive change never happens by accident. It always happens on purpose. On purpose, I had to speak out loud that God loved me and accepted me as He says in His Word. On purpose, I had to say that I am the righteousness of God as He declares in Scripture. Through persistence and the power of His Spirit backing up His Word, the love of God and a true sense of being righteous have become strong realities in my life today. Regardless of what your behavior presently appears to be, **on purpose** you must begin to call it what God says it can be.*

Have you ever watched a "whodunit" mystery? Many times all the evidence seems to point to one particular person. Then just before it ends, the truth surfaces that proves the prime suspect is innocent and someone else is the culprit. This is kind of what happens in our walk with God. The evidence of your behavior may be pointing in a particular direction—that you're imprisoned by porn and always will be. But that is not true!

God says otherwise! He is the all-knowing Eternal One who sees your end from your beginning. He is in your future and already knows how it turns out. Yes, you presently have behaviors and mind-sets that have to catch up with the truth, but that doesn't change the truth. Regardless of your behavior, He calls you victorious! He says that in Christ you are righteous—in Christ you are more than a conqueror. He not only sees you free from the prison of porn, but also helping others find their way to freedom.

Man of God, agree with Him. **Say what you want to see.** Anything that God says about you in His Word is true—even if you don't see it right now. "God is not a man, so he does not lie. He is not human, so he does not change his mind. Has he ever spoken and failed to act? Has he ever promised and not carried it through?" (Numbers 23:19 NLT) God loves you! He believes the best about you, even when you can't see anything but your sin. Begin to open your mouth and call the things that do not exist as though they do. You'll be amazed by what happens!

Walk It:

Along with letting God's Word dwell in you richly, He wants you to speak it faithfully. He says to call the things that do not exist as though they already do—to say what you want to see. Speaking His Word turns your mouth into a flamethrower and a sledgehammer in the realm of the spirit. When you speak the Word over your life, over your situations, and against the enemy, energy and life are released. Satan's lies are incinerated and your flesh's cravings are crushed. Try it. You have nothing to lose... only freedom to gain!

Study It:

Jeremiah 23:28-29; Matthew 4:1-11; Luke 4:1-13; Romans 4:17; Ephesians 5:1; Hebrews 4:12. Also check out the confession scriptures listed in the two endnotes.

Apply It:

1 When the temptation to look and lust comes knocking at your door, how have you responded in the past? What is the Holy Spirit showing you in this lesson that you need to do differently?.

_____

_____

_____

_____

2 Carefully read the account of Jesus' battle against Satan in Luke 4:1-13 (Matthew 4:1-11). What is the Lord showing you about the enemy and your fight? How can you apply this wisdom in your life?

_____

_____

_____

3 God says speaking His Word is like a hammer that breaks in pieces rocks of stubborn resistance. Are you dealing with any stubborn, ungodly thinking, speech, or behavior? If so, what is it? What scriptures can you find to speak over your life and against the enemy to see this broken?

_____

_____

_____

To help you find scriptures, do a "Keyword Search" for related verses at www.biblegateway.org.

4 Something very powerful is happening inside you when you open your mouth and _say what you want to see_ in your life. Carefully read Psalm 45:1 and Proverbs 7:1-3. What is the Lord showing you about your _tongue_ and your _heart_? What do they represent? How does this motivate you?

_____

_____

_____

Related scriptures: Proverbs 3:3; Jeremiah 17:1; 2 Corinthians 3:3.

5 What is your greatest takeaway from this chapter? What scriptures, principles, or ideas exploded in your heart? How are you challenged? What action(s) is the Holy Spirit prompting you to take?

_____

_____

_____

Things I Want to Remember:

Pray It:

"Father, please forgive me for allowing laziness and feeling foolish to muzzle my mouth. I want to experience the full flow of Your power and freedom from sexual sin. Holy Spirit, I ask You to recall to my mind the scriptures I need to speak over my life, over my situations, and against the enemy. When the time comes, help me not to just think about them but to open my mouth and speak them. Empower me to call the things that do not exist as though they do. Make my mouth a flamethrower and a sledgehammer against the enemy and my flesh. In Jesus' name, Amen!"

ONE BROTHER TO ANOTHER

"...Our supernatural set of weaponry comes directly from God. ...Because this weaponry has its origin in God, it is vital for us to remain in unbroken fellowship with Him in order for us to continually enjoy the benefits of our spiritual armor. If we break fellowship with the Lord, we step away from our all-important Power Source. ...Your unbroken, ongoing fellowship with God is your absolute guarantee that you are constantly and habitually dressed in the whole armor of God."

—Rick Renner[1]

Dressed to Kill

Step 20

WEAR YOUR ARMOR

Put on all of God's armor so that you will be able to stand firm against all strategies of the devil.

Ephesians 6:11 NLT

By now you know you are in a war. It's not just against your flesh. It's also against an invisible, but very real enemy—Satan and his demonic forces. The war is spiritual, and it has eternal ramifications.[2] God in His infinite wisdom and love has provided you with powerful spiritual weapons with which to win. And as a soldier in God's army, you are commanded *to wear your armor.*

The apostle Paul became well acquainted with the armor of a Roman soldier during his imprisonment in Rome. Through him, God says, "Stand your ground, putting on the belt of truth and the body armor {breastplate} of God's righteousness. For shoes, put on the peace that comes from the Good News so that you will be fully prepared. In addition to all of these, hold up the shield of faith to stop the fiery arrows of the devil. Put on salvation as your helmet, and take the sword of the Spirit, which is the word of God. Pray in the Spirit at all times and on every occasion..." (Ephesians 6:14-18 NLT).

Something important to note: Your spiritual armor is called the "armor of God" (see Ephesians 6:11). What's the significance? In his incredible book *Dressed to Kill*, Greek scholar Rick Renner explains:

> "...Notice the phrase 'of God.' This little phrase is taken from the Greek phrase *tou theo*.... Simply put, this means our supernatural set of weaponry comes directly *from God*. God Himself is the Source of origin for this armor. ...Because this weaponry has its origin in God, it is vital for us to remain in unbroken fellowship with Him in order for us to continually enjoy the benefits of our spiritual armor. If we break fellowship with the Lord, we step away from our all-important Power Source."[3]

Again, we see it is all about relationship. Fellowshipping with the Lord clothes you in your spiritual armor. Let's briefly take a look at each piece and learn its significance and relevance in your fight for freedom.

Buckle Your Belt of Truth

The first piece of armor mentioned is the *belt of truth*, and rightly so. It's the foundation and most important piece of all. As we have learned, the belt of truth is the *logos*, or written Word of God. All other pieces of armor—the breastplate, the shoes, the helmet, the sword, and the lance (prayer)—are *inseparably connected* to it. Without a commitment to spend time in the Word, you have no ability to understand, receive, or use God's righteousness, peace, salvation, or *rhema* words from His Spirit.

Interestingly, what you may not know is that the Roman soldier's belt had a metal extension that hung down to cover and protect a man's reproductive organs. Are you seeing the spiritual connection? This fact alone should speak volumes to you on the value of God's Word. It supernaturally protects your sexual purity and gives you the ability to reproduce every Christlike quality in your life. As you are intimately connected in relationship with God's Spirit, you have the power to walk in freedom from porn and produce the Spirit's fruit. The belt of truth—your Bible—is the only visible piece of armor. As you read, study, meditate on, and memorize Scripture, you will have all the other pieces of weaponry.

Strap on Your Breastplate of Righteousness

The next important piece of armor is the *breastplate of righteousness*. The Roman breastplate was made of overlapping strips of sturdy metal that started at the shoulders and went down the front and back of the soldier, in some cases to his knees. These strips, resembling the scales of a fish, were held together by metal rings and provided excellent protection and ease of mobility.

The breastplate guarded a man's vital organs, including his heart. In addition to being a defensive piece of weaponry, it was also an *offensive* piece. The more a soldier wore his breastplate, the shinier it became. Metal rubbing against metal created a high luster. Like the blinding light of the sun reflecting off a metal building, soldiers who regularly wore their breastplates gave off a blinding reflection of the sunlight in their enemy's eyes.

What does all this mean? Wearing your breastplate means walking in an awareness of your righteousness in Christ and relying on Him (see 2 Corinthians 5:21). This awareness and reliance protects your vital organs, especially your heart, or emotions. It guards you from things like feelings of false pleasure as well as condemnation, guilt, and shame. The more aware you are of your righteousness in Christ, the brighter His Sonlight will shine in your life, and the greater the blinding effect it will have on the enemy.

Tie Tightly Your Shoes of Peace

The soldier's shoes were deadly. They were made of steel and consisted of two parts: the shoe itself and the greaves. A greave was a solid piece of metal that ran from the ankle to the top of the knee and wrapped around the calf. Greaves allowed the soldier to go through thorny, rough terrain unharmed. They also protected his shins. A favorite tactic of the enemy was to repeatedly kick his opponent until his leg broke and then decapitate him once he fell to the ground. Wearing greaves prevented this.

The shoe itself was also made of steel and had one- to three-inch nails protruding from the front, back, and bottom. Standing in these shoes, a soldier was not easily moved. His feet were firmly planted. And if an enemy got in his way, he was ordered to stomp them to death and keep on walking. God symbolically identifies these killer shoes as *peace*.

When you're walking in the peace of God, you can go through the toughest temptations untouched. Peace firmly plants you in Christ, enabling you to stand immovable against the enemy and not be bruised or broken by his attacks. Yes, he will try to push you back into the prison of porn. And if that doesn't work, he will try to get you to give up your peace through holding on to unforgiveness. But don't give in! Eliminate those little foxes! Pursue peace and let it guard your mind and emotions. "And God, our source of peace, will soon crush Satan under your feet..." (Romans 16:20 GNT).

Lift Up Your Shield of Faith

The Greek word for *shield* in Ephesians 6:16 is *thureos*, a term used to describe "a wide, tall door."[4] That's what the Roman soldier's battle shield looked like—a door that covered him from head to foot. In most cases, the shield was made of several layers of animal hides woven together and mounted on wood. It was extremely strong and durable. To care for his shield, a soldier would rub oil into the leather every morning. This kept it soft, pliable, and slippery, preventing enemy arrows from penetrating. Then, just before battle, he would soak his shield in water. This saturation quickly extinguished the enemy's flaming arrows. A soldier who neglected his shield was a soldier courting death.

Faith is your shield! In order to keep your faith vibrant and healthy, you need the "oil" of the Holy Spirit. The oil represents His anointing that comes as you sit in His presence. He keeps your faith soft, tender, and pliable. Without the anointing of the Spirit, your faith will become dry, inflexible, and fall apart during times of temptation. Soaking one's shield in water represents you soaking in the "water of the Word" (see Ephesians 5:26). As you read, study, meditate on, and memorize the Word, your faith is saturated with strength, enabling you to extinguish the fire of impure desire from the enemy.

Like all the other armor, your faith is inseparably linked to your relationship with the Word of God. When not in use, the Roman soldier's shield rested on a small clip attached to the belt. This signifies that *your faith rests in the Word of God*! In order for your faith to abound, God's Word must abound—it must dwell in you richly. Remember, faith comes by hearing, and hearing by the Word of God (see Romans 10:17). Without the Word, there is no faith.

My brother, nurture your faith! Seek the anointed presence of the Holy Spirit regularly. Saturate yourself in the Word. If you have become discouraged and have stopped believing that God is at work in you, pick up your shield and begin walking forward in faith again! When your faith is strong, God's power is activated and you are shielded from the enemy's attacks.

Put on the Helmet of Salvation

The soldier's helmet was extremely strong, heavy, and impenetrable. It was made of metal and had two wide strips extending down its sides to protect the soldier's cheeks, ears, and jaws. It not only tightly encased his head, but also covered him to the base of the neck, protecting him from being decapitated by his enemy's battle-axe.

Wearing your helmet of salvation means having an iron-clad understanding of what your salvation through Christ provides. Without your helmet, you place yourself in position to be decapitated by deception. With your helmet, you "...have the mind of Christ (the Messiah) and do hold the thoughts (feelings and purposes) of His heart" (1 Corinthians 2:16 AMP).

How do you wear your helmet? Learn all there is to know about your salvation in Christ. Let the Word of God dwell in you richly! Ingrain on your brain all that Jesus died to give you, especially His freedom from sexual temptation. Take the scriptures provided in each chapter and commit them to memory—especially those that the Holy Spirit makes alive to you. He will renew your mind and fortify your faith as you spend time in His presence and in the Scriptures.

Wield the Sword of the Spirit

Your most aggressive piece of weaponry is the sword of the Spirit. The Greek word used for *sword* here is *machaira*. It was nineteen inches of razor-sharp, double-edged terror. After a Roman soldier stabbed his opponent, he would twist his sword while it was still in the gut and then remove it, often spilling his enemy's entrails. This sword was deadly and highly feared.[5]

Symbolically, this is the kind of sword God has given you and He wants you to use it against the enemy. As we learned, the sword of the Spirit is a *rhema* word—it is something specific and powerful that the Holy Spirit speaks to your heart. Many times this is a specific scripture He makes come alive. Remember, the Spirit is your Teacher who recalls to your mind the things God has said in His Word and spoken to you directly (see John 14:26). When the need arises, He reaches into the reservoir of scriptures you've stored in your heart and pulls out the right one at the right time.

When not in use, the Roman sword slipped into a sheath on the left side of the soldier's belt. Again, this signifies the sword of the Spirit's dependence upon the belt of truth. God's devil-defeating rhema Word (the sword) comes from the logos (written) Word.

Interestingly, the sword—God's Word—is described in Scripture as *double-edged*, which is the Greek word meaning "two-mouthed." God spoke the Word first when it was recorded in Scripture. He is the first mouth, or edge, of the sword. When you and I speak His Word, we become the second mouth and edge.[6] The full power of God's Word is not released in your life until it is spoken from your lips. So learn to speak the rhema Word and lethally stab the enemy with the sword of the Spirit!

Hurl Through the Air Your Lance of Prayer

The final piece of your spiritual armor is represented by the Roman soldier's *lance*. While the word lance is not specifically mentioned in

Ephesians 6, its spiritual counterpart is, and that is *prayer*. Lances came in numerous sizes and acted much like a javelin or spear. They were primarily used to battle the enemy from long distances. A soldier who knew how to effectively use his lance could deal a death blow to the enemy from far away.[7]

Just as there were numerous kinds of lances, you have numerous kinds of prayer with which to battle your enemy. Each serves a specific purpose. When you know how to pray and make prayer your first response, you can sabotage many of Satan's schemes *before* he has a chance to set them in motion!

How Do You Wear Your Armor?

As I said at the opening, *fellowshipping with the Lord clothes you in your spiritual armor.* As Pastor Renner powerfully puts it, "Your unbroken, ongoing fellowship with God is your absolute guarantee that you are constantly and habitually dressed in the whole armor of God."[8] So stay in relationship with Jesus. He will teach you how to wield your sword, walk in peace, and utilize every piece of weaponry to its fullest. You'll be dressed, blessed, and ready for battle!

Encouragement from the Heart of a Woman

Man of God, all your spiritual armor is priceless and powerful! The piece I'd like to focus on, though, is the breastplate. It is vital for you to grasp that you truly ARE the righteousness of God IN Christ. In this journey of life, we sometimes fall and/or relapse into old, unhealthy habits. If this happens to you, know that God does not put you in a spiritual "time-out" chair. There is no need for penance, because you can't work your way back into right relationship with God or pay for your mistakes. Repentance—turning away from wrong behavior and turning toward God who has the power to change you—is the answer.

*One of the things I remember as Vincent and I were in the thick of walking out our freedom and healing is the time when he perpetually felt condemned. Vincent is a man who wholeheartedly **loves** God—it's what attracted me to him 25 years ago. And because of his strong love for God, he never wanted to disappoint Him. Satan took advantage of the tenderness of his heart and tried to use it against him. Every time Vincent stumbled or fell, the enemy would condemn him, and Vincent would identify with guilt and condemnation rather than the freedom that Jesus died to give him.*

I noticed that as long as Vincent identified himself as guilty and condemned, his behavior followed suit. Therefore, I began to encourage him to take a leap of faith and trust that he was indeed free because of what Jesus did for him—that he was (and is) righteous because of Jesus. As this truth penetrated his thinking, I began to see true freedom take root and grow.

You see, Man of God, Jesus is the reason we are righteous. Don't overlook this elementary fact. We never outgrow elementary truths. Two plus two is always four, even when we're doing higher levels of math. In other words, you have to believe—really believe—that you are righteous, and your righteousness does not depend upon your behavior but upon Jesus. What He did through His death and resurrection changed you and me forever. It changed our eternal home and the way we can live on this earth.

I encourage you to take a leap of faith and put all of your hope and trust in what Jesus did for you. His Word says that He'll never leave you or forsake you. The word never means just that—never. There is nothing you can do to separate you from God or negate what Jesus did. The enemy is a liar. Your identity is not based on your feelings or behavior. It is in Christ. Abide in relationship with His Spirit, and wear your armor. I call you RIGHTEOUS!

Walk It:

You are in a war and God has provided you with powerful, spiritual weapons with which to defeat the enemy. The armor He has given you includes the belt of truth, the breastplate of righteousness, the shoes of peace, the helmet of salvation, the sword of the Spirit, and the lance of prayer. These supernatural weapons come directly from God and are activated as you abide in fellowship with Him. So stay in relationship with Jesus, and you'll be dressed in your armor, ready for battle!

Study It:

Ephesians 6:10-18 **Truth:** Psalm 119:30; 2 Timothy 3:15-17; Hebrews 4:12; James 1:21 **Righteousness:** Psalm 119:40; Romans 1:17; 3:21-22, 28; 1 Corinthians 1:30; 2 Corinthians 5:21; Philippians 3:8-9; Isaiah 61:10 **Peace:** John 14:27; Romans 14:19; Philippians 4:6-7; Colossians 3:15; 1 Peter 3:11; Isaiah 26:3 **Faith:** Romans 10:17; 2 Corinthians 5:7

Apply It:

1   Of all the armor, the *belt of truth* is most important. In your own words, share how it's inseparably linked to all the other weaponry (your righteousness, peace, faith, salvation, rhema word, and prayer).

_____

_____

_____

_____

2   Have you *lost your peace*? Is your heart (emotions) guarded by God's *righteousness*? If any of your armor seems to be missing, pause and pray, "Holy Spirit, what has happened? Have I done something that has caused me to be disarmed? What do I need to do to put on my armor again?"

_____

_____

_____

_____

3   Every man entering the Roman army was actually *measured* for his shield to make sure it covered him completely. Meditate on Romans 12:3. What does this verse speak to you about your faith?

_____

_____

_____

4   How has the Holy Spirit equipped you with His *sword*—what *rhema* words has He given you that have really helped you to defeat the enemy's attacks of sexual temptation? Write them out.

_____

_____

_____

If you don't have any rhema words or would like some additional ones, pause and pray, "Holy Spirit, please reveal to me Your rhema words with which I can defeat the devil's sexual temptations. Lead me to them as I read and study Scripture. In Jesus' name, Amen."

5   What's your greatest takeaway from this chapter? What scriptures, principles, or ideas exploded in your heart? How are you challenged? What action(s) is the Holy Spirit prompting you to take?

_____

_____

_____

Things I Want to Remember:

Pray It:

"Father, thank You for this eye-opening lesson and the empowering gift of Your armor. Please help me to abide in relationship with You so that I can stay dressed and ready for battle. Teach me how to wear the belt of truth, which is Your Word, and put on the breastplate of righteousness. Show me how to stand and walk in peace and move forward with faith as my shield. Help me to guard my mind with the helmet of salvation by continually growing in my knowledge of all that Jesus died to give me. Holy Spirit, empower me with Your sword—Your rhema words— and teach me how to pray in any situation I face. In Jesus' name, Amen!"

ONE BROTHER TO ANOTHER

"You are an overcomer. You possess the seed of the One who endured the greatest opposition ever encountered. His strength is in you! His nature is yours. You were not made to quit, draw back, falter, or compromise. You've been blessed with the amazing grace of God. No matter how great the adversity against you, view it as a steppingstone to propel you to the next level of rulership!"

—John Bevere[1]

Relentless

NEVER GIVE UP!

Never give up. Eagerly follow the Holy Spirit and serve the Lord. Let your hope make you glad. Be patient in time of trouble and never stop praying.

Romans 12:11-12 CEV

Have you ever felt like giving up? I can hear many of you yelling, "Yes!" I have wanted to give up more times than I can count, and I have never wanted to give up more than during the writing of this book. Our marriage, children, finances, health, and countless other things have come under attack like never before. I cannot express in words how overwhelming the desire to quit has been. I say this for no other reason than to let you know you are not alone, as the enemy would want you to think.

"Every step you take toward God in obedience will always be countered by opposition from the enemy." That is what my friend Bob Martin told me years ago as I started my journey out of the prison of porn. The enemy does not want to lose ground, so he will step up his attack once he sees you are serious about being free. Overwhelming you from every angle is a common strategy he uses to try to get you to quit.

In an attempt to get your flesh to agree with him, Satan repeatedly speaks key phrases to your mind like...

"But...I want to look at it."

I've heard this too, but it's a lie. The real you and the real me does *not* want to look at porn. The real you is the new you—the new man created in Christ (see 2 Corinthians 5:17). "For we are God's masterpiece. He has created us anew in Christ Jesus, so we can do the *good things* he planned for us long ago" (Ephesians 2:10 NLT). This is the truth.

Realize the enemy's greatest disguise is *you*. That is, he feeds you thoughts in the first person, saying things like "*I am* depressed. *I am* afraid," and "*I want* to look at pornography." He whispers these "I am" statements because they can more easily fly under your spiritual radar, and they're easier for your flesh to agree with. But you can learn to recognize and reject these lies.

Again, you need to *say what you want to see*. Do you want to see victory? Than speak it. Say, "No, I don't want to look at pornography and I will not look at it. The new, real me wants to be clean. The new, real me wants to eat what's on my plate. The new, real me wants to enjoy sex that's God-created and God-approved. You're a liar, Satan! In the name of Jesus and on the authority of His Word, take your filth and be gone!"

"But...I have fallen and sinned again!"

Yes, there may be times when you fall back into sin. I did. It's part of the process. I'm not condoning it or trying to speak failure into your life. I'm just giving you a reality check. You didn't get where you are overnight, and you probably won't get free that way either.

Change comes through choices. **The first and most important choice is to live daily in relationship with Jesus.** All other choices—choices to starve your flesh, feed your spirit, avoid the scenes of temptation, etc.—come out of the strength of Christ's Spirit living through you. Remember, victory will come, *but not in your own strength.*

"But Vincent, I've fallen into the same sin again. What am I supposed to do?" Admit it, confess it, and repent. Receive God's forgiveness and go on. He's faithful when we are faithless. He's faithful in spite of how we feel. He's faithful in spite of the enemy's accusations of condemnation. God is faithful—period.

As my uncle Frank has repeatedly told me, "It's a faith *walk*, not a faith pole vault." Victory is experienced one step at a time. When a baby is learning to walk, what does he often do? That's right, he falls. As you're learning to walk in the freedom Christ paid for, you too will fall at times. But just like that baby, you need to get up and keep trying until you get it. "For though a righteous man falls seven times, **he rises again**..." (Proverbs 24:16 NIV).

You will find your footing. Your spiritual legs will be strengthened. As the prophet Habakkuk said in the midst of his overwhelming circumstances, you can say:

"The Lord God is my Strength, my personal bravery, and my invincible army; He makes my feet like hinds' feet and will make me to walk [not to stand still in terror, but to walk] and make [spiritual] progress upon my high places [of trouble, suffering, or responsibility]!"

—Habakkuk 3:19 AMP

"But...It's too hard! I'll never be free."

That's just what the enemy wants you to believe and say, but it's *not* true. God says, "Obeying these commandments is not something beyond your strength and reach" (Deuteronomy 30:11 TLB). He has given you the capacity to hear and obey His Word.[2] You can break free and live free from the prison of pornography because you can do *everything* through Christ who empowers and infuses you with inner strength![3]

Remember, the greatest remedy against pornography is intimacy with Jesus Christ. It's all about relationship. As you abide in Him, you will be infused with inner strength. As you let His Word dwell in you richly and say what you want to see, you will outlast the enemy and not quit.

God says He "is able to keep you from falling away and will bring you with great joy into his glorious presence without a single fault" (Jude 1:24 NLT). "God's your Guardian, right at your side to protect you—shielding you from sunstroke, sheltering you from moonstroke. God guards you from every evil, he guards your very life. He guards you when you leave and when you return, he guards you now, he guards you always" (Psalm 121:5-8 The Message).

God says, "Since the day you were born, I have carried you along. I will still be the same when you are old and gray, and I will take care of you. I created you. I will carry you and always keep you safe. Can anyone compare with me? Is anyone my equal?" (Isaiah 46:3-5 CEV) "God the Father has his eye on each of you, and has determined by the work of the Spirit to keep you obedient through the sacrifice of Jesus. May everything good from God be yours!" (1 Peter 1:2 The Message)

Friend, draw upon God's keeping power and rest in it! Read these incredible promises again and again until they become a part of you. Don't run *from* Him—run *to* Him. Don't give in to the desire or feeling to quit. At one point in Jesus' ministry, many stopped following Him because things got tough. When they did, Jesus turned to the Twelve and asked if they would turn away too. I love Peter's answer: "Master, to whom would we go? You have the words of real life, eternal life"

(John 6:68 The Message). If you turn away and quit following Jesus, what would you go back to? By all means, "stay with God! Take heart. Don't quit. I'll say it again: Stay with God" (Psalm 27:14 The Message).

Encouragement from the Heart of a Woman

Without question, there were times I wanted to give up on our marriage during our journey. There were moments when I wondered if Vincent would ever be truly free. Disappointment, anger, and hurt feelings plagued both of us. And many times neither he nor I thought we could go on. However, I am so grateful we didn't give up! I am so thankful we didn't miss experiencing the many happy times we have shared since then and continue to share. God has blessed us more than I could have ever imagined. Honestly, the Vincent I am married to now is not the same Vincent I married 23 years ago. God has changed him so much that it is as if I am married to a different man!

Listen! Can you hear what the Spirit of God is saying? He's saying, "Don't quit! I will walk with you and not leave you. I love you, and you are totally Mine. You are going to make it!" Man of God, listen to Him, not the voices of defeat, condemnation, or fear. Jesus has already paid for your freedom. Come forth, Man of God! Come forth in power, freedom, and authority!

God has great plans for you and your wife. Trust Him. He does not show favoritism (see Romans 2:11). The freedom and healing that He has brought to Vincent and me He will not withhold from you. Push through. Victory is surely yours because of Jesus (see 2 Corinthians 2:14). See yourself for who you really are! You are the righteousness of God in Christ—the temple of God's Holy Spirit! The same Spirit that raised Christ from the dead lives in you! Surrender yourself to Him and stand firm daily.

I'd like to pray this prayer for you:

"Dear Father, thank You for this, Your son, and his heart to please You. I pray for total and complete freedom and restoration for him and his wife. Holy Spirit, please wrap Your loving arms of grace and strength around him, his wife, and their children. Thank You for leading them into victory and healing. Thank You for Your patience and loving kindness toward them. Thank You that the situation they are in has not caught You off guard, nor is it too big for You to turn around. Thank You for the wonderful future You have for them. I pray that You fill them with everlasting hope and strength to make it through every challenge. You are truly an amazing Father. I bless them with eyes that see, ears

that hear, and hearts that respond to Your will and Your ways. In Jesus' Precious, Holy, and Matchless name I pray, Amen!"

Again, thank you, for allowing me the privilege to speak to you through these pages. I'm expecting you to succeed in everything you do. Your freedom will bring freedom to others. I call you blessed, restored, free, and useful in the hands of Almighty God!

Walk It:

Every step you take toward God in obedience will always be countered by opposition from the enemy. He'll do anything he can to get you to quit your quest for sexual purity. But don't do it! If you fall into sin, run to God in prayer. Admit it, confess it, and repent. Receive His forgiveness and go on. Victory is experienced one step at a time. Remember, the greatest remedy against pornography is intimacy with Jesus. Choose to live daily in relationship with Him, and His Spirit will help you make all the other necessary choices to walk in true freedom.

Study It:

Don't Quit: Proverbs 24:16; Romans 12:11-12; 1 Corinthians 15:57-58; Galatians 5:1; 6:9; Philippians 3:13-16; 2 Timothy 3:14-17; Hebrews 10:19-25, 35-39; 12:1-3; James 1:12; 5:11; 1 Peter 4:1-3; Revelation 3:10-13 **The Lord is Your Strength:** Psalm 121; Isaiah 46:3-5; Habakkuk 3:19; Jude 1:24

Apply It:

1 Pause and pray: "Holy Spirit, what lies of the enemy am I believing and speaking that cause me to want to quit so easily? What truths from Scripture can I memorize and speak to reject them?"

_____

_____

_____

_____

_____

_____

2 Meditate on the verses in the last section of the chapter: Jude 1:24; Psalm 121:5-8; Isaiah 46:3-5; 1 Peter 1:2. What is God speaking to you? How do these verses encourage you to _never give up_?

_____

_____

_____

_____

_____

_____

3 What is your greatest takeaway from this chapter? What scriptures, principles, or ideas exploded in your heart? How are you challenged? What action(s) is the Holy Spirit prompting you to take?

_____

_____

_____

_____

_____

_____

Pray It:

"Father, sometimes I feel so overwhelmed by the struggle with this temptation and the things going on in my life that I do want to quit. But I know in my heart that's not the answer. Quitting will only give the enemy what he wants. Please forgive me for listening to and believing his lies. Let the promises of Your Word become a part of who I am, directing my mind, will, and emotions toward righteousness. Help me passionately pursue my relationship with You, and strengthen my spirit to persevere and never give up. I agree with Your Word: victory over all sin is mine in Jesus Christ! In His matchless Name, Amen!"

Things I Want to Remember:

DO YOU HAVE A RELATIONSHIP WITH JESUS?

The Bible says, "Everyone has sinned; we all fall short of God's glorious standard" (Romans 3:23 NLT). Everyone includes you and me. Thankfully, God didn't leave us without hope, lost in our sin. Out of His great love and desire to be in relationship with you and me, He made a way out through Jesus Christ, His Son!

While "we are utterly incapable of living the glorious lives God wills for us, God did it for us. Out of sheer generosity he put us in right standing with himself. A pure gift. He got us out of the mess we're in and restored us to where he always wanted us to be. And he did it by means of Jesus Christ. God sacrificed Jesus on the altar of the world to clear that world of sin. Having faith in him sets us in the clear" (Romans 3:23-25 The Message).

Why Did Jesus Have to Die?

Jesus died on the cross to pay the price for our sins. Isaiah 53:4-5 declares that "it was our pains he carried—our disfigurements, all the things wrong with us. We thought he brought it on himself, that God was punishing him for his own failures. But it was our sins that did that to him, that ripped and tore and crushed him—our sins! He took the punishment, and that made us whole. Through his bruises we get healed" (The Message).

God is holy—pure, spotless, and without sin. Nothing and no one stained with sin can enter His presence. Through Adam, the first man, sin entered the world (see Romans 5:12-19). The only way we can be restored to right relationship with God and enter His presence again is to have our sins removed. We cannot do this in our own strength, so God, Himself, came to earth in the form of man—as Jesus. He paid the wages for our sins, which is death (see Romans 6:23). He was gruesomely crucified and shed His life's blood to cover the cost of our sins. "For without the shedding of blood, there is no forgiveness" (Hebrews 9:22 NLT).

Jesus Wants to Be in Relationship with You!

Jesus says, "Look! I stand at the door and knock. If you hear my voice and open the door, I will come in, and we will share a meal together as friends" (Revelation 3:20 NLT). The emptiness in your life cannot be filled by porn, sex, alcohol, or drugs. More money, material possessions, and power are not going to cut it either. Only Jesus can heal your soul and make you whole. Today is a great day to invite

Him in! "...Behold, now is the accepted time; behold, now is the day of salvation" (2 Corinthians 6:2 NKJV). If you have never asked God to forgive you of your sins and invited Jesus to come and live in your heart, take a moment and do it now. Just say...

> "Father, I come to You just as I am. I've done many things wrong, and I'm a sinner. I ask You to forgive me of everything wrong I've ever done, and wash me clean. Jesus, I believe You are God's Son. Thank You for coming and dying in my place and paying for my sins. Come and live in my heart. Show me how to live. I need You to lead my life, and I want You to be my Best Friend. Thank You, Father, for hearing my prayer and forgiving my sins. In the name of Your Son, Jesus, Amen."

If you just prayed that prayer, you are now a part of God's family. Welcome! The angels are cheering! We encourage you to share your decision to follow Christ with a trusted friend who is also a believer. We also encourage you to find a good Bible-believing church to attend. God loves you and the best days of your life are ahead. Congratulations!

HAVE YOU RECEIVED GOD'S PROMISED GIFT?

It is vital to understand that the infilling of God's Spirit that took place on the day of Pentecost is different from the initial indwelling of God's Spirit that we receive the day we get saved. The same day Jesus was raised from the dead, He appeared to His disciples and "...He breathed on them, and said to them, 'Receive the Holy Spirit'" (John 20:22 NKJV). Then forty days later, just before He ascended into heaven, He "...commanded them not to depart from Jerusalem, but to wait for the Promise of the Father, '...for John truly baptized with water, but you shall be baptized with the Holy Spirit not many days from now'" (Acts 1:4-5 NKJV).

The baptism of the Holy Spirit is God's supernatural empowerment. The same Spirit that raised Christ from the dead wants to live through you and fill you to overflowing! He wants to strengthen you to live like Jesus so you can say "NO!" to all temptation, including the temptation of porn. The Spirit gives you His amazing grace to live free from the power of sin and be Jesus to the world. Through the Holy Spirit, you have everything you need to live a holy life and advance God's Kingdom on earth.

If you've accepted Jesus as your Lord and Savior but have not received the promised gift of the Holy Spirit, you can do so now. All you have to do is ask! Jesus said, "If you then, though you are evil {have a fallen nature}, know how to give good gifts to your children, how much more will your Father in heaven give the Holy Spirit to those who ask him!" (Luke 11:13 NIV; words in brackets added for clarity). Just believe in your heart that what you ask for will be given to you the moment you ask (see James 1:6,7; Mark 11:24).

Once you ask for the Holy Spirit, you will receive the Holy Spirit. Acts 2:4 (NKJV) says, "And they were all filled with the Holy Spirit and began to speak with other tongues, as the Spirit gave them utterance." The word utterance means "syllables, sounds, or words." While you are praying, you will probably sense a syllable, sound, or word being impressed on your spirit or swirling around in your head. Although the impression may be faint and you may feel silly, speak it out! That's the Holy Spirit. He is giving you the utterance, but you must surrender your lips, tongue and vocal cords to speak what He is impressing upon you.

Are you ready to receive? Do you believe God will give you the empowerment of His Spirit when you ask? Are you willing to surrender yourself to the Holy Spirit? Let's pray…

"Father, I come to You in the name of Jesus. First of all, I ask You to forgive me of any sin that would hinder me from receiving the baptism of the Holy Spirit, including the sin of unforgiveness. By Your grace and as an act of my will, I choose to release anyone who has offended me. I bless them with the best of what You have. Please wash me clean from the inside out with the blood of Jesus.

Now, as Your child, I ask You for the promised gift of the Holy Spirit. You said if I ask You for the Holy Spirit, You would give Him to me. I can't be good enough to receive Him, but because of the blood of Jesus which cleanses me of sin, I boldly and humbly ask You to baptize me in the Holy Spirit. I ask this by faith, and I receive everything You have for me, including the ability to speak in a new heavenly tongue. Now in faith, I will speak in new tongues…in Jesus' name!"

Study It:

BAPTISM OF THE HOLY SPIRIT	MINISTRY OF THE HOLY SPIRIT
Joel 2:28,29	John 6:63; 14:15-26; 16:7-15
Matthew 3:11	Romans 8:11
John 7:38,39	2 Corinthians 3:6
Acts 1:4,5, 8; 2:1-21, 38,39	1 John 2:27

21 STEPS TO BREAK FREE
FROM THE PRISON OF PORN

Steps 1 through 7 enable you to
break free from past patterns of sin.

Step 1	Abide in Relationship with Jesus	John 15:5
Step 2	Admit It. Confess It. Repent.	1 John 1:9
Step 3	Destroy the Strongholds	2 Corinthians 10:3-4
Step 4	Take Control of Your Thoughts	2 Corinthians 10:5
Step 5	Don't Give the Enemy an Inch	Ephesians 4:26-27
Step 6	Avoid the Very Scenes of Temptation	Proverbs 5:8
Step 7	Starve Your Flesh	Romans 13:14

Steps 8 thru 14 empower you to
establish new habits that help you live pure.

Step 8	Feed Your Spirit	John 6:48, 51
Step 9	Submit to God…Resist the Devil	James 4:7
Step 10	On Guard!	1 Corinthians 16:13; Proverbs 4:23
Step 11	Eat What's on Your Plate	Proverbs 5:15-19
Step 12	Live Free from Feelings	Galatians 5:24-25
Step 13	Be Accountable to Others	James 5:16
Step 14	Eliminate the "Little Foxes"	Song of Solomon 2:15

Steps 15 thru 21 position you to
unite you with your greatest defense of all!

Step 15	Stay Filled with the Holy Spirit	Ephesians 5:18; Acts 1:8
Step 16	Remember…It's Not in Your Own Strength	Philippians 2:13
Step 17	Make Prayer Your First Response	Ephesians 6:18; 1 Thessalonians 5:17
Step 18	Let God's Word Dwell in You Richly	Colossians 3:16; 2 Timothy 3:16-17
Step 19	Say What You Want to See (Speak the Word)	Jeremiah 23:28-29
Step 20	Wear Your Armor	Ephesians 6:11
Step 21	Never Give Up!	Romans 12:11-12; Proverbs 24:16

Jailbreak ENDNOTES
PART 1: SETTING THE STAGE

CHAPTER 1: WHAT IS PORN?
(1) Rick Renner, *Sparkling Gems from the Greek* (Tulsa, OK: Teach All Nations, 2003) p. 496. (2) *Pornography* (http://www.britannica.com/EBchecked/topic/470645/pornography, accessed 1/9/14). (3) Definition of Pornography (http://www.oxforddictionaries.com/definition/english/pornography, accessed 1/9/14.) (4) *History of Prostitution* (http://en.wikipedia.org/wiki/Prostitution, accessed 1/9/14). (5) Definition of *Prostitute* (http://dictionary.reference.com/browse/prostitute, retrieved 1/9/14). (6) *History of Porn* (adapted from http://www.britannica.com/EBchecked/topic/470645/pornography and http://en.wikipedia.org/wiki/History_of_erotic_depictions, accessed 1/9/14). (7) Ibid. (8) Statistics on Porn (http://www.xxxchurch.com/extras/stats.html, accessed 1/9/14). (9) "How Big Is Porn?" (http://www.forbes.com/2001/05/25/0524porn.html, accessed 1/8/14). (10) See note 8; also see *Porn Industry, Porn Trade* (http://www.economywatch.com/world-industries/porn-industry.html, accessed 1/9/14). (11) Statistics on *Porn* (http://www.onlineeducation.net/porn, accessed 1/9/14).

CHAPTER 2: READ 'EM AND WEEP
(1) *Pornography: A Human Tragedy*, Tom Minnery, Editor (Wheaton, IL: Living Books, Tyndale House Publishers, 1987) p. 105. (2) Ibid., pp. 31, 269-270. (3) Ibid., p. 37. (4) Ibid., p. 71. (5) Ibid., p. 130. (6) Ibid., pp. 117- 121 (findings on p. 121). (7) Ibid., p. 40. (8) Ibid., pp. 137-139 (findings on p. 139). (9) Ibid., pp. 140-142 (findings on p. 141). (10) Ibid. (11) Ibid., p. 125. (12) Ibid., p. 134. (13) Ibid., p. 123. (14) Ibid., pp. 124-125. (15) Ibid., p. 132. (16) Ibid., p. 39. (17) Ibid., pp. 141-142. (18) Ibid., p. 134. Author's Note: For details of each experiment and highlights of the report, we suggest reading Pornography: A Human Tragedy, Tom Minnery, Editor.

CHAPTER 3: THE ENEMY'S ULTIMATE GOAL
(1) Stephen Arterburn and Fred Stoeker, *Every Man's Battle* (Colorado Springs, CO: WaterBrook Press, 2000) p. 4. (2) Richard Exley, *Deliver Me* (Nashville, TN: Thomas Nelson, Inc. 1998) p. 189. (3) Ted Bundy's Story (http://www.pureintimacy.org/piArticles/A000000433.cfm, accessed 1/9/14). (4) Ibid. (5) Ibid. (6) "The Harmful Effect of Pornography" by American Life League (http://www.ewtn.com/library/PROLENC/ENCYC134.HTM, accessed 1/9/14). (7) Ibid.; additional source: (http://everything2.com/title/the+contents+of+Jeffrey+Dahmer%2527s+apartment, accessed 1/9/14). (8) See note 5. (9) See note 5; additional source: *Pornography: A Human Tragedy*, Tom Minnery, Editor (Wheaton, IL: Tyndale House Publishers, Inc., 1987) pp. 148-151. (10) A21 Campaign, *The Facts* (http://www.thea21campaign.org/content/the-facts/gjekag, accessed

1/9/14). (11) A21 Campaign, *The Problem* (http://neutrinodata.s3.amazonaws. com/a21/userimages/A21%20Website%20Resources-The%20Problem.pdf, accessed 1/9/14). (12) Mark Driscoll, *Porn-Again Christian* (Seattle WA: Mars Hill Church, 2009) p. 35.

CHAPTER 4: SEX: GOD-CREATED…GOD-APPROVED!

(1) "Sexual Fulfillment in Marriage" by Jimmy Evans, Marriage on the Rock [Session 9, DVD Curriculum] Marriage Today, 2012. (2) *Noah Webster's American Dictionary of the English Language* (http://1828.mshaffer.com/d/ search/word,sex, accessed 1/6/14). (3) "The #1 Key to Incredible Sex," by Mark Gungor, Laugh Your Way to a Better Marriage [DVD Curriculum] Laugh Your Way America, 2007. (4) See Proverbs 22:6; Ephesians 6:4.

CHAPTER 5: EVERYONE HAS A STORY

(1) Charles H. Spurgeon, *All of Grace* (New Kensington, PA: Whitaker House, 1981) pp. 48-49, 52. (2) Adapted from *Thayer's Greek English Lexicon of the New Testament* (Grand Rapids, MI: Baker Book House, 1977) Strong's #3540, p. 427.

CHAPTER 6: LIKE FATHER…LIKE SON

(1) Mark and Grace Driscoll, *Real Marriage* (Nashville, TN: Thomas Nelson, 2012) p.155. (2) "The Story Told by 40 Years of Abortion Statistics" (http://www. nrlc.org/news/13/winter13news/abortionstatspage13/, accessed 1/6/14). (3) Adapted from *Noah Webster's First Edition of An American Dictionary of the English Language* (1828), Republished in facsimile edition by Foundation for American Christian Education (San Francisco, CA 1995). (4) See Nehemiah 9:2; Daniel 9:3-4.

CHAPTER 7: YOU ARE WHAT YOU EAT

(1) Billy Graham, *The Secret of Happiness* (Garden City, NY: Doubleday & Company, Inc., 1955) pp. 79-80. (2) "Game On! Here Are the Top Super Bowl Ad Spenders in the Last Decade" (http://www.dailyfinance.com/2012/02/01/ game-on-here-are-the-top-super-bowl-ad-spenders-in/, accessed 1/6/14). (3) See note 1. (4) See Proverbs 4:23; Hebrews 12:1.

CHAPTER 8: THE LOOK IS THE HOOK

(1) William M. Struthers, Ph.D., "Pornography Addiction in the Brain," Enrichment (Summer 2011; The General Council of the Assemblies of God, Springfield, MO.) p. 83. (2) Ibid., p. 82. (3) *Ventral Tegmental Area*, (http://en.wikipedia.org/wiki/Ventral_tegmental_area, accessed 1/6/14). (4) Definition of VTA, (http://en.wikipedia.org/wiki/Midbrain, accessed 1/6/14). (5) See note 1, p. 82. (6) Jonathan Croswell, "How Do I Increase Dopamine Levels Naturally?" (http://www.livestrong.com/article/194748-how-do-i-increase-dopamine-levels-naturally/, accessed 1/6/14). (7) See note 1, p. 82. (8) Stephen Arterburn and Fred Stoeker, *Every Man's Battle* (Colorado Springs, CO: WaterBrook Press, 2000), p. 30. (9) See note 1.

CHAPTER 9: IT'S THE FRUIT OF A DEEPER ROOT

(1) Dr. Archibald D. Hart, *The Sexual Man* (W. Publishing Group, a Division of Thomas Nelson, Inc., 1994) pp. 74-75. (2) William M. Struthers, Ph.D., "Pornography Addiction in the Brain," Enrichment (Summer 2011/Volume 16/Number 3; The General Council of the Assemblies of God, Springfield, MO.) p. 84. (3) Randy Alcorn, *The Purity Principle* (Colorado Springs, CO: Multnomah Books, 2003) p. 47. (4) See note 1. (5) Ibid., p. 75. (6) Ibid., p.76. (7) See Matthew 11:28-30; John 14:26. (8) Adapted from Stephen Arterburn and Fred Stoeker's, *Every Man's Battle* (Colorado Springs, CO: WaterBrook Press, 2000) pp. 63-64.

CHAPTER 10: YOUR FREEDOM HAS BEEN PAID FOR!

(1) Mark Batterson, *The Circle Maker* (Grand Rapids, MI: Zondervan, 2011) p. 170.

PART 2: THE GREAT ESCAPE
21 STEPS TO FREEDOM

STEP 1: ABIDE IN RELATIONSHIP WITH JESUS

(1) Quotes on *Intimacy with God* (http://dailychristianquote.com/dcqintimacy. html, accessed 1/8/14). (2) See John 14:10-11; 17:21-23. (3) See John 16:15; 17:10. (4) See Matthew 14:23; 15:29; 17:1-5; Mark 6:31-32; John 18:1-2. (5) See Matthew 28:20; Hebrews 13:5. (6) John Eldredge, *Wild at Heart* (Nashville, TN: Thomas Nelson, Inc., in association with Yates & Yates, LLP, Literary Agents, Orange, CA, 2001), p. 116. (7) Ibid., p. 121.

STEP 2: ADMIT IT. CONFESS IT. REPENT.

(1) *Fast Break* (St. San Luis Obispo, CA: Parable, 2007) Day 349. (2) Adapted from *Thayer's Greek-English Lexicon of the New Testament* (Grand Rapids, MI: Baker Book House, 1977) Strong's #3340, p. 405. (3) See Ephesians 3:12; 5:26; Hebrews 4:15-16; 1 John 1:9. (4) See Hebrews 9:11-14; 22, 28; Matthew 26:28; Romans 5:9; 1 John 1:7. (5) See 1 Corinthians 3:17-18; 1 Thessalonians 5:23-24. (6) See 12 Corinthians 5:21; Isaiah 61:10; Romans 13:12-14; Galatians 3:27.

STEP 3: DESTROY THE STRONGHOLDS

(1) David Wilkerson, *The New Covenant Unveiled* (Lindale, TX: Wilkerson Trust Publications, 2000) pp. 121-122. (2) Adapted from Rick Renner's, *Sparkling Gems from the Greek* (Tulsa, OK: Teach All Nations, 2003) pp. 918-919.

STEP 4: TAKE CONTROL OF YOUR THOUGHTS

(1) Neil. T. Anderson, *Victory over the Darkness* (Ventura, CA: Regal Books, 2000) pp. 154-155. (2) Adapted from *The New Strong's Exhaustive Concordance of the Bible*, Strong's #2507 (Nashville, TN: Thomas Nelson

Publishers, 1990); and *Thayer's Greek-English Lexicon of the New Testament* (Grand Rapids, MI: Baker Book House, 1977) p. 312. (3) Adapted from *Thayer's* (see note 2) Strong's #1869, pp. 227-228. (4) See Satan's temptation, Genesis 3:1-5. (5) See Luke 10:19; Mark 16:17-18; Matthew 28:18-19; 2 Corinthians 10:4. (6) See note 1, p. 155. (7) See 1 Corinthians 6:18; 1 Thessalonians 4:3-8. (8) See note 1, p. 155. (9) John L. Sanford and R. Loren Sanford, *The Renewal of the Mind* (Tulsa, OK: Victory House Publishers, 1991) p. 57. (10) Ibid. (11) See Luke 24:13-27.

STEP 5: DON'T GIVE THE ENEMY AN INCH

(1) Randy Alcorn, *The Purity Principle* (Colorado Springs, CO: Multnomah Books, 2003) pp. 65-66. (2) Adapted from Rick Renner's, *Sparkling Gems from the Greek* (Tulsa, OK: Teach All Nations, 2003) p. 840. (3) Adapted from *Thayer's Greek-English Lexicon of the New Testament* (Grand Rapids, MI: Baker Book House, 1977) Strong's #5117, p. 628. (4) See note 2, p. 942. (5) See Philippians 2:12; 1 Timothy 6:11-12.

STEP 6: AVOID THE VERY SCENES OF TEMPTATION

(1) Jerry B. Jenkins, *Hedges* (Brentwood, TN: Wolgemuth & Hyatt, Publishers, Inc. 1989) p. 31.

STEP 7: STARVE YOUR FLESH

(1) John Eldredge, *Wild at Heart* (Nashville, TN: Thomas Nelson, Inc., in association with Yates & Yates, LLP, Literary Agents, Orange, CA, 2001), pp. 144-145.

STEP 8: FEED YOUR SPIRIT

(1) Brother Lawrence, *The Practice of the Presence of God* (New Kensington, PA: Whitaker House, 1982) pp. 61, 68. (2) See John 6:35, 48, 51; 14:6. (3) See Mark 10:46-52. (4) See Mark 5:24-34. (5) See Ephesians 3:12; Hebrews 4:15-16; 10:19-23.

STEP 9: SUBMIT TO GOD...RESIST THE DEVIL

(1) *Francis Frangipane* Quotes (http://dailychristianquote.com/dcqfrangipane. html, accessed 1/8/14). (2) Adapted from *Thayer's Greek-English Lexicon of the New Testament* (Grand Rapids, MI: Baker Book House, 1977) Strong's #5293, p. 645.

STEP 10: ON GUARD!

(1) Charles R. Swindoll, *The Quest for Character* (Portland, OR: Multnomah Press, 1987) pp. 27-28. (2) Adapted definition of En Garde (http://www. thefreedictionary.com/en+garde, accessed 1/9/14). (3) See Ezekiel 11:19; 36:25-27. (4) See Romans 12:1-2; Ephesians 4:22-24; Proverbs 16:3 (AMP). (5) See Philippians 4:6-7.

Step 11: Eat What's on Your Plate

(1) Bill and Pam Farrel, *Men Are Like Waffles—Women Are Like Spaghetti* (Eugene, OR: Harvest House Publishers, 2001) p. 93.

Step 12: Live Free from Feelings

(1) John L. and R. Loren Sanford, *The Renewal of the Mind* (Tulsa OK: Victory House Publishers, 1991) p. 29. (2) Adapted from *Vine's Complete Expository Dictionary* (Nashville, TN: Thomas Nelson, Inc., 1996) New Testament, pp. 118-119. (3) See Revelation 12:10; Job 1:6-12; 2:1-6. (4) Adapted from *Thayer's Greek-English Lexicon of the New Testament* (Grand Rapids, MI: Baker Book House, 1977) #2616, p. 331. (5) "The Believer's #1 Enemy," by Joyce Meyer (Life in the Word Magazine, January 2003, Vol. 17, Number 1) p. 6. (6) See Ephesians 1:6-7; 1 Peter 1:18-19; Revelation 5:9.

Step 13: Be Accountable to Others

(1) Richard Exley, *Deliver Me* (Nashville, TN: Thomas Nelson, Inc., 1998) p. 191. (2) Randy Alcorn, *The Purity Principle* (Colorado Springs, CO: Multnomah Books, 2003) p. 87.

Step 14: Eliminate the "Little Foxes"

(1) Explanation of *Little Foxes* found on Song of Solomon 2:15 (Matthew Henry's Concise Commentary, http://biblehub.com/songs/2-15.htm, accessed 1-9-14. (2) Ibid., adapted from Pulpit Commentary section. (3) See Jeremiah 2:13; John 4:10-14; 7:37-39). (4) Quotes on Pride (http://dailychristianquote. com/dcqpride.html, accessed 1/9/14). (5) See John 6:63; 15:5; Romans 7:18; Philippians 3:3; 4:13. (6) Andrew Murray, *Humility* (Fort Washington, PA: CLC Publications, 2006) p. 12. (7) See Proverbs 12:24; 21:25; 20:24; 26:16; Matthew 25:24-30. (8) Richard Exley, *Deliver Me* (Nashville, TN: Thomas Nelson, Inc. 1998) p. 190. (9) See Romans 5:5; 1 John 4:16-17.

Step 15: Stay Filled with the Holy Spirit

(1) See 1 Corinthians 15:6. (2) See Matthew 26:64; Mark 14:62; Luke 22:69; Ephesians 1:19-21; Colossians 3:1; Hebrews 8:1; 1 Peter 3:22; Revelation 4:2-4. (3) See John 14:17, 23; Colossians 2:9-10. (4) See 2 Timothy 3:16; 2 Peter 1:20-21. (5) Adapted from *Thayer's Greek-English Lexicon of the New Testament* (Grand Rapids, MI: Baker Book House, 1977) Strong's #907, p. 94. (6) See Mark 16:17; Acts 2:38-39. (7) See Matthew 1:20; Luke 1:35. (8) See Matthew 4:1; Luke 4:1. (9) See John 5:19-20, 30; 14:10. (10) See Luke 4:14. 18-19; John 3:34. (11) See 1 Corinthians 14:4; Jude 1:20.

Step 16: Remember...It's Not in Your Own Strength

(1) Tony Evans, *Free at Last* (Chicago, IL: Moody Publishers, 2001) pp. 60-61. (2) See John 14:23; Colossians 2:9-10. (3) Adapted from Rick Renner's, *Sparkling Gems from the Greek* (Tulsa, OK: Teach All Nations, 2003) pp. 91-

92. (Author's note: The word *yearn* in James 4:5 in the Amplified Bible is translated "lusteth" in the King James Version.)

STEP 17: MAKE PRAYER YOUR FIRST RESPONSE
(1) Watchman Nee, *Let Us Pray* (New York, Christian Fellowship Publishers, Inc., 1977) p. 11. (2) See Colossians 4:2; 1 Thessalonians 5:17. (3) See Matthew 7:7-8. (4) See Isaiah 40:29-31; Philippians 4:13; Psalm 18:1-3; 27:1; Habakkuk 3:19; Galatians 2:20; John 15:5. (5) See Mark 1:35; 6:46; Luke 5:16; 6:12; 22:39-46. (6) See Romans 7:18; Philippians 2:12-13.

STEP 18: LET GOD'S WORD DWELL IN YOU RICHLY
(1) Christian Quotes on *the Bible* (http://dailychristianquote.com/dcqbible.html, accessed 1/9/14). (2) Adapted from Rick Renner's, *Sparkling Gems from the Greek* (Tulsa, OK: Teach All Nations, 2003), p. 61. (3) Francis Frangipane, *Holiness, Truth and the Presence of God* (Cedar Rapids, IA: Arrow Publications, 1999) p.56. (4) See John 1:1, 14. (5) See note 2, pp. 584-585. (6) See Philippians 4:8; 2 Corinthians 10:5; Romans 6:14. (7) See Ephesians 4:27; Proverbs 5:8 (AMP). (8) See Psalm 119:11; Deuteronomy 6:6; 11:18. (9) See John 17:17; Ephesians 5:26. (10) See James 1:21; Romans 1:16. (11) See Romans 8:16-17; Ephesians 3:6; 1 Peter 3:7. (12) See Acts 10:34; Romans 2:11. (13) See James 4:6; 1 Peter 5:5; Psalm 84:11.

STEP 19: SAY WHAT YOU WANT TO SEE
(1) Dr. Paul Yonggi Cho, *The Fourth Dimension* (Plainfield, NJ: Logos International, 1979) pp. 70-71. (2) See John 14:26; 16:13-15. (3) See Matthew 5:28; Proverbs 5:8; 6:26-28; Isaiah 54:17; James 4:7. (4) See 2 Corinthians 5:17, 21; Romans 6:6, 12, 14; 8:37; Galatians 2:20; Ephesians 4:27; James 4:7.

STEP 20: WEAR YOUR ARMOR
(1) Rick Renner, *Dressed to Kill* (Tulsa, OK: Teach All Nations, 2007) pp. 187-188, 191. (2) See Ephesians 6:12; 2 Corinthians 10:3-4. (3) See note 1, pp. 187-188. (4) Ibid., adapted from p. 347. (5) Ibid., adapted from pp. 405-406. (6) Ibid., adapted from pp. 416-418. (7) Ibid., adapted from pp. 436-440. (8) Ibid., p. 191.

STEP 21: NEVER GIVE UP!
(1) "Never Give Up!" *Relentless Curriculum*, DVD Session 12, by John Bevere (Palmer Lake, CO: Messenger International, 2011). (2) See Psalm 40:6, the Amplified Bible. (3) See Philippians 4:13, the Amplified Bible.

Also Available...

Real Life Answers
Finding Direction for Everyday Challenges
available in e-book and print
www.newfieldscreativeservices.org

Other Resources Written by Vincent M. Newfield
in Partnership with John & Lisa Bevere

The Story of Marriage (Devotionals and Discussion Questions)

The Holy Spirit: An Introduction (Devotionals and Discussion Questions)

The Fear of the Lord Devotional Workbook

Relentless Devotional Workbook

Extraordinary Devotional Workbook

Honor's Reward Devotional Workbook

The Bait of Satan Workbook

Breaking Intimidation Devotional Workbook

Nurture Workbook

These powerful resources can be obtained at
www.MessengerInternational.org

VINCENT AND ALLISON NEWFIELD

Celebrating Over 20 Years of Ministry
through Writing and Teaching

Vincent Newfield is a *seasoned wordsmith* and communication specialist serving New York Times best-selling authors like Joyce Meyer, John and Lisa Bevere, Rick Renner, Don Colbert M.D., and others.

In addition to his work being published in *Charisma, Ministry Today,* and Joyce Meyer's *Enjoying Everyday Life Magazine,* Vincent has been privileged to create several devotional workbooks in partnership with John and Lisa Bevere including...*The Bait of Satan Workbook, Extraordinary Devotional Workbook, The Fear of the Lord Devotional Workbook, Breaking Intimidation Devotional Workbook, Relentless Devotional Workbook, Nurture Workbook, The Holy Spirit: An Introduction,* and *The Story of Marriage.*

More than a writer, Vincent is also a licensed minister, teacher, and student of the Word, bringing relevant, practical truth to congregations across the country.

Allison Newfield is an accomplished administrator and dedicated mother and wife. Over eighteen years ago, she laid down her commitments to the corporate world and began investing her life in the most impactful position in which she has ever served—motherhood. In addition to overseeing the education of her four children, Allison also functions as project manager for *New Fields Creative Services* and continues to faithfully serve teaching teen girls and helping them develop into women of God.

Vincent and Allison have been married for over 23 years and continue to share their passion for bringing freedom, healing, and restoration to marriages and families.

For more information, visit www.newfieldscreativeservices.com.

Bring *Jailbreak's* Message of Freedom to Your Church or Conference!

Allison and I are bringing this cutting-edge ministry to hurting people across the country. It's our intense passion to see people FREE! We believe this freedom must begin in the house of God. Through practical teaching and sharing our real-life story, we help men and women...

- Understand the science behind porn's addictive nature

- Discover and apply reliable steps needed to break free and stay free from porn

- Receive answers and healing for their marriage and family

Pastors, we are here to support you and help bring freedom to the people you shepherd.

For availability and scheduling, contact us at:
info@jailbreakthebook.com.

"Vincent has consistently proven himself to be a faithful and humble man of excellence and integrity. Whether it is through writing or teaching the Word, I believe he will continue to be a great asset to the body of Christ and a blessing to all the lives he touches."

—Joyce Meyer
President, Joyce Meyer Ministries

"On the outside, you might view the Newfields as the ideal couple. **Jailbreak** is their personal story of struggles and liberation from the enslavement of porn. Clearly, one of the best sources of information on the subject of sexual dependency I've ever read."

—C. R. Kersten
Executive Director, Teen Challenge of St. Louis

"Being a pastor's kid, Vincent possesses a unique insight into the concerns of leadership and has great compassion for the heart of shepherds. He delivers anointed and passionate messages that are remembered long after they have been delivered. He connects with people through his creative use of props that illustrate specific truths. Without question, **Jailbreak** will help and equip many in our society and the church. I highly recommend him as a man of integrity."

—Ed Shirrell
Senior Pastor, Faith Community Church

"Through many years of genuine service to the Lord, my son Vincent Newfield has demonstrated character qualities of humility, compassion, and loyalty. He is also a man of integrity, and I highly recommend his and Allison's ministry. As they share the Word, the Lord's anointing and blessings will follow."

—Frank W. Newfield, Sr. M.A., BCCC
Presbyter, Assemblies of God, Louisiana District

the journey of freedom continues...

www.JailbreakTheBook.com

Blog

Audio Podcasts / Teachings

Free Downloads

Scheduled Events

Recommended Resources:

- Books

- DVD/CD teachings

- Internet filters

- Real-life stories of victory

Follow us on Facebook
https://www.facebook.com/pages/Jailbreak/735933329756371